Irish Women Writers
SPEAK OUT

Irish
Studies

Sanford Sternlicht, *Series Editor*

Irish Women Writers
SPEAK OUT

Voices from the Field

Caitriona Moloney *&* Helen Thompson

With a Foreword by Ann Owens Weekes

SYRACUSE UNIVERSITY PRESS

Copyright © 2003 by Syracuse University Press
Syracuse, New York 13244-5160

All Rights Reserved

First Edition 2003

03 04 05 06 07 08   6 5 4 3 2 1

The paper used in this publication meets the minimum requirements
of American National Standard for Information Sciences—Permanence
of Paper for Printed Library Materials, ANSI Z39.48–1984.∞™

Library of Congress Cataloging-in-Publication Data

Moloney, Caitriona.
Irish women writers speak out : voices from the field / Caitriona
Moloney and Helen Thompson ; with a foreword by Ann Owens Weekes.— 1st
ed.
p. cm.—(Irish studies)
Includes bibliographical references (p.) and index.
ISBN 0–8156–2971–0 (alk. paper)—ISBN 0–8156–3025–5 (pbk. : alk.
paper)
1. Women and literature—Ireland—History—20th century. 2.
Novelists, Irish—20th century—Interviews. 3. Women authors,
Irish—Interviews. 4. Women—Ireland—Interviews. I. Thompson, Helen,
1966– II. Title. III. Irish studies (Syracuse, N.Y.)
PR8733 .M65 2003
820.9'9287'094170904—dc21
2002154365

Manufactured in the United States of America

Contents

Illustrations

Caitriona Moloney earned her Ph.D. in English at the University of California, Davis, in 1995, with a dissertation on women from Ancient Irish myth in Yeats and Joyce. She is assistant professor of English at Bradley University, Peoria, Illinois, and coeditor of *Ireland as Postcolonial,* a special edition of the *Journal of Commonwealth and Postcolonial Studies.* Her current project is a critical book on contemporary Irish women fiction writers.

Helen Thompson, a native of Darlaston, England, is assistant professor of English at the University of Louisiana at Lafayette. She is currently completing a book on the works of Edna O'Brien.

Foreword

ANN OWENS WEEKES

AWAKENED AND COERCED by the liberation movements of the
1960s, authorities everywhere today pay lip service to the justice and necessity of allowing people to speak in their own voices. The hollowness of
the proclamations, however, is evident in a world increasingly controlled
by bureaucrats and businesspeople. Even in the field of Irish literature,
where the repression of women is widely analyzed, the voices of the
women analyzed are rarely heard. Thus, Jenny Beale's groundbreaking
1986 work, *Women in Ireland: Voices of Change,* based on interviews
with twenty-seven Irish women of different ages, backgrounds, and opinions, was widely welcomed by the academic community. Beale's work
was followed in 1990 by Rebecca E. Wilson's *Sleeping with Monsters:
Conversations with Scottish and Irish Women Poets* and in 2001 by Patricia Boyle Haberstroh's *My Self, My Muse: Irish Women Poets Reflect
on Life and Art.* Collected during times of dramatic social and economic
change, these interviews chart women's diverse responses to both change
and tradition. Moloney and Thompson's *Irish Women Writers Speak
Out: Voices from the Field* introducing contemporary fiction writers, is a
much-needed addition to this small collection. Like its predecessors, *Irish
Women Writers Speak Out* reveals a diversity of opinions on questions of
feminism, politics, religion, and publishing; more important, the writers'
reminiscences provide complicated maps of experiences, whose very diversity, while allowing readers to hypothesize the origin of difference,
militates against the critical endeavor of classification and categorizing.
Further, the confident voices in *Irish Women Writers Speak Out* intro-

duce the concerns of contemporary Ireland, concerns that literary criticism has yet to embrace.

The changes that Beale's voices recorded and predicted in 1986 have in large part, despite the best efforts of traditionalists, been effected. Liz McManus, born in 1947, for example, remarks on the fortunate timing of her birth: far from feeling restricted as a Catholic woman growing up in Ireland in the 1960s, she felt, she notes, "part of a generation blessed with good timing (see p. 80)." The Irish society that Edna O'Brien depicted in her 1960 novel *The Country Girls* is now, Liz McManus continues, "unrecognizable and firmly in the past," a view with which the other interviewees, including O'Brien, generally agree. I would argue that the repressive society has not disappeared totally in rural Ireland, but it is no longer so widespread and has been well analyzed already. The writers do not agree, however, on either the value of or the means by which change was effected.

This diversity of opinion, of course, parallels that of women in other countries, reflecting inevitably the writers' experiences. In Ireland, birth dates are as important as roots in shaping the perspectives of women born in the rapidly changing twentieth century. To illustrate, consider the responses to questions of feminism and postcolonialism by some of the best-known women writers who enjoy considerable success, all of whom are college educated. Jennifer Johnston, born in 1930 to well-established Anglo-Irish parents, has little interest in academic feminism or theories of postcolonialism; eccentricity, she believes, was always tolerated in her world, as it can be where people are secure, and her work, while exploring the problems of women, depicts personal rather than gender liberation. Born six years later, Edna O'Brien, who lived in a "very backward part" of Ireland where, despite the transformation in Ireland, "guilt, shame, and sin" still dominate, matured, as did Johnston, before the feminist movement started in Ireland; her perspective is women centered but not feminist: her works usually depict the traps of femininity rather than liberation. Born to an affluent family in 1947, Liz McManus's first years were spent in homogenous, repressive, poverty-stricken Ireland, but she encountered and embraced the student unrest of the late 1960s, her radicalization driven she suspects by "middle-class guilt." The difficulty and tedium of motherhood was lessened for her, as for so many women, by the advent of 1970s feminism, when women of different backgrounds banded together, educating and supporting each other.

The Irish economic revival, which began in the late 1960s, offered educational opportunities to women born to less affluent families. Feminism also awakened these women to the institutional nature of gender repression. Evelyn Conlon, born in 1952, participated in the almost-legendary gender and political conflicts from the 1970s to the present; her work reflects a sophisticated understanding of inequalities and injustices. "I could not see my life as a writer," she notes, "divorced from my life as a citizen" (see p. 25). Éilís Ní Dhuibhne, born in 1954, records the struggle of a child caught between classes, a common occurrence in Ireland from 1945 to 1975, an indication of social change. The "adolescent feeling of being ashamed of your own parents," is not necessarily rural or urban but is definitely a class matter, reports the woman who felt "deprived" in middle-class surroundings, "thanks to the great ambition and hard work and energy" of her mother (see p. 104–5). Similar struggles appear in her work. Awakened through activism or academia to the injustices of gender, class, and creed, principled writers cannot hide behind veils, cannot *not* reveal the inequities in the societies they depict.

But if, as Jenny Beale notes, the feminist movement, the product of economic and social change, itself fueled further change, those further changes, I suggest, now in turn fuel their own freedoms, including young women's disinterest in feminism. Born in 1962, Anne Enright is more interested in the experimental and imaginative than the thematic: exploring the relationship between words and the world, she faults Irish prose for clinging to the "world in an underconfident way" (see p. 55). Fiction is not fact, so why not, she asks, allow a table to sprout wings and fly. Suggesting that she ignores gender restrictions, she adds that she cannot be a woman all day: "the work of it is far too strenuous. It's too boring" (see p. 63). Born in 1969, Emma Donoghue seems to take feminism as a given. She rejects the equation of lesbian writing with narrative subversion and delivers her "new" lesbian material in "comfortingly old-fashioned forms" (see p. 175). Neither Enright nor Donoghue feel burdened by Irish colonial history: Enright attended graduate school in England because she was offered funds there. Donoghue, who describes herself as a privileged, confident Dubliner, rejects the idea that she left

Dublin because of homophobia; she, too, simply was offered more funding in Britain. Their unquestioning belief in their freedom and ability to experiment in writing and in life mark Enright and Donoghue as, if not postfeminist and postmodern, postidentity-crisis-ridden Ireland.

Still influential in Irish life, church, state, and family no longer dominate Irish lives liberated by economics, education, and social reforms. Gender equality has yet to be achieved in politics and economics, as well as religion, but many writers today perceive race and class as more pressing injustices. No longer homogenous, Ireland, whose principal export for so many years was people, now looks askance at immigrants from Eastern Europe, Asia, and Africa. The discriminations once practiced against the Irish in England and the United States are now practiced in Ireland, perhaps by those who also fear for their own livelihoods. The fear is not irrational: despite the extraordinary economic success of the 1990s, benefits from the Celtic Tiger have hardly been fairly shared. Indeed, Ireland had the dubitable honor in the 1990s of coming second only to the United States in the gap between the incomes of rich and poor. Irish writers, their own imaginations nurtured by a history of colonization, immigration, and discrimination, seem more troubled by these immediate problems than by what many see as academic or historic concerns. The task is to see Ireland as it is, not as it was. Ivy Bannister, a writer who moved to Ireland in 1970, recalls that when she first traveled from New York to Dublin, she felt she was "moving backward in time to a more gracious world." Now, however, she finds little difference between New York and Dublin, though a "huge difference" between New York and the Irish countryside, or we might note, between Dublin and the Irish countryside (see p. 148–49).

In introducing the contemporary Irish scene to American readers, this collection performs a very valuable service. Despite the distinctiveness of the Ireland depicted, the problems are similar to those current in Western Europe and the United States and different, yet hauntingly familiar. More important from a literary and critical viewpoint, the volume introduces a broad spectrum of excellent writers, some well known in the United States, others not yet discovered. Readers, their interest piqued by the interviews, will delight in the comprehensive bibliography of primary and secondary sources in this essential guide, not only for new readers but for all students of Irish fiction.

Acknowledgments

MANY HELPED US on the road to this book with road maps, sign posts, and simply places to rest. First, the writers themselves have made this collection possible, and their enthusiasm and encouragement have made it worthwhile. Our thanks to the writers and critics whose words do not appear in this book. We are indebted to Ailbhe Smyth's facilitation and support, helping us contact writers and providing a space for our meetings. Her tireless efforts to encourage those working in Irish women's studies and her own stellar contributions to the field are an inspiration. Our thanks go to Tracy Anderson, Kevin Phipps, and Maria King at Bradley University who typed, collated, researched, and compiled the manuscript, generally keeping us organized.

Helen would like to thank Nathan Moore, department chair (recently retired), and William Lawson, college dean, formerly at Alabama State University (now at Tennessee State University), for bending university policy regarding foreign travel and supporting her trip to Ireland for the Celebrating IrishWomen Writers Conference in 1999; thanks should also go to Patrick Morrow who gave her the keys to the car by suggesting she organize the Irish women writers panel. His suggestions have given her academic career fruitful and interesting trajectories. Helen is deeply indebted to him and to Joyce Rothschild for their unwavering support and friendship. Thanks also to friends and colleagues at the feminist reading groups Helen has belonged to in Auburn and Montgomery, Alabama: Ruth Crocker, Mary Cameron, Louise Kateinen, Pauline Scott, Susan Roberson, Jennifer Fremlin, E-K Daufin, Shirley Jordan, and Faye Cobb, to name just a few of the wonderful women with whom she has supped. They have been a source of comfort and inspiration as she juggled life, teaching, and research, and they helped her keep her sense of humor, even at her most harried. To Helen's new colleagues at the University of Louisiana at Lafayette, thanks for such a professional yet nurturing environment in which to produce the collection. Particular thanks go to Darrell Bourque and David Barry for their generous support of this project. To her husband, Ron Watts, thanks for giving her the space and quiet to write, and generally keeping her grounded. She dedicates the book to Matthew and Rachel.

Caitriona dedicates this book to her family, the Moloney, Murray, and Roche clans, especially her father Sean Moloney, M.D. (15 February 1917–20 April 1993)] and her nephew William T. Newton (17 October 17, 1982–3 January 2001).

Without the generous and enthusiastic support of Bradley University and my colleagues in the Bradley English Department through grants, research, and travel funds, this work would not have been possible. The National Endowment for the Humanities Institute on Postcolonial Theory and Literature led by Reed Way Dasenbrock and Feroza Jussawalla was invaluable in getting this project off the ground. Thanks also go to the Bradley University librarians, especially Laura Corpuz and Meg Frazier, for helping with interlibrary loan and internet technology.

Thanks are also due to my mother, Una, aunts Ala and Moni, and to many relatives and friends for excellent hospitality and conversation: Sheila Newton, Eileen Wee, Francis Bennett, Margaret Andrews, Eileen Barratt, Colleen O'Neill, Pam Demory, Marcia Kent, Karen Pratt, Bev Lauderdale, and Cathy Dunn. Thanks are also owed to Fionnuala and David Cook for their generosity and introductions, and to Éilís Ní Dhuibhne, whose energetic assistance was invaluable. To Bob and Becky Tracy for the privilege of their friendship, to Margaret MacCurtain for a significant third-year honors history tutorial, to Ailbhe Smyth, Ann Owens Weekes, and Sandra Gilbert, to Michael Hoffman, and to Kathleen Kovach and Dan Schmidt for finding that fax.

We both thank Amy Farranto, our excellent editor at Syracuse University Press.

Introduction

CAITRIONA MOLONEY AND HELEN THOMPSON

THIS BOOK EMERGED from a series of interests, meetings, projects, and controversies over the last five years. We met in 1997 while participating in a panel organized by Helen on Irish Women Writers at The Commonwealth and Postcolonial Studies Conference. Also on the panel were Kelli Malloy and Ailbhe Smyth, director of the Women's Education, Research and Resource Center (WERRC) at University College, Dublin. Both the panel's content and its locale pertained to the direction our work would take in combining feminism, postcolonialism, and Irish studies.

The paucity of Irish studies at postcolonial conferences, and vice versa, mirrors a similar marginalization of women's writing that occurs at the highest levels of Irish literary criticism. This exclusion corresponds ironically with a groundswell of interest in Irish women's fiction in the public and in the academy.

This dichotomy became obvious in 1998 when Caitriona received a fellowship to a National Endowment for the Humanities institute in London on postcolonial theory and literature. The scions of high postcolonial theory who participated in that institute demonstrated a staggering lack of interest in women's literature, especially Irish women's writing (even if they were Irish). A chasm seemed to exist between theory and literature. Many postcolonial writers also attended that institute and indicated by their lively critical sense of their art that they were far from "dead." Encouraged by that institute to pursue the literary conversation between critic and writer as a new way to infuse life into theory, Caitriona met and spoke with Jennifer Johnston and Evelyn Conlon. The institute affirmed that "postfeminism" was premature, and the resurgence of the "Troubles" in Northern Ireland that summer unfortunately confirmed the relevance of a postcolonial approach to Irish studies.

Unlike Caitriona's Ph.D. dissertation on Yeats and Joyce, Helen's dissertation was about Edna O'Brien. Helen too had worked on a canonical figure—Samuel Beckett—before she "discovered" Edna O'Brien, Jennifer Johnston, Mary Lavin, and Kate O'Brien. In her attempt to publish her dissertation on O'Brien, which won the National Women's Studies Association Book Manuscript Award in 1996, Helen has been asked by reviewers and publishers to defend the validity of writing about O'Brien at all, an argument Caitriona has not encountered in publishing her dissertation work on Yeats and Joyce. These experiences awakened the concerns with feminism and postcolonialism that emerge in these conversations with new and important Irish women writers.

This work was also inspired by the controversy over the publication of the first three volumes of the *Field Day Anthology of Irish Writing* in 1991. This monumental work spans medieval and postmodern Irish literature while managing to include very few women writers. These three volumes, and the subsequent volumes 4 and 5 on women's literature conceived as an afterthought, epitomize the territorial attitudes and "gender-blindness" we had encountered since our doctoral research (Ní Dhomhnaill 1999, 4). Critical inattention to Irish women's writing meant that it was difficult to teach Irish women writers and to publish criticism about them. *Field Day*'s marginalization of women writers was also our own, and we wanted to articulate a common grievance.

This book was also facilitated by the Celebrating Irish Women Writers Conference organized by Ailbhe Smyth in Dublin in 1999 as an international reply to the insult of *Field Day*. Having discussed such a conference back in 1997 on our postcolonial panel, we felt in a small way that we had contributed to its realization. Writers and critics from all over the world converged on Dublin in May of 1999, invading what Ní Dhomhnaill called the "misogynistic bardic club" of Irish letters (4). The conference presented writers and critics side-by-side, creating a space for productive critical conversations such as those that appear in this book. So, this collection of literary conversations developed from critical and pragmatic concerns to showcase contemporary Irish women writers, a timely move in light of *Field Day*'s glaring omissions.

Our list of writers grew from Evelyn Conlon, Jennifer Johnston, and Edna O'Brien to include conference participants and writers recommended by Ailbhe Smyth, Margaret MacCurtain, Dermot Bolger, and Éilís Ní Dhuibhne. We also included Irish-American writers Valerie Miner, Catherine Brady, and Maura Stanton to expand the concept of Irishness beyond the island and into the diaspora. These writers differ in style, concerns, ages, and reputations; however, they share a focus on women's issues and Irishness. Although these writers employ a variety of genres, we are primarily concerned with their fiction because of our own interests in narrative as well as our desire to fuel the growing critical interest in Irish women's fiction, where attention falls behind that paid to poetry.

These conversations were conducted through a variety of strategies: in person, by telephone, by fax, and by email, a process reflecting the preferences of the authors and the availability of travel funding. Caitriona conducted her interviews in Ireland, England, and Mendocino, California, while the majority of Helen's were conducted at a distance. While the methods were different, the responses are in no way hindered by these differences. Face-to-face discussions may be more spontaneous and conversational, but written responses benefit in that the writers have more time to consider their remarks and know that nothing will be lost in translation. Of course, the overall editing process levels these differences to the point that the two methods are indiscernible.

With the inevitable exceptions, our preparation included reading the entire canon of each writer's fiction. We wrote questions, generally sent to the writers in advance, that came from the texts and focused on identity issues through the lenses of gender and nationality. This process has produced a collection of diverse voices and perspectives that offers a sense of the writers, their work, and their concerns about their own identities as Irish women writers. Transcripts have been extensively edited and reorganized, often with the cooperation of the writers. For the sake of consistency and coherence, we have removed the spontaneous and organic flow of conversation, editing out redundancy, false starts, and grammatical errors, in short, all the things that hinder clarity of meaning. Some authors edited their own work, changing or removing responses. This process allowed writers to clarify their meanings and add new ideas so that these critical conversations reflect their authentic voices. All spelling has been Americanized according to the practice of our publisher.

Deciding on an organizational method for the collection presented all the problems of Irish studies in miniature. In order to give readers some guidance in distinguishing the versions of Irishness represented by the writers, we divided them into two sections. This naturally was a near impossible task, and undoubtedly many other rubrics would have worked equally well, or badly. The problem of categorizing reproduces the essentialisms that our collection questions; however, we eventually named our divisions according to geography. Our first section includes writers whose Irishness is determined by birth or residence, and our second section groups writers together who were not born in Ireland, or do not live there, or both. This decision has its own problems, particularly because it overlooks the mobile and fluid possibilities of all identities. The section introductions that follow problematize the construction of identity that arises in our conversations.

The diverse group of fiction writers represented here mirror some of the contradictions of our own backgrounds: Caitriona was born in Ireland but has spent most of her life in the U.S.; Helen was born in England but has been partially educated in and now lives in the U.S. Our conversations center on the Irish cultural contexts from which writing is produced: the women's movement, legal changes, and attitudes toward the Catholic Church, as well as the concerns women have negotiating family and work, publishing, and the literary establishment. Attitudes toward canonicity focused on the *Field Day Anthology of Irish Writing,* whose initial exclusion of women's writing often elicited fervent responses.

Surprisingly, Ireland's historical relationship to Britain and the utility of a postcolonial paradigm in that context emerged as very controversial. We had not expected such a wide range of opinions regarding this topic. These reactions have complicated in very fruitful ways our own understandings of Irishness and our own subjectivities as Irish-American and British scholars in the field of Irish studies.

Local Irish Identities

Introduction to Part One

CAITRIONA MOLONEY

EVELYN CONLON, Miriam Dunne, Catherine Dunne, Anne Enright, Jennifer Johnston, Liz McManus, Cláir Ní Aonghusa, Éilís Ní Dhuibhne, and Mary O'Donnell talk about fiction, gender, nationality, and religion in Ireland.

The writers in this collection talk mainly about their fiction and their lives as writers; the conversations do, however, gravitate toward issues which bring them into dialogue with each other, issues that are important for the field of Irish literature. Gender and nationality's intersection is an axis that defines Irish women's writing as a genre. Many of the generalizations made about male literature and national identity do not hold true for women's writing. Two editors introducing new collections of Irish literature, Caroline Walsh and Colm Tóibín, demonstrate this disparity. In her introduction to *Virgins and Hyacinths* (1993), Walsh writes that "in reading dozens of new short stories for this collection it was at times quite startling how the same common experience was thrown up again and again . . . themes echoed one another in story after story, confirming each other, questioning one another; making a dialogue" (6–7). Tóibín, in introducing *Soho Square 6: New Writing from Ireland,* on the other hand declares that the authors in the volume "have nothing in common except a beginning under the same sky, the same uncertain weather. And there is no collective consciousness, no conscience of our race, no responsibilities, no nation singing in unison. Instead, diversity, the single mind and the imagination making themselves heard" (9). Perhaps a valid distinction between the traditions of male and female writers exists:

3

whereas the men's literary tradition has long been acknowledged and contemporary male writers are in revolt against it, the women's tradition has been buried and hidden, and women writers are only now demonstrating a relationship to it. Women have been oppressed by the Irish state and the church in ways that separate their experience from men's, and their fiction is more likely to express common themes.

Eavan Boland in *Object Lessons* argues that women writers have traveled "from being the object of Irish poems to being their author" (1995, 140). Geraldine Meaney counters that this assumption results from the invisibility of Irish women writers throughout history. Whatever the reason, women writers have been excluded from the critical landscape in Ireland, due to a fiercely patriarchal literary tradition that only acknowledges male writers as having significance or even as having existed at all. Writing by women is often unavailable and out of print, so their critical reputation even among feminists wanes. Recovery of unknown or underappreciated writers is still an important task for feminist critics of Irish writing.

Contemporary Irish women writers have met with mixed success in their journey to authorhood: in the publishing houses and the bookstores, women writers are experiencing a renaissance. But, in academia, literary criticism, and journalism, women writers still do not get anthologized, critiqued, or reviewed with the same attention Irish men receive. Nuala Ní Dhomhnaill, in her opening address to the 1999 WERRC Conference on Women Writers, advanced a psychoanalytic theory for "the hysterical male outbursts masquerading as literary criticism which have heralded the emergence of women's voices in literature" (1999, 4). She argued that male critics' "tone-deafness" to women writers came from a Freudian mother-son dyad with roots in a masculinist construct of the bardic male writer that requires the suppression of the female, a construct that sees women writing as "a threat to being on the basic level of self-image or primary narcissism" (4). Ní Dhomnhaill's theory partially explains the necessity for and evolution of volumes 4 and 5 of the *Field Day Anthology of Irish Writing,* volumes devoted to women's writing. After ten years, volumes 4 and 5 were finally released in 2002. Many of the writers in this collection responded to the Field Day story, and their reactions partially explain women's exclusion from Irish letters. The immediacy of this story (volumes 4 and 5 released in 2002) indicates that the problem is not yet safely in the past.

We asked most of the writers we interviewed about the *Field Day* controversy. Writers living in Ireland were familiar with the story and had something to say about it, sometimes off the record. The scandalous episode functions well as a touchstone for women writers' general relationship with publishing and criticism. The first three volumes of *Field Day* included so few women writers—for example, only five women poets in the twentieth century—that it sparked an ongoing controversy and engendered subsequent volumes labored over by Irish women writers and academics eventually published by Cork University Press. The controversy is emblematic of women's larger struggle to appear publicly as writers and artists. Although Irish women writers command considerable space in bookstores in Ireland and the U.K., they can still be almost totally excluded from an anthology of Irish literature that spans the medieval to the postmodern. They are still left out of critical collections and college curricula, and the official Irish literary tradition is considered homogeneously male. The litany of Yeats, Joyce, Synge, Wilde, Beckett, Kavanagh, and Heaney endures, punctuated only occasionally by an apologetic mention of Lady Gregory or Lady Wilde. The names of the great Irish women writers—Maria Edgeworth, Emily Lawless, Edna O'Brien, Kate O'Brien, Jennifer Johnston, Mary Lavin, Elizabeth Bowen—with rare exceptions, do not pass the lips of male Irish critics.

After the appearance of the first three volumes, and their egregious omission of women writers, the *Field Day* editors agreed to a fourth volume. Many women academics were enlisted as editors and spent the better part of ten years on the project. There was a considerable difficulty in finding a publisher for the women's volumes. Negotiations with Norton, *Field Day*'s North American distributor, dragged on for three years before the project moved to Cork University. The extensive delay around the publishing of volumes 4 and 5 caused much frustration, as it allowed other critics to "scoop" women who had worked on *Field Day* for years and could not publish their research elsewhere. Women writers and critics were divided about strategy regarding volumes 4 and 5. Ailbhe Smyth believed that *The Field Day Anthology* should have been boycotted and left "womenless" as a statement. Eavan Boland is quoted in the *Irish*

Times as saying that the *Field Day* is "post-colonial project," and its omission of women "continues the exclusions for which it reproaches the original colony"; Boland said the debate was "at the heart of Irish literature now." Ann Enright expresses considerable anger about *Field Day*, stating that although she did not withhold her contribution, she should have. Evelyn Conlon regrets the "exclusivity" but believes that volume 4 was "the lesser of two evils" (private correspondence with C. Moloney, 4 August 2001). The comments and opinions of fiction writers Conlon, Ní Dhuibhne, Enright, McManus, Ní Aonghusa, and O'Donnell on this controversy illuminate many elements of women's issues with Irish literary culture.

Conlon is generally optimistic about the possibilities for friendly relations between men and women; however, she sees the Irish literary critical scene as decidedly un-woman friendly. Conlon believes that many male critics "do not want to read women or know what they have to say" (see p. 27). Citing the media coverage of Mary Robinson as a case in point, Conlon observes ironically that almost all the BBC shows on Mary Robinson consisted of "four men" speaking; "the BBC and the Irish men certainly didn't look for the women; the Irish women were a well-kept secret. Everybody managed to avoid the whole notion of what the feminist movement had been in Ireland" (see p. 28). Like many of these writers, Conlon points to exceptions, saying that Paul Durcan was "one glorious exception" who complained about the lack of women on these programs (see p. 28).

Ní Dhuibhne is an editor of the folklore section of what she calls the "infamous volume 4 of the *Field Day Anthology*," and she talks about the critical reception of Irish women writers in relevant terms (see p. 111). Ní Dhuibhne, who received a Ph.D. from University College, Dublin, says that as an undergraduate in English literature there "women simply were not acknowledged as having existed in the canon of Anglo-Irish literature" (see p. 113). This absence of women from the critical landscape is contradicted by women writers from the past whose work is being recovered as well as by the huge number of women writers currently selling in the bookstores.

Anne Enright's response to the story is characteristically emphatic: "That's all bollocks. . . . *The Field Day Anthology* got it so spectacularly wrong that anyone would know that they had no credibility. . . . This is one of the reasons why Ireland would drive you mad" (see p. 56). Ultimately, Enright prefers not to dwell on the injustice; she says she can't be a feminist all day; it's too much work, and the strain is not good for her writing. She does say, however, that events like *Field Day* cause her to market her work toward an English or American audience: "Why not go where you are liked?" she asks (see p. 54). Enright remains ambivalent about her own participation in volume 4; although she does appear in the volume, she feels she ought not to.

Mary O'Donnell considers the Field Day's "reprehensible act" of omitting women to be part of a larger problem: men don't read women's fiction, unless "they are particularly open and smart" (see p. 120). McManus further comments that the editors of *Field Day* were indifferent to women's response to the omissions, contributing to the eight-year delay in the publishing of the women's volumes, which she calls a "whitewashing exercise" (see p. 120). Ní Aonghusa feels that the "scandal" of *Field Day* occurred because "men like . . . Seamus Deane didn't disregard women writers—they just never saw them or considered them" (see pp. 99–100). She is optimistic that this represents an old school and that things are changing.

In many ways the *Field Day* story represents the problems women writers have encountered in their careers. They are separated from "real" literature because of their gender, whether or not they choose this separation. Some writers are angry about this and others overlook it, but women's role in society is inescapable for writers who are women. The cultural constraints placed on Irish women as mothers and wives have silenced women through the generations, creating a submerged invisible history that emerges to animate the fiction of these writers. Dermot Bolger, in his introduction to the *Vintage Book of Contemporary Fiction*, makes explicit the connection between motherhood and women's writing careers that has for so long been invisible and unstated. He notes that Mary Beckett "abandoned writing for twenty years after moving south while she raised her children" and that Van Mulkerns "underwent a similar (if not as total) silence while rearing her family" (1993, xxi). He observes that "the role of women in Irish family life in the past has to be a factor in the relatively late debuts of writers like Mary Leland (44), Jen-

nifer Johnston (42) or Maeve Kelly (46)" (xxi). Every writer in these conversations talks about writing within and around issues of marriage and
motherhood.

Jennifer Johnston chose writing as a career partially because her children were young and she wanted to be "unavailable at home" (see p. 66).
She sees the relationship between women artists and their families as difficult because some husbands and sons "expect constant service from
their wives and mothers" (see p. 72). Johnston suggests a class element to
the conflict, arguing that her mother, actress Sheela Richards, was a
"working woman," and that her class, "the gentry," tolerated eccentricity and accepted women artists (see p. 73). Conlon theorizes that society's
construction of gender influences the way women with children are allowed to behave, specifically in regard to the arts. Society places such an
inordinately huge burden on women as mothers—they are responsible
for children's emotional, psychological, intellectual, and academic development—that women are stifled in other areas. In heterosexual relationships, gender difference is exaggerated to enhance sexuality, but this
difference can be a disability for women. Conlon says that society conve-
niently believes that "women really want to have children." What is
more often the case, Conlon believes, is that women "fall" into motherhood and are shocked "by the implications" and "bury" them so they
can get on with life (see p. 22). Since writing involves a process of un-
burying, it can profoundly conflict with that type of motherhood.

Catherine Dunne sees herself as part of a younger generation of
women writers who were liberated from the constraints of traditional
Irish motherhood by the women's movement. Dunne says her "generation had access to contraception, which definitely gave us an enormous
amount of control over our lives," because such feminists as Nell Mc-
Cafferty brought condoms down from Belfast. Her generation gritted
their teeth "to juggle career and family" (see p. 32). Miriam Dunne comments that "Given that Jane Austen died at the age of forty two, one
wonders how she would have fared as a writer if she hadn't broken off
her engagement to Bigg-Withers, who went on to marry someone else
and had ten children" (see p. 47).

McManus also talks about the pressures of motherhood, career, and
writing: she began writing when staying home with her three small boys,
a process that "put iron in my soul" (see p. 78). She relied on feminist

groups to learn about other women in similar situations. Unlike most other women in this collection, McManus sees a positive aspect to the Catholic role in Irish motherhood, saying that because of the importance of mothers in Irish culture, the Catholic Church emphasized the education of women. McManus sees her generation, at college in the 1960s, as well-placed to effect change in the way motherhood is defined in Ireland through reform of laws about divorce, birth control, and equal pay for women. Ní Aonghusa is also optimistic about the current generation of working mothers in Ireland, saying that men's behaviors and attitudes have changed. She sees husbands of her generation doing domestic work and genuinely liking women, contrary to men of her father's generation, whom she believes, "neither respected nor liked women" (see p. 91).

Éilis Ní Dhuibhne and Enright both discuss the Irish cultural construction of femininity and motherhood. Ní Dhuibhne, herself a professional, a wife, and a mother, believes gender is constructed in the way boys and girls are treated in schools. Enright talks about her interest in the "iconized mother figure in Irish literature," often "dead" because "the men can't actually write them" (see p. 61). In her novel, *What Are You Like?* Enright splits that figure into two characters—one dead, the other living—and examines the guilt and anger of the mother-daughter relationship. She says the problem concerns the daughter "trying to separate, to become someone else" (see p. 61). Acknowledging the historical silencing of women's voices, Enright poses the writer's problem this way: "When women have been silent so long, you have to read the silences really urgently. The silences and also the illusions and slippages" (see p. 63).

The question of identity, ethnic and national, appears frequently in these interviews, as it does in the literature of these writers. Irishness in all its variants carries considerable controversy. Much as some of these writers prefer not be known as "Irish writers," some admit Irishness is a market niche and one route to success. Enright says, "Irish writing is a healthy business, and we are all members of the firm" (see p. 57). Irishness is always at least a bifurcated entity; within Ireland, the usual suspects for binary opposition include North/South, Catholic/Protestant, rich/poor, Nationalist/Unionist, urban/rural, Gaelic/English. Outside Ireland in the diaspora a plethora of hyphenated identities compete for Irishness: American-Irish; Canadian-Irish; British-Irish; Anglo-Irish (in

Ireland and in England); and more. For the purposes of this collection, we have decided to divide our writers into two categories (as useful as any) based on domicile. On the basis that proximity is the greatest factor in relationships, it seems valid that those writers who actually reside within the borders of Ireland (in a optimistic spirit, North and South) have a different experience than those who live in America, Canada, or the U.K. The distinction often deconstructs when global travel and the extended families produced by immigration are introduced into the equation. So, it is a marriage of convenience.

Controversy over "Irishness" parallels issues within postcolonial theory and the question of whether Ireland shares characteristics with other countries previously colonized by England. The subject of postcolonial theory raised considerable controversy amongst the women we interviewed, a few agreeing that Ireland fits the paradigm, others quite passionately opposed. Conlon—a citizen of the diaspora whose sister lives in Oakland, California, and whose novel, *Glassful of Letters,* is partially set in New York—feels connected to Caribbean writer Jamaica Kincaid's "A Very Small Place," an analysis of what happens when the colonizers leave. Like Ní Dhuibhne, Conlon sees nationalism's valorization of Gaelic language, football, and music as a backlash to "having doffed your cap and felt subservient for all those years" (see p. 126). While Conlon objects to the idea that the Irish themselves were colonizers, she does see the Catholic Church's role in British imperialism as a form of colonization.

Enright sees her relationship with England primarily as a writer's access to a market to "sixty million people who will buy," and to reviewers such as Penelope Fitzgerald of the *Times of London,* who understands her work better than the *Irish Times* (see p. 62). But Enright also sees Irish nationalism as having given Irish people a sense of class unity that set them apart from the British; ironically, she does not include the North in that unity. Artistically, Enright's main stance on nationalism is "I can't be Irish all day; it's too much of an effort" (see p. 63). Johnston, like Enright, would prefer to eschew all labels except "writer." Like fellow northerner Edna Longley who equates postcolonialism as "starry-eyed lit crit from the USA" in *The Living Stream* (Longley 1994, 175) Johnston believes that postcolonial theory is "an academic exercise that may have relatively short-lived duration" (see p. 73). However, in terms of national identity, Johnston accepts the title "Irish writer," saying, "What else would I be? I am Irish. Everything I know is about Ireland" (see p. 74). Johnston's statement is especially significant as she lives in Derry (or Londonderry), a border city that exemplifies many of the contradictions of Irish identity—British/Irish; North/South; Catholic/Protestant; and unionist/nationalist.

Ní Dhuibhne applies postcolonial theory to internal conflicts in Ireland. Talking about her novel *Dancers Dancing*, which was short-listed for the Orange Prize, Ní Dhuibhne describes her protagonist Orla as representing "the postcolonial Irish who are ashamed of their Irishness" (see p. 104). Ní Dhuibhne believes that contemporary Irish society, particularly in Dublin, would happily look away while their Gaelic ancestry died off, although they are too politically correct to actively kill it off. However, if the European Union saw it as a valuable commodity, they might resurrect it. Ní Dhuibhne sees elements of postcolonial identity such as duality and duplicity resulting from the necessity of two personas, one for the colonizer and another for home. She sees a certain shame and self-loathing resulting from collaboration with colonial administrators by "castle-hacks," immigrants' interactions with the English, Scottish, Americans, as well as rural immigrant's feelings moving to urban Ireland. Like Conlon, Ní Dhuibhne sees reactions to colonization as essential components in national identity: "Irish nationalism constitutes a backlash against everything that's British" and so has created a society that is "rigidly Catholic, censorial, and punitive" (see p. 115).

The writers we interviewed often disliked the term "postcolonial," while accepting some of its premises as "ex-colonial" or "anticolonial." Catherine Dunne considers Ireland's "difficulties of learning how to self-govern" a result of "being a colony and victims of imperialism" (see p. 37). Similar to Ní Dhuibhne, O'Donnell sees an Irish characteristic duplicity as a result of colonization; although she feels connected to Salman Rushdie's work and the political problems of Kenyan women, she rejects the term "postcolonial," interpreting it to mean the "retention of all the characteristics of the former colonizer" (see p. 123). Living in Monaghan, a border county, O'Donnell feels she benefited from contact with British and European culture that was blocked in the South. On the other hand, examining the deeds of her parents' home, O'Donnell is struck by the reality of absentee landlords and the economics of colonization. She too sees colonization's causing a "sense of unworthiness, inadequacy, a lack of confidence" in Ireland until recently (see p. 122). Like Ní Dhuibhne and O'Donnell, McManus connects the colonial experience with the Irish character, saying, "the ruses and stratagems of the powerless and dispossessed are still part of the Irish psyche" (see p. 82). A politician herself, McManus easily segues from the topic of postcolonialism to the Troubles in the North, problematic, as its colonialism is more present than "post."

The intersections of Irish identities that occur in the North illuminate the complexities of Irishness. Even the names associated with identity in the North—the six counties, the North of Ireland, Ulster, Northern Ireland—reveal subtly different political positions.

The writers we interviewed naturally held different views on the North related somewhat to their location. Johnston lives in Derry, a border city, and she believes that the culture of "hatred and violence" in the North has to "color the way we look at the world, the way we write books" (see p. 68). O'Donnell, from Monaghan, a border county, believes that "the question of Irishness is overzealous in the region" (see p. 121). Catherine Dunne, on the other hand, argues that even in a border town like Dundalk, for many people the Troubles "hasn't touched their lives at all" (see p. 36). Dunne believes that Ireland's process of "growing up" requires deromanticizing nationalism.

McManus sees economic cost as the reason the South does not pressure England to relinquish the North, and she sees terrorism on both sides caused more by poverty than politics. Ní Aonghusa also sees Northern problems as primarily economic, citing European Union participation, noticeably absent in the North, as a key factor of economic progress in the South. Ní Aonghusa feels that Northern feminism lags behind the South: "Nationalists aren't famous for being wildly pro-women, but . . . Unionists are about thirty years behind the republic" (see pp. 88–89). Also a resident of Dublin, Enright admits a reluctance to dwell on the North: "My generation is sloppy about the North. It has gone on too long, too boring, too horrible" (see p. 61). However, Enright comments on the Troubles and the arts, saying that Northern theater audiences are dramatically bifurcated. Judging the *Irish Times* theater awards in 1998, Enright noticed that Catholic audiences approve of characters becoming IRA terrorists, and Unionist audiences "laughed at some really hideous jokes about Catholics always squealing when you shoot them" (see p. 62). As Johnston says, the Troubles are "the background to all our lives," and "the border is a state of mind and little by little that state of mind must change" (see p. 68).

Varieties of Irishness extend beyond Ireland into the diaspora. The writers in this collection have important ties to England, Canada, and America. Without making any pretensions to inclusivity or universality, these interviews often speak about these complicated hyphenated relationships from the point of view of the Irish who stayed on the island. Frank McCourt's portrayal of Ireland in *Angela's Ashes* often emerged as a touchstone for feelings about the Irish image in America. Asked about *Angela's Ashes,* Enright responded by talking about McCourt's second novel, *'Tis,* and its portrayal of Ireland as a "peasant European hell" that Americans felt lucky to have escaped. Enright feels this view of Ireland appeals to immigrants who want to confirm their choice by an extremely abject portrayal of the past. O'Donnell found the procession of calamities in *Angela's Ashes* uninteresting, although she believes that the "poverty, or the awfulness" of the story was valid and a useful challenge to "rose-tinted stuff about 'old Ireland' " (see p. 129). Asked about American's view of Irishness, Johnston theorized that Americans oversimplify Irish issues: "my vision of Ireland is too complex for some Irish-Americans" (see p. 68). On the other hand, Conlon, whose most recent novel is set in the U.S., says she often feels "that America is just a part of Ireland" (see p. 21).

Even more dramatically than the U.S., England figures largely in the fiction of these authors. Enright, while acknowledging that poor Irish were discriminated against when they went to England for work, now sees England primarily as a place where her work is received positively. She sees the balance of power between England and Ireland shifting and English workers now appearing on Irish construction sites. Enright feels that being Irish is an advantage to a writer because until recently, nationalism surmounted class differences within Irish society, whereas "English fiction is so caste bound " (see p. 62). For a different reason, Ní Dhuibhne also sees Irishness in exile as an advantage for a writer. Ní Dhuibhne feels that migration of any kind, within Ireland or to the U.K. or the U.S., creates a doubleness of vision and perception that is useful to a writer. She is "increasingly interested in this duality and ambiguity of my own personality, which is very typically Irish" (see p. 105). Ní Dhuibhne's new collection of short stories, *The Pale Gold of Alaska*, deals with the "dislocation and being an outsider, which has the advantage of making a writer of you" (see p. 105). Johnston suggests that the English view of Irishness can have a negative affect on a writer. She considers *Shadows on Our Skins*, which was short-listed for the Booker Prize, to be "not a very good book." Its popularity in England, Johnston explains as its satisfying "the kind of 'Irishness' that people in England like" (see pp. 71–72). Enright responds to Johnston's "kind of Irishness" by saying that all writers want to avoid stereotypes, including those about the Irish. As does the role of immigration in general, England's affect on Irish writers continues to be complex and contradictory.

Like England, the Catholic Church exerts a pervasive influence on Irish culture and writers. Most of the writers in this section see the Catholic Church as a negative influence, although most agree that its hold is waning. Several writers attribute this decline to recent revelations of abuse of children and women within Catholic institutions and scandal among the clergy. Catholicism impacts women's lives and writing around sexuality and its concomitant political issues of birth control, abortion, and divorce. Another less commonly noted issue raised by these writers concerns Catholicism's usurpation of spirituality and mysticism within Irish culture.

Ní Dhuibhne characterizes nationalism as having created a society "frightened of every sexual impulse and of writing" (see p. 115). She talks about a recent spate of revelations "of the sadism in our society in the past," and she blames the priest, in whose name the abuse was perpetrated, but who "keeps his hands clean" (see p. 113). Ní Dhuibhne advocates exposing and acknowledging these abuses so they do not happen again. Conlon also talks about priests' behavior, specifically the Bishop Casey scandal, saying that many women in Ireland had been asked out on a date by a priest but "it was the thing that nobody ever discussed" (see p. 25). Catherine Dunne also talks about recent "cases of child abuse and other appalling behavior" as a factor in the diminished power of the church (see p. 34). Ní Aonghusa talks about a past where "women could be incarcerated in mental institutions if unmarried and pregnant" (see p. 93).

Clerical hostility to women's sexuality is seen by some of these writers as the reason for state legislation banning divorce, birth control, and abortion, except the last, all now legal in Ireland due to long feminist battles. Ní Aonghusa talks about the 1995 divorce referendum, seeing divorce as a "necessary evil" (see p. 87). Conlon talks about her interest in adoption and its possible complications. Her short story "Birth Certificates" develops some less obvious implications of the Catholic Church's booming adoption business in babies of single mothers.

The writers interviewed here note the ironies of traditional Catholicism, prohibiting sexuality for women while mandating motherhood. Conlon believes that readers assume women writing about sexuality are speaking autobiographically rather than using their imagination and consequently censor them. Seeing it as a sign of "how far we had *not* come," O'Donnell was disappointed by the critical reception of *Virgin and the Boy,* feeling that most Irish reviewers were distracted by its sexuality and could not accept women writing about "their bodies" (see p. 119). McManus talks about the damage done to Protestants who married Catholics by the Ne Temere papal decree. McManus also sees a postcolonial aspect to the domination of the Catholic Church, saying that the codes and strictures set by the church were "impossible" and "rigid" and contributed to a cultural "subterfuge" (see p. 82). Enright sees a connection between a Catholic worldview, "you spend a very fixed amount of time looking at a dead man on a cross," and a sexual aesthetic resembling that of the Renaissance, half in love with death (see p. 59). In discussing *The Elysium Testament,* O'Donnell suggests that Catholic domination of Irish culture has occluded spirituality and mysticism.

I hope this introduction whets readers' appetites for the ideas and fiction of the nine writers that follow. Some are well known, others are not, but reading these interviews will reveal surprising aspects of the writers and their work and encourage readers to visit, or revisit, their novels and short stories.

Works Cited

Boland, Eavan. 1998. Interview by Eileen Battersby. *Irish Times,* Sept. 22, 14.
———. 1995. *Object Lessons: The Life of the Woman and the Poet in Our Time.* New York: Norton.
Bolger, Dermot. 1993. Introduction to the *Vintage Book of Contemporary Fiction,* i–xxviii. London: Random House.

Conlon, Evelyn. 1993. *Taking Scarlet as a Real Colour.* Belfast: Blackstaff.

Longley, Edna. 1994. *The Living Stream: Literature and Revisionism in Ireland.* Newcastle upon Tyne: Bloodaxe Books.

Meaney, Geraldine. 1997. "Territory and Transgression: History, Nationality and Sexuality in Kate O'Brien's Fiction." *Irish Journal of Feminist Studies* 2, no. 2 (winter): 77–92.

Ní Dhomhnaill, Nuala. 1999. "A Spectacular Flowering." *Irish Times,* 29 May, The Arts 4.

Tóibín, Colm. 1993. Introduction to *Soho Square 6: New Writing from Ireland,* 8–9. London: Bloomsbury Publishing.

Walsh, Caroline. 1993. Introduction to *Virgins and Hyacinths.* Dublin: Attic Press, 5–10.

Evelyn Conlon

Interviewed by

CAITRIONA MOLONEY

Claus Gretter—Frankfurt—Germany

BORN: Monaghan, Ireland, 1952
EDUCATED: Maynooth College (B.A. and H.Dip)
RESIDES: Dublin
GENRES: Fiction, drama, screenwriting, nonfiction
AWARDS: Arts Council Bursary for Literature (1988 and 1995), European Script Award (1989), Arts Council Award (1989), writer-in-residence for Dublin City Library and counties of Kilkenny, Cavan, and Limerick

Evelyn Conlon has had a long career as an activist, taking a major role in the feminist struggles of the recent past, including those over divorce, birth control, Mary Robinson's election, and equity for women workers. She has published two novels and four collections of short stories. Conlon's fiction exemplifies many of the dualities that trouble Irish culture and literature; having spent considerable time in America and Australia as a writer-in-residence at writer's institutes and retreats, she has a strong sense of how Irish identity is enmeshed in the diaspora. Conlon's fiction also addresses the complications imposed on identity by movement: the traditional exile and escape paradigm, as well as relatively new variables in the migration story, asylum-seeking refugees and returning Irish emigrants. For example, in her darkly humorous story of the pope's visit to Ireland in 1972, "The Park," from her collection Taking Scarlet

17

as a Real Colour, *Conlon makes clear the inevitability of escape to America. Immigration is juxtaposed with the ultimate confinement, prison, because those characters who do not immigrate are jailed for protesting the constraints of Irish Catholicism.*

Her epistolary novel, A Glassful of Letters, *counterpoints several elements of Irish identity: letters of a political prisoner, letters from a recent immigrant to New York, and letters from an Aer Lingus flight attendant who leaves and returns. Conlon's evolving "Irishness" is created on several stages simultaneously; the condition of being separate from, but connected to, an "other" identity seems to be the normal state of Irish life, on the island and in the diaspora.*

Conlon's fiction avoids didacticism because of her multifaceted style and her ironic wit. Reviewers say her prose is "clearsighted, rigorously unsentimental" and that it manhandles time (Gaisford 1993, 26). She is complemented for an Irish narrative voice "that laughs with a lump in its throat" (Potter 1993, 33). While decidedly a citizen of the Irish-American diaspora, she is not an apologist for all things American. Her new novel takes a hard look at capital punishment in the United States. Whether confinement is cultural, religious, domestic, or political, Conlon's sympathies are always with the prisoner. I interviewed Evelyn Conlon at her home in Dublin in the summer of 1998.

◆ ◆ ◆

MOLONEY: Your work challenges stereotypes about women and motherhood; what kind of reaction does that get in Ireland?

CONLON: One of the reactions that I've always got from my work has been, "Oh, there aren't people like this." I've always found that *totally* amusing because I'm surrounded by them. In *Taking Scarlet as a Real Colour,* I wrote, "Susan, do you think that we're ordinary women? A man ran the Late, Late one night and said that there were no ordinary women on the panel. He wanted an ordinary woman like his wife, but his wife is probably like us, Susan, and he doesn't know it." Very often when I'm being accused as a writer of having created characters that don't exist, it is because people haven't *seen* them, but they're there.

MOLONEY: *A Glassful of Letters* becomes controversial when the political prisoner, Senan, comes into the book; he changes everybody's lives. The novel could be seen as a nonpolitical book, but shifting the lens slightly, it's a very political book.

CONLON: Yes, it is. One time I was giving a class lecture and I was talking about writing letters. I have always been very interested in the notion of how people write letters, and if they write letters. I asked the people in this class if they wrote letters, and one man said "Yes." He wrote a letter once a week. And I said, "Extraordinary, to whom?"

"To my brother." "What an amazing relationship. Where's your brother?" And, of course, the minute I had asked the question, I knew that his brother had to be in prison. In no other way would a man write his brother every week. I began to think of prison as a place where the letter still lives; because the book is about letters, there had to be a prisoner.

MOLONEY: Have you been criticized for your position on the early release of political prisoners?

CONLON: Writers are pilloried for not dealing with an issue and if they deal with it, it's like it's put under a microscope to see which side they're taking, which has been very difficult because, surely the writer should be allowed to be ambivalent, because a character should be allowed to be ambivalent the way a lot of people are. So, what was valuable to me as a writer was that because *A Glassful of Letters* was in letter form, I was able to let people have the argument. Nobody, in fact, supports Senan's politics, even perhaps himself. The letters allow the others to have a discussion they could never have face to face. Connie and Bernard are more sympathetic to Senan's plight, while insisting they don't agree with his politics. Fergal is over the top anti-his politics, and anti-him, which may not just be about Connie writing to Senan. The fury may be about Connie writing to any man. He felt, in a way, that this prisoner was going to become a big part of her life, which he resented. So there was a personal thing going on there as well.

MOLONEY: Well, he was right. Senan was the good news and the bad news. *A Glassful of Letters* both explodes and reaffirms some stereotypes about romance; Helena, the Aer Lingus flight attendant, for example, picks her man for very down-to-earth reasons and then he turns out to be a great lover.

CONLON: I think she's just quite realistic and grateful about the fact that this man of whom she now thinks the world, a wonderful father, didn't bowl her over in the beginning. She admits that she did think about things like the fact that he would fit into her life and into her job, and that he wasn't over possessive, that he didn't need her all the time. I think what she does is pick him out. She does "fall in love" with him, as we call it. But people are encouraged to fall in love with people whom they see will be able to fit into their lives.

MOLONEY: One of the novel's many topics is the difference between friendship and romance.

CONLON: The book is about friendship between men and women. I do actually believe that men and women can be friends, although it's rare. If you look at the way romantic love is portrayed, there is an acceptance in some quarters that difference is a large component, that romantic love wouldn't be there without the clash, that sex depends on that edge of difference between people. Within homosexual relationships, the edge of difference is because the two people *are* different, but within heterosexual relations we depend on the fact that the other person is of the opposite sex in order to make that difference.

MOLONEY: A *Glassful of Letters* is written in an epistolary style with third-person narration. How did you decide on this structure and technique?

CONLON: I first became attracted by the notion of letters when I had read an Italian writer, Natalia Ginzberg's novel, called *The City and the House,* about two brothers. One of them has gone to America and the other is in Rome thinking of joining him. I fell in love with that novel and began to play around with the notion of letters. Then, I became very interested in the fact that letters are gone really, or are going. Now it's telephones, faxes, emails, whatever. None of those things are going to keep or people don't keep them. We don't print out our email, fax paper won't last, and letters are going. In "Petty Crime," a story in *Taking Scarlet as a Real Colour,* I say, "all children should have a letter from their father to their mother that they can find some day when they're rooting through boxes looking for something else."

MOLONEY: The epistolary style is only as interesting as its letter writers, and your book has a panoply of fully developed characters writing letters. Bernard, for example, is very complex. How did you develop Bernard's character? Does he come out of any previous work?

CONLON: No. But I thought of him first. I began to think about him when I was writing the story "The Un-deathing of Gertrude," where the widower Eddie McGivern is alone and thinking about his wife. And then I became interested in the notion of glass and people working with glass. So, in fact, the beginning of the book was him, really.

MOLONEY: Why did you decide to make Helena a flight attendant for Aer Lingus?

CONLON: Letters are associated with emigration, so I wanted somebody who was going to have to leave the country, but wasn't continuously away. So Helena was in and out, but was never away long enough to be an emigrant. She was out of the country often enough and on such a regular basis that it made her view things quite differently.

I also wanted a way to write about America. Those of us who have had aunts and uncles in America actually feel that America is just a part of Ireland. Not all the time, but we feel, for instance, familiar with the criticisms of America. And then, of course, we criticize America as if it's our own. And that's what makes us different from the majority of Americans, who don't like criticism.

MOLONEY: Is any one character privileged as the narrator of *A Glassful of Letters?*

CONLON: No, I don't think anybody's privileged. There are different views. Bernard is older, so there's a certain wisdom of age, and he mentions that at one stage about it being important, but other than that, nobody is privileged.

MOLONEY: Desmond, Connie's husband and Bernard's son, is a somewhat problematic character, isn't he?

CONLON: Desmond is a bit tongue in cheek, this idea that somebody would be fucked up because their parents loved each other too much. I mean everybody's going around talking about their parents not loving each other and not loving them. But here they were, this wonderful old couple who really loved each other and the son is there, and he is thoroughly fucked up.

MOLONEY: You wrote about motherhood in a book review in July, 1998, that "women were expected to make enormous sacrifices for the well-being of their children . . . the mother is also in charge of the child's emotional stability and psychological development . . . [and] driving their offspring towards intellectual and academic achievement" (18). Does the novel comment on motherhood through the two women characters, Connie and Helena?

CONLON: Well, they're very different kinds of mothers. One of them, Helena, very specifically says that she thanks God for the wisdom that came from nowhere. She knew to keep her job was the only way that she could have a decent relationship with her child. And she is also quite determined that she will never have more than one. Connie sort of slid into motherhood. There's a story about that in my first book, *My Head Is Opening,* called, "As Good a Reason as Any." I think society has a notion about why women have children. It is handy to believe that women really want to have children. Quite often women fall into it and then are so shocked by the implications of motherhood that they actually bury a lot of it, because if they don't bury it, it's very dangerous to their everyday living. Connie actually says things in those letters to Fergal that she would not say to Helena, another mother. Fergal is much more in tune with the difficulties that Connie is having as a mother than Helena.

MOLONEY: What are you working on now?

CONLON: Well, I'm getting together *Telling: New and Selected Short Stories,* which will be out in spring 2000. I'm now beginning another novel, as well.

MOLONEY: Do you feel like talking about the new novel?

CONLON: I shouldn't. But I have a fair idea of where it's going. One of the central themes is capital punishment. I've gone to the States and spent about three weeks doing a lot of research into capital punishment; then, sometime later, I shifted the story back to Ireland, although the American component is important. I'm now basing it on a man who was hanged here in the forties for the murder of a woman which he quite obviously did not commit. Some of it is based on him, but there will be an American component at some level, but, again, I don't *really* know yet. I'm going into this room for six months, and we'll see what happens.

In the new novel, the woman who was murdered was the sort of woman mentioned in *Taking Scarlet as a Real Colour.* She was a prostitute and had many children by different fathers from around the area. She was murdered and this man was set up. A solicitor has written a factual book, which gained very little currency or discussion. There should be a movement to have this man pardoned posthumously. When my book comes out there might be. The story is told through the eyes of a grandniece who comes across the facts after her parents have died, never having been told before.

MOLONEY: The title story of your collection of short stories, *Taking Scarlet as a Real Colour,* addresses the issues of sexuality and difference between men and women; why does that story have two titles?

CONLON: At the end of my first collection of short stories, *My Head Is Opening*, I had quite a political monologue. This woman sitting in a bar, speaking to a woman called Susan, letting off steam about everything. But when I went to do the story at the end of *Scarlet*, I very much wanted to write about women and literature, and the way their voices and lives are excluded from literature. I also wanted to write about women writing, particularly about sex. If a man writes about sex, it can be his imagination; if a woman writes about sex, nobody will believe that she hasn't had that experience. And, again, even if this man had sexual experience, that's okay, whereas it's not okay for a woman. So, I wanted to write about that difference, and it just came to me the way I would do that was to use the same monologue. In *Telling: New and Selected Short Stories* again I've used a monologue to Susan. The first one was, "Did you hear?" and then it was, "And also, Susan," and the third one is, "Furthermore, Susan."

MOLONEY: Who is Susan?

CONLON: The imaginary woman we need to address.

MOLONEY: I think an American audience needs some background to understand "Birth Certificates"; could you explain the history of adoption in Catholic Ireland? And how that relates to the story?

CONLON: "Birth Certificates" is based on the old notion of adoption in which the person—usually the single mother—was encouraged to give her child up, and she never saw that child again. In the story, a woman is helping children to find their natural mothers, and a young woman journalist is fascinated by what she's doing. The boyfriend is unusually negative and uncharacteristically extremely aggressive about this work and doesn't want her doing it. Eventually he admits that he has been adopted, and the twist in the tale is that they help him to find his mother, and it's the woman's mother as well. So, in fact, they're brother and sister, and they have been together as lovers.

MOLONEY: Do you think the Irish system of adoption has created situations like this in Ireland?

CONLON: Well, I think in a small place it could happen. Cousins, first cousins could certainly marry. We have now moved beyond that and the government actually pays people to do this work. Some part of my stories—very small parts—are actually based on things that did happen. One small piece in that story is a woman in a bed in the hospital, she's just had a baby, she's giving it up for adoption, she doesn't want to touch the baby then eventually she does, and then she won't leave it down.

And that actually happened. When I was having my second child, the young woman in the bed beside me was giving her child up for adoption, and I have never suffered so much as I did that five days being beside that woman. I thought it was unbelievable.

MOLONEY: By her parents?

CONLON: By her mother. Her father didn't know. She had been sent to Dublin, and this was all being done in absolute secrecy, and one can only presume that everybody's life was going to be hell if the father knew. It was just one of the most horrendous things I'd ever seen. It put me off adoption, I can tell you, for the rest of my life. Now, I know that there are other ways of doing it, but I found that too appalling. And it was cruelly contrasted by a woman in the bed opposite me, who was seventeen, having a baby, and her parents were going to rear that child as if it was their own, letting the child know that their daughter was the mother. It was just extraordinarily open. And that was happening six feet away from this unfortunate young woman, who was beside me.

MOLONEY: It's a Catholic issue isn't it, because abortion was illegal and a sin. Speaking of Catholicism, you are quite critical of the Catholic clergy in "The Last Confession." Why did you decide to narrate that from the brother's point of view?

CONLON: Because sometimes I love writing as a man. I have never had a brother myself, and perhaps I have a romanticized notion of what brothers would be like. Writing as the brother means that I sometimes feel that I can leave my own baggage behind me. He's sympathetic, and he loves his sister dearly.

MOLONEY: His sister's activities—seducing priests and then publishing the pictures in the newspaper—seem very radical. How would they have fit into the political climate of the seventies?

CONLON: Those of us who were involved in the feminist movement in Ireland in the 1970s were considered quite deranged. I remember the first time I spoke in public was in the Mansion House at the banning of *Spare Rib,* the London feminist magazine. An issue of it had been banned because it contained abortion information, and we had a public meeting, at which we sold copies. We were putting ourselves out there—to be arrested. We did things like stand at the top of Grafton Street and sell condoms. I had my name taken and was cautioned.

Now my male colleagues never had to do those things. They, of course, would say that I didn't have to do them either. I, however, feel that I did. I could not see my life as a writer divorced from my life as a citizen of this place, who wanted to shift it forward a bit. We all talk about Bishop Casey at the moment, but before the Bishop Casey thing broke there were numerous women in Ireland who could tell you about having been touched up by priests and whatever. And, in fact, there had been an article written a number of years before about a group of women sitting around one night, and there wasn't one among them who hadn't either had a date with a priest or been asked to go on a date by a priest, but it was the thing that nobody ever discussed. Anyway, I wrote "The Last Confession" and it was published in the *Sunday Tribune* before the Bishop Casey thing happened.

MOLONEY: How does that compare with feminism today?

CONLON: Well, there's this great tragic thing: young women don't want to know anything about feminism, and they think they have it all. They're in for some terrible shock ten years or more down the road. The feminist movement was very strong in the 1970s and early 1980s; there were also women who didn't want to have anything to do with it. What did we do? We wore dungarees. We didn't wear bras. All those wonderful stereotypes. And we hated men, supposedly.

I mean, the irony of all that was that among the feminist movement, many women were the first women to discuss having good sexual relationships with men. I mean, they were far more interested in the notion of the relationship with men than some of their nonfeminist sisters were. So, there was lots of stereotyping. But, one of the things that's different now is that a lot of the young women have got jobs, and other freedoms, as the result of those huge fights, but *they really* don't want to know that. And one of the reasons, of course, is that they don't want to think about the history of feminism, because they *want* to know that they've got their jobs on merit. They *have* got their jobs on merit, but the point about it is that without all the fighting that was done, they would *not* have got their jobs: merit or no.

MOLONEY: How did men fit into the feminist movement in those days?

CONLON: Well, certainly in the seventies when we worked within "women only groups" or, as I always said, "all women," there would have been some very supportive males in Ireland. Not a huge number, but very supportive—and let me say there were all the usual arguments that took place in the States as well, but they were quite more intense here, because of the size of the country. I remember when we had the first "Reclaim the Night March." Some of the men who were supportive were extraordinarily annoyed that they were not allowed on the March (the whole issue of the March being that it was about women being able to walk down the street on their own). It was quite difficult to get that across. You have some politicians now—mostly Labor Party politicians—claiming that they were active in feminist movements like the Divorce Campaign when they weren't. They were not. They ran a mile, but did eventually come on board. But it's the usual thing: the politicians take over what actually happened, when the fighting is done, and don't give credit where it is due.

MOLONEY: How do you see feminism and postcolonialism intersecting?

CONLON: The "postcolonial people" have never dealt with the issue of women. They may claim that they understand the issue of women, but that's because they are good at reading the tracts; they do a quick read over and say that they know it. They don't. In fact, they know less about how women are viewing the world than the so-called average man.

MOLONEY: Is there a sense in which "Irishness" is being overdetermined in the culture for export as a commodity? Commodified in a way that fits some stereotypes? Is that connected to postcolonialism?

CONLON: Oh, you could talk about that all night. *Yes.* It's at times extraordinarily gauche. And yet in a way, the postcolonialists would say that this is an automatic and inevitable result of having doffed your cap and felt subservient for all those years, and then suddenly coming into one's own, and that everything that happens which is positive—like football—is celebrated; it doesn't have to be literature. It doesn't have to be dance. It's anything that is asserting one's final adulthood. And, in a way, I accept that. Jamaica Kincaid's essay "A Very Small Place" looks at what happens when colonizers leave. In her mind the class of people who take over are the people who have allied themselves closest with the colonizers. I think, in a way, Ireland is in extraordinary turmoil at the moment. On the one hand being very positive and on the other quite negative.

One of the things that's going to be very *interesting* over the next few years is the whole issue of racism against asylum-seeking refugees coming in for the first time; Ireland is doing well economically, and people don't want to share it, but if they want to share it with anybody, they want Irish people to come back home. Some Irish people when they went to other places have been extraordinarily racist. At home in Ireland we have not had to deal with that. We were never a colonizer, so therefore we didn't have large numbers of people outside the Irish tradition owning Irish passports. We certainly didn't have people who weren't white coming to Ireland; in fact no one came, because why *would* you be coming to Ireland? There was no work. Irish people were *leaving*. But now that's changed, and for the first time we will actually have to examine *how* we behaved in other countries.

MOLONEY: You say Ireland was never a colonizer, but some colonized people, specifically Nigerians, feel they were colonized by the Irish in the English colonial service and in the Catholic missions.

CONLON: Not quite true, because the number of Irish people who had jobs in the colonial administration was minimal. But, I would say that they have a point with reference to the missions. Being a missionary is in a sense being a colonizer; you essentially feel that your way of life is better than the locals. But it's not in another way, because you don't own the land of the colonized. The colonizer *owns* the country, and *owns* the wealth, and *owns* whatever, whereas the missionary doesn't. But what the old-fashioned missionary *did* do was destroy the beliefs of the indigenous population.

MOLONEY: Speaking of the artificial construction of ideological difference, what do you think about the notion of "women's writing"?

CONLON: They don't talk about men's writing. They talk about writing and they talk about women's writing. In other words, there's writing. There's *real writing* and there's women's writing. I'm exhausted by it. I just feel that women read men. Women are much more educated and precise readers. They know the writer is a man or a woman. They read it. Men don't want to read women, because they actually don't want to know how they view the world—obviously some men. Everything I say about men, it's *some* men, but on an off day, I mean almost all of them. Certainly among academics. Many of them do not want to read women or know what they have to say. They obviously do not want to be informed by them, and they don't want their education to be furthered by them, unfortunately. Because, if they did, they'd be out there reading and teaching them. And I think that it's not just the women writers who suffer as a result of this.

MOLONEY: I recently listened to a lecture by a very big name in the Irish studies literary critical establishment, and afterward in the questioning he admitted that he didn't know any contemporary women writers in Ireland. Your name was mentioned, and Jennifer Johnston's, and several others, and he said, "I don't know any of those names." I don't think it was a problem for him; he wasn't going to run right out and buy those women and read them.

CONLON: And Ireland is particularly bad for that. I think the students, both male and female, suffer all the time when they do not examine the work of a woman. You know, in America, the place is big enough for a certain enthusiasm. Certainly at times within Ireland as a woman writer, you think: "How did I ever let myself stay here?" And a lot of women leave. Julia O'Faolain's work is never spoken about here or the work of Leland Bardwell. When some of the men will include women's work, they only include a narrow type of work by women to make absolutely sure that they're not touching any of the work that raises questions about themselves.

In Ireland, things have changed so enormously in some ways, and yet other things stay the same. I remember when Mary Robinson was elected president, many, many BBC programs were being done on her and on practically all of them, there were four men. On some of them, there were three men and one woman—and I really have to say it—not the best women. But, you know, the world is a small enough place for gossip: a man, who's a friend of mine, overheard one of the cultural "gurus" in Ireland being asked in a BBC studio, "what Irish women would discuss such and such," and he said, "There aren't any." The BBC did not go out and look for Irish women to discuss the issue. They took the usual stable of men, with one glorious exception: I know that Paul Durcan raised the question about one program because there weren't enough women on it. There may have been other exceptions, but essentially the BBC and the Irish men certainly didn't look for the women; the Irish women were a well-kept secret. Everybody managed to avoid the whole notion of what the feminist movement had been in Ireland. How much Mary Robinson had been absolutely encouraged by feminists to live the life that she had lived, to work the way that she had worked. I'm not saying that she was dependent upon feminism, but at a certain point in her life, certainly at the beginning of her career, that's where she got her moral support. So that when she was elected, it's amazing that this was never discussed.

MOLONEY: Could it be that an early feminist background can be a liability later on in a successful career? Has that been the case with your first novel, *Stars in the Daytime,* which was published by Women's Press?

CONLON: But this is the old question, you know. It's the old question, and one of the terrible things is that essentially after a certain length of time, women writers wanted to leave the feminist presses and go into the mainstream. There was more money, and they were tired of being branded, and they were tired of not getting reviews because they had been published by a women's press. And yet, they would never have got their work started if the women's presses hadn't published them, because the men's presses—which is exactly what they were—would never have published women. So, it's one of those dilemmas, like people not wanting to say that they're a feminist writer. I don't think you can be a "feminist" writer, I think you're a writer. I am a writer who is a feminist. And, my consciousness as a feminist affects the sort of things that I enjoy writing about.

Courtesy of Edmund Ross, Dublin, Ireland

Catherine Dunne

Interviewed by

HELEN THOMPSON

BORN: Dublin, 1954
EDUCATED: Trinity College, Dublin
RESIDES: Dublin
GENRES: Fiction, nonfiction, poetry
AWARDS: Short-listed for Bancarella Italian Booksellers' Prize (1999), short-listed for Kerry Ingredients Book of the Year Award (1998)

Catherine Dunne has lived in the same Dublin suburb all of her life. A schoolteacher by profession, she has published four novels, all of which have been well received. Dunne has also been active politically in the abortion and divorce referendums.

Like her favorite writer, Jane Austen, Dunne writes about small enclosed worlds that constitute domesticity. She also situates her writing within the context of contemporary Ireland, a rapidly changing culture and one in which women have been able to adopt increasingly more diverse roles, making her version of the domestic tradition one that is highly politicized. While her stories are grounded in the realities of Irish life, she does experiment with form. For example, in The Walled Garden *she blends epistolary form with conventional narrative; in* In the Beginning *she recreates the book of Genesis; and in* A Name for Himself, *she writes from the perspective of an emotionally damaged man who becomes abusive and violent toward his wife.*

Particularly, her novels reflect Ireland's growth in the last thirty years: its new affluence, its openness to discussion of social problems, its painful revelations of abuse and dysfunction, and its loosening ties between church and state. For example, In the Beginning *(1997) responds to and endorses the success of the 1995 divorce referendum. Her work also explores the problems that arise from this liberalization of the culture, the limited coping mechanisms for change, and the need for the Irish national identity to mature.*

Dunne's female characters exist within traditional roles of wife and mother but are played out in untraditional ways. For example, Alice, in The Walled Garden *(2000), is an independent single mother who chooses not to remarry after the death of her husband. The novel refutes the notion that the feminist movement since the 1960s has been solely responsible for imbuing women with agency and self-direction.*

Catherine Dunne is currently on leave from her teaching profession. Her latest novel, Another Kind of Life, *was published in 2002. I interviewed her at her home (also the birthplace of Bram Stoker) in Dublin.*

•   •   •

THOMPSON: How does your generation, coming of age in the 1970s, differ from preceding ones?

DUNNE: I think we were the first generation of girls who saw ourselves going on to university. Girls three or four years before that, even though so-called middle class, couldn't. Girls had been expected to finish school, do a commercial course—typing and shorthand—and get a job. So our generation started to replace that mold.

THOMPSON: Were you benefiting from the women's movement?

DUNNE: I think it was in 1971, my penultimate year, and feminism had just exploded. In one of the first battles we put up a poster for a debate about burning your bra and we got into severe trouble with the nuns. One didn't mention that one wore a bra. So feminism was slowly filtering down even to a very small community on the north side of Dublin. We missed the 1960s because we were too young, but we hit the very early 1970s, which was our blossoming time.

THOMPSON: So you didn't consider yourselves trailblazers?

DUNNE: We were too young to be involved in the contraceptive train, as it was called, along with Nell McCafferty and all of the front line feminists who brought condoms down from Belfast. But we gained from it. Our generation had access to contraception, which definitely gave us an enormous amount of control over our lives.

THOMPSON: How accessible was contraception?

DUNNE: Not freely available, but you could find your way to getting it when you needed it, and it made a huge difference. Women who are three or four years older than me had their first babies when they were in their early twenties. But, girls of my generation who have been to school and colleges didn't have babies until our late twenties or thirties. And while an incredibly difficult thing to juggle career and family, most of us did it through gritted teeth because we were damned if we were going to give this up!

THOMPSON: How would you define your feminism?

DUNNE: For me, feminism is recognizing that the world in very subtle ways is not the same for women as for men, but accepting that each half of the human race should have the same rights as the other. I wonder sometimes about people who say the battle has been won and now it's the men's turn. That's crap. However, little things have changed, but sadly, men have disimproved.

THOMPSON: Was your first novel, *In the Beginning,* inspired by the divorce referendums?

DUNNE: In 1986, Dennis, my husband, and I were doing pro-divorce referendum work. I was struck to my core at people's stories about how relationships had failed, the struggles to maintain a ridiculous pretense that everything was okay, or to separate and put up with public opprobrium. What struck me was all these stories and people were "ordinary," the same story repeated over again.

Out of that experience of that campaign I came up with four stories of four friends, which was far too ambitious. I got it to about forty thousand words and then I threw it in the bin. It was too wide a canvas.

THOMPSON: How did it find shape?

DUNNE: In 1993, about three years after I won a poetry competition, I worked really hard on Rose's story. I took every spare minute and it became an obsession. I took a career break in 1995 and ironically by the time the break started, the first draft was finished.

THOMPSON: What poetry competition did you win?

DUNNE: I won third prize in a poetry competition for the Gerard Manley Hopkins Summer School. It was a watershed, the first time anything I'd written had been publicly acknowledged.

THOMPSON: Did you not send out your work at all before that?

DUNNE: I used to send in short stories on a regular basis to David Marcus, who wrote an Irish writing page in the *Irish Press*. Although he didn't publish them, he'd send them back always with comments and that feedback was enough.

THOMPSON: How did *In the Beginning* come to be published?

DUNNE: Roddy Doyle, who was a colleague at work, said he'd like to see the manuscript; he thought it was terrific and recommended his publisher look at it. Jonathan Cape in London took it.

THOMPSON: Tell me about the structure of *In the Beginning*.

DUNNE: Well, my motivation was for once I wanted to see a female God! I just thought it would be an interesting idea to mirror the creation of the world in the creation of a new space after the old structure of the family has broken down. So the seven-day metaphor was the change from the old male God into the female God.

THOMPSON: Rose's journey, just making it from one day to the next, is very real.

DUNNE: There's probably not as much depth and complexity to her character as I would have liked. I'd probably write a different book now if I were to go back and do it.

THOMPSON: I think we see Ben only at his worst, don't we?

DUNNE: I got a bit of flack over Ben for not being an entirely sympathetic male character. The book was deliberately entitled *In the Beginning,* and the only reason the scenes from the marriage are there is to show why it has come to an end, why a new beginning is necessary. When the crisis happens—not the ending of the marriage but the way in which it ended—he takes away his wife's choices and power and control. Unfortunately, I have seen men behave like that.

THOMPSON: Does Rose blame herself?

DUNNE: In the flashbacks I wanted it to be perfectly obvious that the marriage probably hadn't existed for quite some time, a phenomenon I had seen with many friends. When the break-up happened, the marriage had been deteriorating for so long that it was a relief that it was over. The recovery time was astonishingly quick except for the guilt, which was focused on children, the guilt that goes with any sort of major failure in your life.

THOMPSON: Is this Catholic guilt?

DUNNE: Her guilt isn't "Catholic guilt" precisely because of the contemporary time when the book is set. I get tired of reading the rural Irish mother who's basically paralyzed by guilt, the martyr. That stereotype doesn't accurately reflect the experience of a huge proportion of Irish women.

THOMPSON: Has this guilt evaporated from the Irish psyche?

DUNNE: The church does not have the authority, and its iron grip is relaxing, even in rural areas where it would be much more conservative. There have been so many cases of child abuse and other appalling behavior that I don't think the church will ever be the same again. Church and state are not separated to nearly the degree that they need to be, but they are separating psychologically in people's minds. I think people don't take as much crap as they were fed.

THOMPSON: So times are better for women?

DUNNE: Yes, but the battle still remaining to be fought is access to abortion or at least the right to choose. People still seem to be quite comfortable exporting the problem. Five thousand women every year travel to anywhere else rather than here for abortions.

THOMPSON: Where do you stand?

DUNNE: I don't think abortion is a good thing, and it astonishes me that people think if we have abortion everyone will want one, as though it's some nice way to spend a free weekend. I won't even call it a necessary evil, but it's certainly a necessary process.

THOMPSON: How much of a difference would it make if abortion became legal?

DUNNE: I'm sure some people would still prefer the anonymity of England. But not everyone rushed out to get a divorce as soon as it was available, and I can't see legalization encouraging people to have abortions who wouldn't have already gone to England. It means more honesty in the situation, and the people who are traumatized enough can have their needs looked after at home rather than exporting the problem.

THOMPSON: Yes, it is also rather hypocritical.

DUNNE: One of the hypocrisies I find so hard to handle is that the "child-centered" culture—particularly now when there's not nearly the same sort of stigma attached to having a child out of wedlock—seems to extend only to the unborn, not to children in institutions run by the church and paid for by the state who suffered awful abuse at the hands of their guardians.

THOMPSON: Is this kind of abuse what inspired you to write *A Name for Himself?*

DUNNE: I was trying to subvert the reader's expectations and some people were disappointed that it was not Rose Part Two. And we all knew families like young Farrell's; they were a big portion in every community and as representative as the happy church-going mother and devoted father.

THOMPSON: Would you say that also, in light of these abuse stories surfacing, you are also exposing the underside of Irish masculinity?

DUNNE: I think people looking in from the outside see people as smiling and reciting of poems at the drop of a hat, all these stereotypes. There's also truth to the darker bits which people aren't too keen to explore.

THOMPSON: Are we to sympathize with Farrell?

DUNNE: I wanted to look at the dark side, over a man's shoulder so that we get his view of the universe. I wanted to make him a sympathetic character, but I wanted there to be a point where the reader suddenly sat back and realized that Farrell was beginning to inhabit a completely different reality. Some critics have called it a descent into madness, but I'm not interested in pinning it down. I was interested in looking at how people who appear so ordinary on the outside, and who appear to have everything sorted out, but you don't know what is actually going on behind that ordinary face.

THOMPSON: Is it dysfunction or is it to do with the way men are socialized within the family?

DUNNE: One of the differences between men and women is this lack of emotional vocabulary. When things get to the really unbearable pitch, women have a bottle of wine with a girlfriend and let it all out and we're fine. Men don't seem to have that kind of mechanism. So for Farrell, the lack of an emotional vocabulary and the violence of the family upbringing converge in his character and spiral out of control. But again, that spiraling takes place beneath a completely ordinary facade.

THOMPSON: Can you explain how you shaped Grace's character?

DUNNE: No matter how afraid she was, and even though it was a tremendous struggle for her to escape from her father and husband, she did it; she did find her strength, and she did have art college to go back to. That's a testament to the kind of growth I have seen women capable of in the most appalling circumstances.

THOMPSON: What was your inspiration for Grace?

DUNNE: This goes back to my experience teaching school. There are many families that have seven or eight children, and in some cases the father is not up to much. Those kids would arrive at school everyday darned and patched, the clothes perfect, even though there was no money. There was a huge investment by the mother. Now I have only one son and it's a struggle enough. Anybody who manages to survive with seven or eight with no back up from the other parent and turns out great kids, and manages [as] well to be self-actualizing in as much as their circumstances allow them, I just admire them enormously.

THOMPSON: Farrell's violence is a part of the political violence, and also he mentions feeling close to the border. Is there a connection here between family and the "Troubles"?

DUNNE: He was working in Dundalk, a very Republican town close to the border where access to guns would be easier than in Dublin. Also I wanted to make the point that for many people here it doesn't matter how close or how distant they were from the border, it hasn't touched their lives at all. And that to me is sad.

THOMPSON: Farrell hasn't been touched by the Troubles?

DUNNE: Well, you've got the armchair nationalists who'll treat you to political discussions in the pub; you've people who do work committedly for change and for cross-border cooperation; and then you've people for whom the Troubles mightn't be happening at all, who have come to the point where they don't want to know about it because it's been going on so long, it's so appalling to contemplate, the suffering has been so acute, and it has been on our television screens night after night after night. And Farrell is one of those.

THOMPSON: Do you think it is important to remember?

DUNNE: I think so, yes. We are the product of thousands of years of tradition; in order to embrace change you don't need to throw all of that away. I was actually remembering some appalling poetry I wrote when I was twelve for the fiftieth celebration of the Easter Rising here in 1966. Nationalist fervor was everywhere. Everyone was caught up in this whole romantic celebration of Ireland's struggle for freedom, seen through rose-tinted spectacles and good equals Irish and bad equals British. The other bits of Ireland were nicely glossed over by this romantic celebration of brave heroes. Clinging to an idealized version of the past makes it easy to blame someone else. The more I think about it, the more I realize we are in a very painful process of growing up.

THOMPSON: How do you think Ireland will come of age?

DUNNE: We have all of the difficulties that go along with being a colony and victims of imperialism and the difficulties of learning how to self-govern. We are what we are, warts and all, and certainly we need to remember, but not to remember in order to hold grudges.

THOMPSON: In some ways tourism, which has helped to globalize Ireland, has also led to perpetuated myths of Irishness.

DUNNE: I sometimes feel very sorry for tourists coming here. They will land somewhere notoriously unfriendly and are so deeply shocked that they go away thinking this isn't the Ireland they thought existed. The burden for Irish people is this reputation of Ireland as virtuous, saintly, scholarly, family oriented, and all this stuff and reality, of course, is quite different.

THOMPSON: How prevalent now are images of Ireland as a woman?

DUNNE: I really have to think about that, which in a way answers your question. All the images of Ireland as woman come from the past—the bardic tradition where Ireland was a woman who had to be wooed and won; Ireland as mother, Caithleen Ní Houlihan, who changes from hag to radiant queen once young men die for her in political insurrection. Side by side with passive images of the blonde, lovely *speirbhean* of eighteenth-century Gaelic poetry, we have the warrior queen Maeve, the pirate Grace O'Malley, and the enigmatic Deirdre of the Sorrows. The more active and forceful icons, however, tended to be overshadowed by the passive, mournful, suffering feminine figure. In fact, the Celtic temperament tended to be equated with the feminine principle—in other words, unworthy of, and unsuitable for, self-government! A useful little ploy for the colonizer, I suppose!

THOMPSON: Do these images still have currency?

DUNNE: Today, the national TV's symbol for the millennium was an ethereal, Enya-like figure, rising mystically from the sea. The Tourist Board used the voice of Dolores O'Riordan from the Cranberries to support one of its most recent campaigns, but really the most predominant image of Ireland is now that of the dreaded "Celtic Tiger." The Tiger—an image many of us are getting heartily sick of—is aggressive, technological, forward looking, entrepreneurial, and rich. It has pretty sharp claws, too, and isn't the best at looking out for its weaker cubs.

THOMPSON: What strikes me as a common thread between your three novels is a highly politicized domestic tradition.

DUNNE: Well certainly I've always had a fascination with the ordinary. *In the Beginning* grew out of the politicization of ordinary grief and ordinary pain; and in *A Name for Himself* I also have a natural affinity with the underdog; and in *The Walled Garden* it is the different expectations between mothers and daughters. My fascination with domestic details comes from the first author I really fell in love with: Jane Austen. So much of a society is reflected in the claustrophobia of family relationships going through conflict. So, while you don't set out to write about politics, if you're dealing with people obviously they have to reflect the society they come from, even if you reject that society.

THOMPSON: Edna O'Brien said the same thing when I asked her about her work.

DUNNE: I don't think you can write about people without having political concerns. I think the mother in *The Walled Garden* might be unusual, as probably my own mother was in that generation. Alice's being left a widow heightens the realization that women as well as men need to be economically independent, a reflection of what my generation is realizing much more profoundly than generations before us.

THOMPSON: Especially with the success of the 1995 divorce referendum.

DUNNE: No matter how bad marriages were people stuck together and that just doesn't happen anymore. Some people say that society is collapsing, but I say it always was. People collapsed together under the same roof rather than separating and setting up on their own.

THOMPSON: Yet, the novel seems more focused on Alice's story.

DUNNE: Beth actually started off as my main character. I wanted her to be liberated, making her own way, bringing up a child on her own, and so on. I also wanted her to have a complex relationship with her mother, which again was very typical of my generation. But Alice took over and she elbowed Beth out of the way completely. And when I saw what was happening, I thought, why wouldn't the older woman be the stronger one? It's simplistic to think we're the generation with the strength; older women have managed to overcome their circumstances and should be admired because they succeeded in a society which was far less tolerant.

THOMPSON: How was your mother atypical of her generation?

DUNNE: I remember people turning around in astonishment as my mother and her two sisters—women in their late sixties—walked into a fund-raising party in 1983 for the first abortion referendum. People assumed that if your mother's generation had a take on this particular issue it would be to vote no. My mother and her sisters knew it's not as simple as that.

THOMPSON: You didn't think it strange that they were politically active?

DUNNE: Not at the time, and they were not highly politicized women. Their lives were quite traditional, but they thought for themselves and they didn't swallow the stuff that was fed them. They would have all left school very early and been working in shops from the time they were fourteen or fifteen, but they never lost interest in the issues of the day. They were quite happy to stand up and be counted on issues that their peers would not have approved of.

THOMPSON: While Farrell in *A Name for Himself* can't get away from his past and it damages him, for Alice and Beth the past heals and brings them together.

DUNNE: I think the difference, again, is emotional articulacy. Farrell is unable to discuss his past—he can't come to terms with it, and history for him is crippling. With Beth, it is forced upon her through the silent conversation. Articulating the difficulties and the hurts helps people come to terms with their history. Your history doesn't have to be a prison.

THOMPSON: As you created characters in *The Walled Garden,* did you try to balance sympathetic male and female characters?

DUNNE: I didn't do it to balance them. Olive just grew as she was. She was quite a minor character to start with and then she got under my skin and took on her own momentum. It's well that she balances Ben in that she is as nasty as he was, and yet I hope I create in her an equally realistic picture. I suppose I indulged the nastiness in the character of Olive; she doesn't seem to have any redeeming features. I cannot stand the idea of a person being ambitious for anybody else. Her upper-middle-class desires are only fulfilled through her husband. She buys into the whole philosophy that the man's job is the important one and women can bask in the reflected glory, which I don't admire.

THOMPSON: That attitude still has widespread currency and is a problem even for women with careers.

DUNNE: The lasting inequality of household management being women's responsibility is a problem. I think we bring some of it on ourselves when we accept a responsibility nobody else expects of us. I'm trying to learn how to negotiate my way around it to realize that if the shopping isn't done or meals haven't been prepared, nobody is going to be offended with me. It's a process of learning my way out of those old ways. I remember Mary Morrissy talking about this at one stage. She said for no discernible obvious reason women start later in terms of writing than men do. Not just women who have children, either; it's all women. I think women allow themselves to be distracted more than men do. The temptation that sometimes cleaning the toilet is infinitely preferable to sitting down to the terrible blank screen exists.

THOMPSON: What about inequalities in publishing?

DUNNE: I think probably in many ways, the writing business is a pretty equal one. If the manuscript is good, as a particular publisher defines it for their particular market, then it's good and the sex of the writer doesn't make that much of a difference. But in terms of carving the space out of the universe, it is far more difficult for women.

THOMPSON: Certainly carving out a space in Irish letters is tough. What do you think about the *Field Day Anthology*?

DUNNE: Half an answer would be I'm waiting to see how volume 4 will attempt to right the wrongs of volumes 1, 2, and 3. The other half is it should never have happened in the first place, that so many women writers through the centuries were either ignored or had their work considerably underrepresented. I remember the lively public controversy at the time of publication, and I imagine that the debate is far from over. It seems that writing, like so many other areas of life, is not a level playing field. I was recently fascinated by an American academic's work in examining the critical response to Seamus Heaney and Eavan Boland's work, at a time when their careers were at a very similar stage. Heaney was lauded for his manly imagery—twelve different words for soil and associated implements! Boland was harshly criticized for all the different words she used for fabric—too trivial, too domestic! Too female? I believe that academic publications such as *The Field Day Anthology* have a duty to challenge established assumptions, not perpetuate them. One of these comfortable assumptions seems to be that women's work is not as weighty or as significant as men's. In that sense, I feel that the *Anthology* has been another opportunity missed.

THOMPSON: Who do you like to read?

DUNNE: I have so many favorites that that is a very difficult question to answer! In terms of influence, Margaret Atwood was a woman whose work I read at just the right time for me—she had an enormous impact. So did Jane Austen. Anne Tyler, Roddy Doyle, Carol Shields, John Irving, Emma Donoghue, Deirdre Madden—just to mention the top layer of my bedside table! Also recent favorites include Suzanne Beirne, Jay McInerney, and Nicola Barker. I couldn't possibly draw up any sort of definitive list—and that's the joy of reading, for me, the constant discovery of other voices, other stories. However, I try not to read contemporary fiction when I'm writing, because I'm terrified that someone else's words will leach onto my page.

Miriam Dunne

Interviewed by

HELEN THOMPSON

BORN: Dublin
RESIDES: Sherkin Island, County Cork, Ireland
WORKS: Writer and silversmith
GENRES: Fiction, poetry, children's stories, articles

Miriam Dunne was born and raised in Dublin, and after living in London and almost moving to New York, she now lives on a small island in County Cork. She started writing in London after trying a variety of night classes and finally ending up in a writer's workshop. Her first novel, Blessed Art Thou a Monk Swimming, *was published in 1997.*

Dunne's novel follows a tradition where the difficulties of an Irish childhood are humorously tackled, surmounted, and left behind, usually by emigrating. Anne Haverty says that Dunne's novel is "a spirited reprise of early Edna O'Brien" (1997, 37). Indeed, her protagonist, Marian, is reminiscent of O'Brien's Caithleen (from The Country Girls Trilogy*) in that they are both naïve in a world that is rigidly against any form of female self-expression and self-knowledge.*

Yet Marian has far more will than Caithleen. Unlike her predecessor, she works against her disinterested parents to educate herself, to learn about sex, and to leave Ireland. Further, she is less guilt-ridden than Caithleen.

Dunne has a polished wit. The pathos created by the appalling con-

ditions in which Marian lives is softened by often grotesque humor. For example, Marian's gullibility in believing that the secrets of sex exist in the Hail Mary ridicule her shameful lack of knowledge, as does her confession that she believes men have white periods and women have red ones. The humor does more, however, than lighten Marian's load; it also critiques a culture that allows young girls to be so utterly unprepared for the roles they are socialized into. Hence, Dunne's humor does what Theresa O'Connor recognizes as a hallmark of the Irish woman writer's comic vision, she "engages in witty negotiation with established patriarchal, colonial, and nationalist orthodoxies" (1996, 4).

She is presently working on some short stories and a sequel to her first novel, which will chronicle Marian's further adventures in London. I interviewed Miriam Dunne during the Irish Women Writers Conference in Dublin.

◆　◆　◆

THOMPSON: Are you related to Catherine Dunne?

DUNNE: No. The name Dunne is the Irish word for brown and is as common in Ireland as Brown is in England or the United States.

THOMPSON: How did you come to be living on Sherkin Island?

DUNNE: I needed to get away from London; also it is a very economical place to live with few distractions.

THOMPSON: What is it like living there?

DUNNE: It's remote, beautiful, wild, a good place to work, especially in winter when there are no distractions.

THOMPSON: You told me you live in quite an old house.

DUNNE: The house is over two hundred years old. It was built by the British when they were expecting a Napoleonic invasion. When we came first there was no road up to the house, no water or electricity.

THOMPSON: Do you think you'll stay there?

DUNNE: That's a bit like asking me will I stay with my family. The island is home. It's the longest I've ever been anywhere. In the past for economic reasons we had to divide our time between London and the island. This went on for twenty-six years. Now it's a relief to be in the one place. However I wouldn't mind a base on the mainland. With the last ferry at 5:30 in the winter, it'd be nice to stay out now and again without having to stay with friends.

THOMPSON: But you were brought up in Dublin?

DUNNE: Dublin suburbs at the foot of the Wicklow Mountains.

THOMPSON: Are you Catholic?

DUNNE: I was brought up a Catholic. I went to a convent boarding school. I wasn't expected to go on to university; you had to be exceptionally bright for that if you were a girl. The money was for the boys as the future breadwinners. In those days girls generally stopped working when they got married. Civil servants were required to.

THOMPSON: Did you find Catholicism oppressive?

DUNNE: England's colonization ended two or three generations ago. Since then we've been trying to shake off another form of colonization, the Catholic Church, which has had a far more damaging effect on Irish society and culture.

THOMPSON: So Catholicism has been a more powerful and oppressive force in Ireland than the British?

DUNNE: The only enduring legacy of the English, as in America, is their language, which has given Irish writers instant access to the world stage. It would be difficult to imagine Joyce, for example, writing *Ulysses* within the confines of a native Irish language. And, perversely, it has been its success on the universal stage that has given present-day Ireland its renewed sense of nationhood and self-confidence.

THOMPSON: What was it like for you going to a convent school?

DUNNE: I was a bit like Marian in that I was expelled from several schools, for something trivial like complaining about the food. I was doing it on behalf of my class. I was a "disruptive influence," which was a cover for not achieving academically. I thought I was dumb, but really I was disturbed. I came from a dysfunctional family. The obvious next question for you to ask me is why my family was dysfunctional, but I don't want to go into that.

THOMPSON: What were your parents like?

DUNNE: My mother was a frustrated housewife. My father dealt in antiques. They seemed ancient to me. The gap between the generations then was much greater. My parents married late and they had me in their forties. My mother loved playing the piano and dressmaking. She was always mourning her lost youth and how she could have married someone much better than my father. My father worked six days a week and he didn't get home till eight at night trying to make enough money to keep us all going, so I hardly ever saw him.

THOMPSON: Did you have postsecondary education?

DUNNE: No college, apart from endless night classes in London for mature students. Reading was my education.

THOMPSON: What did you take night classes in?

DUNNE: I took night classes everywhere in almost everything.

THOMPSON: Did you work while you were in London?

DUNNE: Temporary jobs to make money.

THOMPSON: What does Syd, your husband, do?

DUNNE: Playwright and architect.

THOMPSON: Which one did he pursue in London?

DUNNE: Playwriting with architecture when royalties were scarce.

THOMPSON: What's the writing process like for you?

DUNNE: I write everything down in longhand first, then if it's any good I'll type it up. I stop working on it when I'm not improving it anymore but only making it worse.

THOMPSON: Do you have difficulty getting started?

DUNNE: I have to sit down everyday to see if there's anything coming in. There's always something, or you can improve on work done the day before. The sleeping process helps somehow; I work things out in my unconscious. I met a writer once who said she had to have two glasses of wine before she could get started, which would be disastrous for me.

THOMPSON: What's it like working at home?

DUNNE: It's difficult. There are so many distractions. I don't know why but people tend not to take your work as seriously as they would if you worked away from home. The obvious solution would be to have somewhere to write outside the home. Sometimes I borrow a friend's house when they're away if I'm desperate.

THOMPSON: What are the ages of your children?

DUNNE: Eighteen, twenty-seven, and thirty-two.

THOMPSON: You must have found it difficult with three children.

DUNNE: Yes, but then I had them at five- and nine-year intervals. I got such a shock with the first one it took me five years to get over it. I didn't realize it would be a twenty-four hour a day responsibility. When I had the second it wasn't so bad. It was difficult though; sometimes I had to force myself to work. I remember my youngest putting his hand under the door and waving it round and wriggling it. I was terrified he'd get stuck but I was determined not to go to him. Needless to say I didn't get much work done.

THOMPSON: When we set up the interview on the phone, you mentioned something about Edna O'Brien. You said that she got rid of all of her emotional entanglements in order to write. What did you mean?

DUNNE: At first it used to irritate me that she had all these doomed relationships that she appeared to wallow in. I thought maybe she was doing it to use as material for her writing rather than getting stuck in the one relationship. But on reflection I think her actions are based on the blueprints she had with her parents, especially her father. I think her emotional entanglements were getting in the way. They were too disruptive and she couldn't sustain a relationship; she probably found there were more emotional returns from writing about them.

THOMPSON: Do you have to relinquish temporarily the part of yourself as a mother and a nurturer in order to write?

DUNNE: Yes, but if you have a young child it's impossible to shut off completely. A part of you is always tuned in to listen out for any danger. Though I remember my mother-in-law, a musician, one of the rare women who worked in those days, telling me she was going to rehearsal one day on the bus, when she saw my husband, a boy of six, belting into town on his bicycle. She was so afraid of being late for work and losing her job that she didn't do anything about it. She said she'd carry the guilt to her grave.

THOMPSON: Do you think women today have to be less single-minded?

DUNNE: Yes, my generation, and the generations that came before. But my daughter's generation is a lot more focused. They have more choices than we had. They can conceive and rear children on their own. They don't have to get married. They don't need men to father their children.

THOMPSON: Did your husband, Syd, ignore fingers under the door when he was writing?

DUNNE: Yes, and I admired him for it. I think it's wonderful to be so immersed in work that it takes you over completely. I can do that now, but when I was younger I felt totally inadequate. I thought Syd had all the talent and I'd help him by looking after the kids, etc., so he could get on with it. But that's ridiculous, a total cop out on my part.

THOMPSON: Because of domestic concerns, being a full-time writer seems more difficult for a woman.

DUNNE: I think things are getting better for women. They have more control over their lives because of better child-care facilities and more flexibility in the workplace. Women can choose now whether or not to have children, and how many and when. Given that Jane Austen died at the age of forty-two, one wonders how she would have fared as a writer if she hadn't broken off her engagement to Bigg-Withers, who went on to marry someone else and had ten children. Can you imagine what it must have been like in those days? Every time you had sex you could get pregnant.

THOMPSON: So it's better for women in Ireland now?

DUNNE: Yes, for two reasons. The decline of the Catholic Church and in particular its perception of sex as a form of sin. Also, the liberation of women's sexuality through the introduction of contraception. This was initiated by the women themselves very much against the opposition of the clergy and the government of the day.

THOMPSON: Have you been part of the women's movement in London or in Dublin?

DUNNE: Not in any formal sense, however, I do share some of their aspirations. But also I see great vulnerability in men. I like men. I can't really separate them from women. As boys they are not encouraged to express their feelings. Like women, they can be oppressed. When I was growing up, men were just as much victims of the system as women. Most of them were trapped in jobs they hated for life. Now, their role is less defined. There's no such thing as jobs for life. Middle-aged men are encouraged to retire early. They are made redundant both at work and within the family. Boys compared to girls are underachieving in school. The suicide rate for boys has become an epidemic.

THOMPSON: I want to ask you about your heroine, Marian, in *Blessed Art Thou a Monk Swimming*. She has tremendous spirit despite the fact that she doesn't have a good sense of herself. She has confidence and naïveté.

DUNNE: I think Marian accepts her limitations as a person and rightly ascribes them to her circumstances. She also has the insouciance of youth and the cheerful optimism that something better will turn up.

THOMPSON: You find comedy even in the bleakest situations. Where does that humor come from?

DUNNE: It's a lot to do with one's attitude to life, strategy for survival. Life is made up of tragedy and comedy. The Irish have historically a sense of humor in which tragedy and comedy are closely related. Take O'Casey's *Juno and the Paycock* for example where scenes of outrageous comedy are followed seamlessly by scenes of extreme tragedy. I think comedy is the traditional survival tactic of the temporarily defeated.

THOMPSON: Marian's father has a very strange relationship with his daughter. Are there are suggestions of incest?

DUNNE: The mother is unable to respond to him as a man, so his affections were displaced onto his youngest daughter.

THOMPSON: Doesn't the relationship result from a warped sense of sexuality?

DUNNE: Young girls test their sexuality in the safe, protective situation of the family before they go out into the world. The father was not emotionally and sexually mature enough to recognize this.

THOMPSON: Did the O'Dea's marriage fail because it was sexually dysfunctional?

DUNNE: Sex becomes more important if it's not working. The Catholic Church's restriction of sex to procreation only meant that couples when they reached their forties generally slept in different rooms. I remember only quite recently the pope declaring it was a sin for a man to look at his wife with lust.

THOMPSON: What did your mother teach you about sex?

DUNNE: Apart from warning me that men were only after "the one thing," my mother never mentioned sex. Sadly, she didn't see it as a gesture of love. She couldn't even explain to me about my periods. When my first child was born and I was breastfeeding, she came into the room sideways so she wouldn't have to look. Afterward, she gave me a peck on the cheek and said the whole thing was a "funny business."

THOMPSON: How are your women characters different from each other and traditional women?

DUNNE: Marian is holding out for something better than the life around her. She doesn't want to end up like her sister or mother. Mags for all her sham sophistication will probably settle for this in the end. Mags accepts that all relationships between men and women are essentially loveless and will probably settle into the suburban scene like Marian's mother.

THOMPSON: Why does she go to London?

DUNNE: Because she was crazy about Clair and would have gone with him to the North Pole if necessary. He was the only person who made any sense to her, especially after her father died. She's trusting her instincts and taking the risk.

THOMPSON: What were the reviews of your novel like?

DUNNE: Uniformly excellent.

THOMPSON: Why did you choose an English publisher?

DUNNE: It gives you a wider range of options.

THOMPSON: What has your experience of the publishing world been like?

DUNNE: Very positive and encouraging.

THOMPSON: Have you written in other genres besides fiction?

DUNNE: Poetry, short stories, articles, and children's stories.

THOMPSON: Who do you read?

DUNNE: Flannery O'Connor. I have her complete works by my bed, and I read her all the time. Then there's Sylvia Plath, E. M. Forster, and of course Vladimir Nabokov.

THOMPSON: There are some surface similarities between Edna O'Brien's *The Country Girls* and *Blessed Art Thou a Monk Swimming*— the pairs of female characters, Baba and Caithleen and Mags and Marian, in particular.

DUNNE: That turns up all the time in literature, Don Quixote and Sancho Panza or Holmes and Watson or the obvious alter personae Dr. Jekyll and Mr. Hyde.

THOMPSON: Do you consider O'Brien an influence on your writing?

DUNNE: Every writer that I have admired has influenced me to some degree. My strongest influence is Flannery O'Connor, although I think this is not apparent in anything I have ever written. I believe that good writing can only result from the development of a strong or well-defined personality of one's own. Certainly I admire Edna O'Brien's work greatly. It would be difficult for any Irish woman writer to ignore the impact of her work during the repressive Ireland of the 1960s.

THOMPSON: What is the literary scene like in Ireland?

DUNNE: Living on an island I've very little idea.

THOMPSON: You're not part of a writer's group or workshop?

DUNNE: No, but it is nice to exchange ideas with other writers from time to time.

THOMPSON: What do you think of the *Field Day Anthology?*

DUNNE: I'm looking forward to see how other writers respond. I can't comment. I haven't seen the anthology.

THOMPSON: On the phone when we arranged the interview you told me that you spend six months of the year writing and six months making jewelry. How did you get into jewelry making?

DUNNE: Yes, I design and make jewelry. I think my feelings for jewelry began in my childhood when my mother got out her jewelry box and we went through the pieces together. I feel sometimes that this was the only time I ever got really close to my mother.

Anne Enright

Interviewed by
CAITRIONA MOLONEY

Courtesy of Martin Murphy

BORN: Dublin, 1962

EDUCATED: Trinity College (B.A. Modern English and Philosophy) University of East Anglia (M.A.)

RESIDES: County Wicklow, Ireland

GENRES: Fiction, screenwriting, drama

AWARDS: Rooney Prize (1991), short-listed for the *Irish Times*-Aer Lingus Literature Prize (1992), the Whitbread Award and Kerry Ingredients Listowel Prize (2000), *What Are You Like?* won the Encore Award (2000).

Even though Anne Enright was born, raised, and still lives in Dublin, she has spent time in London and Vancouver. She has worked in television and theater and studied creative writing under Angela Carter. She has published one collection of short stories, The Portable Virgin *(1991), and three novels,* The Wig My Father Wore *(1996),* What Are You Like? *(2000), and* The Pleasure of Eliza Lynch *(2002).*

Enright's fiction rewards the reader's intellectual engagement, and her humor juxtaposes incongruous elements in ways that upset entire belief systems. In the title story, "The Portable Virgin," virginity and portability are conjoined to suggest a radical theoretical construct; but on a literal level, a portable virgin is a plastic statuette of the Virgin Mary that people place on the dashboards of their cars.

Enright conflates the genres of journalism, history, film, and fiction to problematize our records and memories of the past. Her short story "Historical Letters" addresses an absent lover who was in Dublin in 1914, New Orleans in 1926, the Spanish Civil War in 1935, Moscow in 1937, and Berlin in 1989. Enright uses newspapers to intersperse bits of journalistic information into the plot of her novel The Wig My Father Wore *to portray history—fragmented and deconstructed—and similar to the present. In this novel she also uses film techniques of fast cutting and rewind to intersperse three plots. The novel's style resembles the remote channel-surfing behavior that television watchers are familiar with, again suggesting that television's influence is more total and structural than what is communicated by the content of individual shows.*

In her novel What Are You Like? *twins separated at birth articulate themes of loss, exile, and multiple identities. The novel itself is based on the lost limb phenomenon of Irish life, when almost every Irish family has a phantom member who immigrated to England, the U.S., Australia, or New Zealand. The novel has been described by critics as "an allegory for the contemporary political situation in Ireland" (Ettler 2000, 13).*

Anne Enright was working on a new novel about mothers when I interviewed her at her home in Dublin.

◆   ◆   ◆

MOLONEY: Could you tell me about your background and how you became a writer?

ENRIGHT: I grew up in the suburbs of Dublin, went to school in Dublin and in Canada for two years, came back to Trinity College, and then went on to the University of East Anglia and did the M.A. in creative writing with Malcolm Bradbury and Angela Carter. They offered me some money, so I took it. And I wanted to meet Angela Carter. I was working at the time in fringe theater in Dublin and when I came back, I got a job in television as a producer/director in RTE (Irish television). I worked there for six years and then left to write again; most of the time I was there I was working on a show set in a bar where anything either fictional or real could happen. It was a very busy mixture of chat and sketches, where anything can happen, sketches and pieces of art or literature. I stayed on it for four years.

MOLONEY: What did you write during that period?

ENRIGHT: I wrote *The Portable Virgin;* then I realized that I couldn't possibly continue writing and working full-time because the schedule three nights a week live was very hectic. Besides the show was running into trouble with the authorities, and we were taken off the air. So I left, and I've been writing ever since. I wrote *The Wig My Father Wore* and a couple of screenplays that came to nothing and a couple of plays for Dublin New Theatre, and various other time-wasting activities, until I sat down and started this last book, *What Are You Like?* which took me another three years.

MOLONEY: Could you describe your writing process?

ENRIGHT: Well, I work all the time, and I tend to distill rather than expound my work. Rather than build a book, I tend to grow it. In *The Wig* I also attempted to layer the images as if I were a painter. I wouldn't have the overall design before I started applying the color. I'd work on a corner of it, get the corner really perfect, and then wonder, what do I do now? It's an organic process. I'm quite anxiety laden as a result. The story starts to make demands as I am writing it. Some writers call this "the characters running away with the story." I prefer to say the words I put down provoke and demand further meanings—and my job is to find out what these might be.

It is common to all writers, this feeling of trying to follow rather than create the plot, the sense of getting something "right" or "not quite right"—I mean, if it's all made up then anything could be "right"—but it isn't. I tend to redraft and redraft and redraft; although I wouldn't actually rework if the first draft doesn't start humming. I like it to talk to back to me a little, and I like it to surprise me.

MOLONEY: What kind of a place is Ireland for a writer? Some of the writers we are talking to have left, or felt like leaving Ireland, to live in England, America, or Canada.

ENRIGHT: Well, I am on the plane tomorrow morning now to New York, and I'm hoping to have a nice time there. The airport road is the most important road in the country and it's just out there.

MOLONEY: What makes Ireland a difficult place for a writer?

ENRIGHT: In 1985 when I finished my degree and went to East Anglia, the moral climate of the country was so clammy and confining and unpleasant, with the referenda about divorce and abortion. For a woman of my generation, the break between the old and the new Ireland happened in my head; it was a confusing and disturbing time. So it was really important to get bloody out of the place. I didn't have a great time in England; I found it lonely and antisocial. I leave Ireland as much as possible, but I am also quite happy here. It's possible to build a life here, and only at times is it really annoying.

MOLONEY: Why annoying?

ENRIGHT: Just the simplicity of the reception that you get in other places, say in the English press; I've been reviewed by Penelope Fitzgerald in the *London Review of Books:* she's a Booker Prize-winning author, she is very grown up, she's very proper, she is the real thing. She gives me 1,500 words, not a hugely intense or passionate review, but it's all there. You get a review in the *Irish Times* by somebody who you have never heard of, who patronizes you, who assumes a high and academic tone, and writes like they've got a dose of piles, basically. And that's very annoying. You get a fresh look elsewhere with no baggage. So why not go where you are liked?

MOLONEY: Do you think the situation for writers is changing in Ireland?

ENRIGHT: I think the frustrations a writer has in Dublin are the same as the frustrations in London, that the smallness of the place mitigates against freedom of discourse. People get hemmed in and frustrated wherever they are, but Ireland has great advantages. You have colleagues in Ireland. You bump into people in the street, you bump into people at a book launch, there are very few "inner rooms." You can complain about Ireland being small, but it also can be quite livable. In most good writing, there is an argument taking place, and to keep the argument going, it's good to be in fairly close contact with the enemy.

MOLONEY: Could you talk about how reading other writers has affected your work?

ENRIGHT: I read all the Americans, the big guys like Cormack McCarthy I love. He is a brutish sort of male writer, a wonderful stylist. As far as the men in Ireland are concerned, I am engaged quite seriously in a conversation with them, and I don't write like any of them, so that's all fine. The conversation becomes more apparent in the next book, particularly the section of the dead mother.

MOLONEY: What are the issues in that conversation?

ENRIGHT: The relationship between words and the world. I sometimes feel that men over forty don't read fiction. Some of them write fiction but they'd be embarrassed to be seen reading a novel on a train. They prefer things to be real. Therefore a lot of male language is drained of metaphor or even image, and there is an impulse toward journalistic prose. In Irish terms, that impulse is then left by a kind of lyricism and music in the best writers, but it's still not enough for me. I also feel that Irish prose tends to cling to the world in an underconfident way. This is a table, this is a chair. The table is not going to sprout wings and fly out the window. The world should be very ordinary and not be doubted. Make fiction as close to fact as possible. But I don't think that fiction is fact. I feel like saying, you made it up, admit that you made it up, and you can make anything up. But as I say, it's a conversation; as I go along, I am doing less and less overt making up of things. I am making it closer to the credible.

MOLONEY: How about contemporary Irish women writers?

ENRIGHT: Well, I read Irish writers about two years after their books come out, as we are all in the same business I wait until a book has stopped being some kind of marketing artifact or item of conversation. I am not going to say anything about Mary Lavin, Edna O'Brien, and Elizabeth Bowen, because secretly I have avoided all of them all of my life and I don't think I ever will read them. It's the kind of thing of making your own way. But if you look at writers like Jennifer Johnston and Julia O'Faolain, they had famous fathers; they were somebody before they even tried to be somebody. Edna O'Brien is remarkable in that she wrote and got out. She is the exception to all of those rules. The class of women who wrote were rich; they had that confidence built in already. But Edna O'Brien is the great, the wonderful mistake in all of that scheme of things, that she did it.

MOLONEY: Can I ask you about the literary canon in Ireland today, for example, *The Field Day Anthology* and the controversy over its relative absence of women?

ENRIGHT: That's all bollocks; that has no credibility. *The Field Day Anthology* got it so spectacularly wrong that anyone would know that they had no credibility; therefore it doesn't matter. They did get it so spectacularly wrong, so that's bunk.

MOLONEY: But those people are still around; Seamus Deane, for example, is virtually the dean of Irish literary criticism.

ENRIGHT: Yeah, you'd think they'd die, but they just keep living. There is a world elsewhere. This is one of the reasons why Ireland would drive you mad.

MOLONEY: Is it easier for male writers to recognize talent in other men than women?

ENRIGHT: Oh sure. You find it even in the bookshops, that they don't sustain the women's list. They will have books of variable quality by any number of male writers and they will keep them. They will keep Jennifer Johnston, but they won't keep Clare Boylan. It kills Clare Boylan and it kills Julia O'Faolain, but that anger is of no use to my work at all.

MOLONEY: Virginia Woolf said something similar, that the Brontë's work was ruined by their anger.

ENRIGHT: It doesn't help me get up in the morning—it's just so oppressive, so overwhelming, if you started thinking about it; I have seen people deteriorate under that kind of strain. There's nothing worse than the emotion that this is not fair. So what I do is, I write essays for the *London Review of Books,* a very estimable, prestigious publication, and my work gets some kind of seal of approval.

MOLONEY: I've enjoyed your essays in the *Irish Times.*

ENRIGHT: No, that's just hack journalism.

MOLONEY: But they are good, especially the one recommending everyone in the North become a Protestant.

ENRIGHT: That's just fun; but if you are talking about how to get into the establishment, there are more comfortable places out of Ireland which are both establishment and welcoming. It is absolutely true and you must say that I think *The Field Day Anthology* was such total bollocks that its credibility is shot.

MOLONEY: I hear Cork U.P. is going to publish the fourth volume on women's literature.

ENRIGHT: They wrote to me and asked me for my biography, and I should have told them "fuck off"; I should do it; I really don't want to be in that book.

MOLONEY: What do you think Joyce's influence is on writers today? Didn't you say, "if Joyce had been a woman, she would have been locked up"?

ENRIGHT: I was delighted Edna O'Brien quoted that; it was wonderful; I'm so pleased with that line, I'm sticking to it. It's so true. Joyce broke all the rules, but you still get a lot of people in Ireland who are very moral about what gets written. You should be writing proper nineteenth-century realism; the novel of ideas is really beyond the current critical situation.

MOLONEY: Is it true that in Ireland all new fiction writers are measured against Joyce?

ENRIGHT: There is a lot of horse shit talked about Joyce in this country, and in yours. I don't think all fiction writers are measured against Joyce (though it was the kind of sneer that destroyed Flann O'Brien in his day). New fiction writers are measured now by the size of their advances. It is almost taboo to suggest that a writer might be wealthy but not good. Irish writing is a healthy business, and we are all members of the firm. The handing down of the crown happens among the poets—Heaney is the descendent of Yeats (via Kavanagh). He reads Yeats's Nobel speech before he writes his own, and all the other nondeified poets go home and eat their own livers, Prometheus-like, for the rest of their lives. "Nearly," in poetry, never won the race.

I don't think you can trace a line of succession in prose fiction in the same way. The nearest thing to deification happens with the Booker Prize, but because it is so commercial, it doesn't quite have the same élan. Dying can help, of course. Perhaps rural realism, of which the most acclaimed current practitioner is McGahern, interrupts the Joyce succession. These writers do not write anything like Joyce, therefore cannot be measured against him. There is a lot of jostling for the top among male writers. I don't think any of them have achieved canonization. Male writers sometimes refer to Joyce as a father/competitor, thereby somehow flattering themselves as being in the same league. As the "old father, old artificer," he smothers them, and renders them powerless. As far as I am concerned, this is a false conversation that takes place entirely between men. I like Joyce. He does not bother me. He was a wonderful writer. He makes me free. I don't compare myself to the dead. I hardly compare myself to the living. I would hope my writing is my own.

I always say that if Joyce was a woman she would have been locked up for writing psychotic, scatological gibberish; for sleeping with the serving classes and getting herself pregnant; for fleeing her native place in a state of hysteria; and all the rest. And when they had locked her up they would have looked at her scrawlings, and if they bothered to decipher them, might have muttered "Hmmm. Pity. Some of this stuff is almost good you know. Some of it has An Effect." This has changed since Joyce's time: women in Ireland no longer get locked up for having sex. I can't vouch for anything else.

MOLONEY: What about the Booker Prize? Jennifer Johnston said the Booker Prize went to the kind of Irish novel that they liked in England.

ENRIGHT: Elizabeth Bowen has a wonderful line about this flirtatious relationship between Ireland and England. Every writer has a way of saying, "I don't write what people want me to write." I remember saying that I am not an Irish writer, because I don't write about the rain, there's no long johns, there's no chickens, there's no whiskey, but that's part of the conversation with Colm Toibin, a pal of mine, who is more of a realist. He says, "I'm not an Irish writer, I'm not funny." Because people ring him up and say, "we need one of you wonderful, funny Irish writers." So, we all suffer from this, we all suffer, and I think that labels are there to be written out of. We choose the one we least like, and say well, I'm not like that. So Jennifer would have an idea of what the English would like in a Irish book, and she is not going to write that.

MOLONEY: What kind of Irish do the Americans like?

ENRIGHT: I didn't read *Angela's Ashes*. I did read *'Tis* and I thought it was like watching somebody hitting themselves and tap dancing at the same time. It was like watching someone in a state of self-destruction, self-despising, entertaining you. I thought of the phenomenon of *Angela's Ashes;* Americans wanted to feel that they all came from some peasant European hell. It wasn't a story about Ireland; it was a story about getting out, of being successful in America.

MOLONEY: Could you talk about realism, or lack of it, in your short story collection, *The Portable Virgin*?

ENRIGHT: Most of the short stories *The Portable Virgin* are extended metaphors, or two terms looking for their final metaphor. They do not use epiphanies, nor do they seek a final Chekovian sense of perspective: they are not anecdotal, or wise. They are trying, by accumulation, to become "themselves," to finish what they started.

MOLONEY: Your fiction is sometimes critical of the Roman Catholic hierarchy. Do you think that the influence of the Catholic Church in Ireland is waning?

ENRIGHT: I think, for anyone reared in that tradition, the problem of God does not go away. The Catholic Church used to enrage me, but doesn't any more. It's been well and thoroughly dismantled. In an audience of Irish people looking at the Graham Greene's *The End of the Affair,* filmed by Neil Jordan, there are still large issues about God because there is a miracle in the middle of the film. The heroine prays to God that if her lover is alive after this bomb blast, she will stop seeing him. There is a miracle: he is alive, so there's a moral thing at the center of it all.

MOLONEY: In America right now people are doing serious muckraking about the Catholic Church, orphanages run by the nuns, and laundry nuns.

ENRIGHT: That's happening an awful lot here. It's nice to be proved right.

MOLONEY: To what extent is *Wig* about religion?

ENRIGHT: It's a Catholic, religious thing with a high degree of morbidity about it as well. If you are reared a Catholic, in youth you spend a very fixed amount of time looking at a dead man on a cross. In *The Wig My Father Wore,* the wig is a fake thing made of real hair, like television, which makes fake programs with real people's lives. It is also tacky, excruciating, cheap, and moving like television. You could think of the angel as a suicide. Instead of "I have been half in love with easeful death," Grace is in love with someone who is at least half "Death." Throughout, the book contrasts a spiritual/ascetic male idea of love, Catholic in origin, with female sexual love, a kind of love that has not been widely explored in fiction, and which includes pregnancy and children as well as sex. Stephen to this extent represents something that is "wrong."

To me, it's just an old-fashioned love story, with a twist. Or a bildungsroman, in reverse, where the main character becomes more innocent as the book progresses. I am very interested by the happy ending, something particularly hard to achieve, in life as in fiction. I am also fascinated by the problem of goodness. I think, when we look back at the literature of the late twentieth century we will be amazed by the pure weight of unpleasantness in male fiction—so guilt driven and excessive. The characters in my novels are damaged, but though they are interested in badness (or evil), they are more interested in/bewildered by, goodness, all part of the same problem. Sometimes, when I was writing *The Wig,* I thought I was like a Victorian male writing about a female "angel" of domesticity, virtue, and grace, who saves the man from opium, or embezzlement, or some other terrible shame, the same old problem but, wherever possible, I like to flick the coin.

MOLONEY: I was wondering if the father's wig was the tree in the middle of the room that everyone notices but no one talks about?

ENRIGHT: The Emperor's new clothes. I don't know. In our house, we talked about everything; very little was unmentioned. There were five kids and they were all very chatty. And my mother was always a great articulator of things. Of course, Dad never said anything. I think the wig is a very sexual object—this big mysterious hairy thing her father has. It might be the equivalent of not mentioning sex. We weren't a particularly repressive household, although there was a gap between a very easygoing family life with a kind of Catholic thing overlaid on it. I notice even now that my mother doesn't really talk about my pregnancy because she's not comfortable talking about these things; she is quite comfortable with the facts of it all—she loved being pregnant, she loved having babies, but is not comfortable with the speech that might accompany that.

MOLONEY: It seems to me that love and death are juxtaposed in the novel in an Elizabethan way.

ENRIGHT: They are almost inextricable, but in the next book, they are absolutely inextricable. Ireland's relationship with death is amazing. There's any number of kept corpses through literature. There's also that whole homoerotic thing from the Italian, Sebastian, lots of martyrs. Lots of dead flesh in my visual imagery.

MOLONEY: The father in *Wig* has a stroke and then seems partially alive, partially dead. Sometimes he seems completely out to lunch, and then other times he gets it dead-on. He knows when the phone is going to ring.

ENRIGHT: That is the first of the mirror image thing; the stroke is like a mirror: left is right, and right is left. He lives on the wrong side of the mirror; the stroke affects half of his face. His verbal stuff is very *Alice and Wonderland,* very *Through the Looking Glass.* "Don't patronize your parents," he says. He is hardwired into it all. My own father was a very gentle and silent man, wonderful for children because of his playfulness when we were young. He was really good at nonsense.

MOLONEY: On the other hand, the mother-daughter relationship seems tortured. The protagonist is always telling her mother to "Fuck off"; what is her problem with her mother?

ENRIGHT: She is, yeah. I don't think my Ma liked this book so much; she likes the next one. I was surprised by the two mother figures in *What Are You Like?* One is dead and one is the stepmother. I am very interested in the iconized mother figure in Irish literature, because the men can't actually write them. They are very often dead, or left out of the narrative. The mother gets half a sentence and there is an awful lot about fathers. And so in the next book, I split that big iconic mother presence, which for the small child is so large and so unfeasible.

MOLONEY: Is that Freud's phallic mother?

ENRIGHT: I don't know if it is the phallic mother; I'm not entirely convinced by Freud, the castrated mother, and all that. I can't be bothered actually. In the next book one woman dies, and that is like the omnipresent dead mother in Irish fiction, never explained, never made manifest or real, and the stepmother, Evelyn, a perfectly likable person who is friends with her children, rears the child who is left, but the child still doesn't get on with her and never forgives her for something. In *Wig* there's so much rage; I shocked myself. I think the sexual difficulty is establishing a difference between the mother and the daughter; the daughter is trying to separate, to become someone else. I don't know whether I want to understand the mechanisms that go on between the mother and the daughter. I don't want to go there yet; there is so much material and kinetic energy.

MOLONEY: Speaking of places you don't go in your fiction, what are your ideas about the current Northern situation?

ENRIGHT: It's terrible; I suppose it's good that the cease-fire is holding. My generation is sloppy about the North. It's gone on too long, too boring, too horrible. I actually have more Northern friends than most people here, because a lot of the artistic community in Dublin fled from the North, a cultural wilderness. The thing you don't know about the North is that they are all too busy buying leather jackets and cars. They don't read; there is money put into the arts, but it is top-down money. It's possible to put on a play, but there isn't bottom-up support because it's so politicized. You write for one community or another, if you are a playwright. I was a judge of the *Irish Times* theater awards last year so I was up there for *Translations;* I realized that I was in the middle of a Catholic audience because there is a line in the end of the play about some twins who are going to go off and become terrorists, and the guy beside me went "hah hah"; the play became quite a propaganda piece in that audience. I had been previously at a Gary Mitchell play—he is from a unionist background from a poor estate—and the chocolate-eating couple in front of me laughed at some really hideous jokes about Catholics always squealing when you shoot them. I'm sure they don't think that; I'm sure they'd rather eat their Malteasers and not be like that.

MOLONEY: Do you think it's useful to think of Ireland as an ex-colony in understanding Ireland's relationship to England?

ENRIGHT: My personal relationship with England is very complicated; the relative strengths of the colonizer and the colonized have shifted so much over the years. For me—and for a lot of people in Ireland—England is an alternative space. So it's not like bringing your prose to Daddy. Its actually just sixty million people who will buy. England is important for all kinds of other reasons, because you can appeal to England as a higher authority, which I do occasionally, by saying Penelope Fitzgerald really likes it, but the *Irish Times* can't get it together. I am moving in my own head more from the periphery toward the center; I used to think that subversion and refusal and tricks and all kinds of play were the ways to slither around the male establishment, but I want to occupy the middle ground as I grow older.

The advantage of being Irish and writing in English is English fiction is so caste bound. If English people put an object into a domestic interior, they are talking about the amount of money people have. They are talking about the class of the people, as if poor people have different emotions than rich people. Now in Ireland, although it's all changing, we were reared not to judge people by their things or class, so you are free to write about people in a way that English people aren't.

MOLONEY: Would Ireland's role as an ex-colony enter into those distinctions?

ENRIGHT: The project when I was growing up was the accomplishment of the nation-state, so we were separate, we were Irish. Poor Irish and rich Irish were part of the same project. Whereas the Brits didn't have that equivalent; they were still aristocrats and working class; now they talk about whether they are Labor or Tory. Irish people always have recourse to Irish identity, which complicates the relationship.

MOLONEY: Do you see yourself as a feminist? Do you have problems with the term? Some people do nowadays.

ENRIGHT: I have no problems with the term at all; I've never had any problems with the term. Neither have I found it to my advantage to go around saying that I am a feminist particularly. There's no point in getting involved in linguistic, ideologist arguments about the term "feminism." But I do stick my outspoken neck out at every opportunity. Someone asked me to do a conference in England recently because they wanted a women's voice, so I said "you don't know me from a hole in the ground, but at this stage, any hole will do." I do take a line on things. The current line is, I can't be Irish all day; it's too much of an effort. I can't be a woman all day; the work of it is far too strenuous. It's too boring, being a woman all day. It needs constant attention; I can't be bothered. As a writer, I don't want to use language that has become ideological because that's a deadener for a writer of fiction. So, I like to keep my politics fluid so that it won't hem in the work.

MOLONEY: Both Johnston and O'Faolain have used mad characters in their novels. Some critics say this figure represents the woman writer's anxiety about writing. Do you find that plausible?

ENRIGHT: Novel narrative is involved in revelation; it's the gap, the awful hole in the text, through which the characters fall. I do think that there is an unsayable thing in the center of a book, and that if you fill it with something too obvious, then you are lost. You have to fill it with something archetypal that has the possibility of being at least two things at once—that energy has to be maintained.

MOLONEY: Is there a madness to your women characters?

ENRIGHT: I'm really interested in the gap, but I see it as part of a feminist aesthetic. When women have been silent so long, you have to read the silences really urgently. The silences and also the illusions and the slippages. Is that madness in my work? Well certainly the gaps, and the slippages, and the jumps, and the uncertain way of making sense.

MOLONEY: Is your protagonist in *The Wig My Father Wore* a madwoman?

ENRIGHT: Yes, of course. And the thing that's mad is that she's working in television. That's mad behavior.

MOLONEY: Has people's thinking been changed by television?

ENRIGHT: The way people structure their books has been changed by television. Things happen faster; it's a three-minute culture. You want to move on; you don't trust the reader to not become bored; you have to get in there fast. Some of the book feels as though it is happening in rewind, and the reader might find it disjointed, though you can't write about television without fast cutting. The book literally does go into rewind at the end, with the frantic studio section. I used to work in TV, and it did make you "use" reality (or people) rather than experience it (or them)—because it is an exploitative medium. It is nice to walk down the street with a soundtrack going in your head; it arranges the scene into a story. But if the soundtrack doesn't go away then you are mad, obviously. Are we more mad? I don't know. The fact of the matter is, I haven't had a television for six years. I don't think they make people happy.

MOLONEY: Have you thought about whether your fiction is post-modern?

ENRIGHT: Actually, when you say postmodern, Colm Toibin, in his *New Penguin Book of Irish Fiction,* says that my work is postnationalist, postmodern, postfeminist, post-everything, which is just a bit of fun I hope.

MOLONEY: I think it is, although I have trouble defining postmodernism.

ENRIGHT: I think the French and the Spanish have a better word than "post," which is either "supaire" or "epaire." "Post" in English means redundancy—afterward. So the Spanish can say "supaire"—modern, meaning even more modern—or "epaire," hyperrealism. The French, when you say realism in France, they all think of Zola, and bits of bodies, and morgues; realism makes me think of rain and cows.

MOLONEY: The problemization and fragmentation of history—particularly women recovering a lost history—seems part of the postmodern paradigm.

ENRIGHT: Well, it's all buried under the wallpaper. We are living in it; it's in bits, it's half-mad, the wallpaper and all the historical bits and scraps which are all real things. That's a menstrual image—we have to rip at the lining of this for something new to happen. In this next book, the mother finally speaks in it, as the nearly last thing, and so another woman's story is finally uncovered.

Jennifer Johnston

Interviewed by

CAITRIONA MOLONEY

Caroline Forbes

BORN: Dublin, 1930
EDUCATED: Trinity College
RESIDES: Derry, Northern Ireland
GENRES: Fiction, drama
AWARDS: Short-listed for the Booker Prize for *Shadows on Our Skins;* Whitbread Award for Fiction for *The Old Jest;* short-listed for Sunday Express Book of the Year for *The Invisible Worm*

Jennifer Johnston is one of the most important novelists writing today in Ireland. She started writing when she was thirty-five years old and has since published thirteen novels; she has a growing reputation and readership in Ireland and the United Kingdom. Critics consider her current work her best: "At the age of seventy, Johnston is at her best, and the essential works are The Invisible Worm, Three Monologues *(1995) and her two most recent novels,* The Illusionist *(1995) and* Two Moons *(1998)" (Kenny 2000, 20).*

Johnston's roots are in the Anglo-Irish tradition; she is the daughter of playwright Denis Johnston and his first wife, Sheelagh Richards, an actress and director. Johnston's work represents the contradictions of Irish identity intelligently and poetically, appealing to readers and frustrating critics. Refusing closure, her novels address the conflicts between revolutionary nationalism and Anglo-Irish ascendancy, Catholics and Protestants, parents and children, men and women, art and culture. Johnston's surrealist style, multiple narrative voices, and overlapping time periods allow her to convey the ambiguity of Irish identity.

Critical work on Johnston focuses on the "Big House" tradition, feminist issues, and the Nationalist/Ascendancy conflict as well as the "Troubles." The question of feminism in her work is complicated by Johnston's nominal rejection of feminism; nonetheless, some critics find evidence of feminist thinking in her canon.

Johnston's canon does embrace the "Big House" theme, the bildungsroman in a politically divided country, and women's conflicting roles. Without subscribing to a neocolonial ascription of "local color" to Johnston's work, one can see the framework of a jaded Protestant Ascendancy contending with an energetic Catholic nationalism, especially in such earlier novels as Fool's Sanctuary *and* The Old Jest. *Confined and isolated by their "big houses," women characters in* The Railway Station Man *and* The Invisible Worm *relocate in "small houses" that counter repression with independence, creativity, and self-expression. Although Johnston's early work reveals some nostalgia for the lost culture of the Ascendancy, the development of her women characters takes her fiction away from Ireland's troubled history and into a more emancipatory world where art equates with freedom and "a room of one's own."*

The bildungsroman—tied to a subtext about "the man with a gun"—is a strong component of Johnston's early work. Some of Johnston's heroines lose lovers to the IRA, to the British army, to IRA bullets fired in error, and to random Provo bombs. Only rarely portrayed positively, the gunman increasingly becomes more unattractive, incompetent, and irrelevant to Johnston's women characters.

I interviewed her at her home in Derry.

•   •   •

MOLONEY: Can you describe how your writing career got started?

JOHNSTON: I was living in London. I was thirty-five; I had two children and suddenly one day I said, if I get run over by a tram, it will be as if I'd never been here. I wanted to do something, and I wasn't trained for anything else, so I started writing. My children were young; I didn't want to be unavailable. Well at times I was unavailable, but I was unavailable at home. I spent four years filling wastebaskets, teaching myself the trade, and then I wrote a book. After I published my first book, I realized that was what I had been put on this earth to do.

MOLONEY: Your first novel is *The Captains and the Kings?*

JOHNSTON: No, that was my second book. My first book was *The Gates* but no one would publish that until after I had published *Captains and Kings*, my second book. I started writing when I was thirty-five and my first book was published when I was forty. My fifth book, *The Old Jest*, was the first book I had written where everything worked. I knew all the characters so well. Nancy was a sort of homage to my mother, who would have been much the same age as Nancy, but no other resemblance, apart from energy.

MOLONEY: The act of writing plays an important role in your novels; how much of this is about your own writing?

JOHNSTON: My writing is much like Helen Cuffe's painting in *Railway Station Man*. She hears voices in her head telling her what to paint. I hear voices telling me what to write. Sometimes I don't want the voices, sometimes I don't listen to the voices, but they are there. I don't plan my writing; I just sit down and listen to the voices. This makes it sound easy. It is not. The voice only points the way. It does not dictate the book.

MOLONEY: Do you work from outlines?

JOHNSTON: Well, I have outlines ... but stories and characters take on a life of their own, and they move from time to time in their own surprising directions. Sometimes I have to run to keep up with them.

MOLONEY: What about writers who say they approach writing like any nine-to-five job? They sit down at their computers at 9 A.M., take a one-hour lunch break, and finish up at 5 P.M.

JOHNSTON: I don't believe them.

MOLONEY: What new writers on the Irish literary scene do you consider promising?

JOHNSTON: I think Sebastian Barry's *Whereabouts of Eneas McNulty* is a stunning book. Colum McCann, Anne Enright, both young prose writers.

MOLONEY: Who would you say your literary influences were?

JOHNSTON: (Johnston gestures around the room, floor to ceiling bookshelves on two walls.) I am always reading contemporary young men and women writers coming out of Ireland today, but they are not influences on me. If I had five books to take away to a desert island for the rest of my life, they would be *Pride and Prejudice,* Chekov's short stories, *Anna Karenina, A Room with a View,* and I think I would have to have *Ulysses.* To teach me a bit of literary courage.

MOLONEY: Is Yeats an influence?

JOHNSTON: Well, I am always quoting Yeats in my books, but no, he was not an influence.

MOLONEY: Joyce?

JOHNSTON: Definitely not.

MOLONEY: How important is the Irish political situation in your work?

JOHNSTON: Well it is important. It is the background to all our lives. It doesn't go away if you shut your eyes. We all live against this background of hatred and violence. It has to color the way we look at the world, the way we write books. The border is a state of mind and little by little that state of mind must change. Not though, in the way people have tried to change it over the last twenty-five years.

MOLONEY: Is coming to terms with Irish political identity part of growing up Irish?

JOHNSTON: Well yes, in my novels about young people—*The Old Jest, Fool's Sanctuary, Shadows on Our Skin, How Many Miles to Babylon*—the protagonists learn about heroism. Real heroism, not fake heroism. Miranda learns heroism from Cathal, who is shot by the IRA for refusing to lead them to Miranda's brother. In *How Many Miles to Babylon,* Alec learns to be a hero by shooting his friend, Jerry, so he won't have to go in front of a firing squad. Alec is then ordered to be executed. He learns that it is more important to be loyal to a friend than loyal to a country.

MOLONEY: Why do think your representation of Irishness has not been as popular in the States as in Britain?

JOHNSTON: I don't think that I portray the kind of Ireland that Irish-Americans want to read about. A lot of people in America see the Northern Ireland problem as a conflict between England and the Republic of Ireland. That is much too simple. My vision of Ireland is too complex for some Irish-Americans; I am not saying who is right and who is wrong in the Irish situation as much as I am trying to write about the complex overlapping of history and personalities involved in being Irish in the past and at the moment.

MOLONEY: I see "Irishness" in your novels as being on the horizon, peripheral. In your writing is there a progression away from questions of "Irishness"?

JOHNSTON: Yes, *Two Moons* is about Irish people. All my books are about Irish people. They are the only people that I honestly know. The focus of the book is not on the "Irishness" of the characters.

MOLONEY: In *The Illusionist*, the protagonist's husband, Martyn, is such an extreme misogynist he seems almost over-the-top.

JOHNSTON: Yes, I had to make Martyn over-the-top in order for people to accept what I was saying. I have received letters and calls from all sorts of people; women call me up and say "that was me . . . you were writing about me." It's not a book that will reach a wide audience, but those it does reach need to have a book like *The Illusionist*.

MOLONEY: Can you compare Stella, the heroine of *The Illusionist,* and Laura, the heroine of *The Invisible Worm*—your two most recent books—in terms of how they cope with bad marriages?

JOHNSTON: They have something in common. A door opens, and they are able to walk through. For Laura, the door is being able to tell her story; for Stella, the door is learning that she is a writer. The difference is Laura stays with her husband and Stella leaves hers, but the important thing is the doors are opened.

MOLONEY: Naming seems to be an issue with your characters, for example Star/Stella in *The Illusionist* and Cathal/Charles in *Fool's Sanctuary.*

JOHNSTON: Well, Stella hates being called Star in the end, but in the beginning she quite likes it. She takes it as a sign of Martyn's love. In the end, it comes to represent Martyn's refusal to allow her to be a writer or a person. Cathal is the Irish for Charles and many people like to use their Irish names here. At that time it was a measure of his commitment to the cause. His parents call him Charlie.

I don't mind being called Jennifer; I don't stand on ceremony with people. I'm fine with people calling me Jennifer. I hate people calling me "Jen" though. That's a family name, and my mother used to call me Jen and indeed so did my father. Now only my brother and my sister-in-law call me "Jen" and that's fine. I used to have an agent who insisted on calling me "Jenny." One time at a big publishing lunch I just spoke up and said, "Please don't call me Jenny. It's not my name." He just laughed and went on calling me Jenny. He's not my agent any more. (That is coincidental.)

MOLONEY: What name do you go by socially?

JOHNSTON: Well around here, I would be introduced socially as Mrs. Gilliland and some people might know I was Jennifer Johnston, but around the town here, with people, I'm Mrs. Gilliland. But everywhere else I would be known as Jennifer Johnston.

MOLONEY: I'd like to talk about *The Invisible Worm*. Although it's your second most recent book, it was the first book of yours that I read and taught.

JOHNSTON: You taught it in the States? I didn't think it was available there. I have not had good distribution from my publishers in the States, which is why I have a new publisher. Doubleday was not the right publisher for me. They were just too big for a writer like me. Starting with *Two Moons,* which will be released September 2000, my books will be published by Headline Review.

MOLONEY: To get back to *The Invisible Worm:* can I ask you about Laura? I have always wondered about the "running woman" symbolism.

JOHNSTON: Well there were going to be two women in *The Invisible Worm*. I started to write the book about two women, one an actress, living in Dublin, the other a woman living in the country and suffering from deep depression. But then Laura took over and demanded that her story be told. The other woman became the woman in the next book, *The Illusionist*. Laura is also the running woman in a way because she is always running away from her life, from the dislocation of it.

MOLONEY: Can you talk about Laura's madness, her agoraphobia? Specifically can you comment on this passage which describes her illness: "It's as if there were a stopper somewhere in my body, and when it is pulled out I become slowly drained of hope, love, confidence, even the ability to feel pain; I become an empty skin; I do not even have the energy to kill myself. I long for the safe, lapping waters of the womb, darkness."

JOHNSTON: She is not so much an agoraphobic as depressed. I do not, thank God suffer from depression, but I have been close to people who do. It just happens; it comes from nowhere; it is not understandable. It overwhelms Laura quite unsought, and she is incapable for weeks of any energy, either physical or mental. Slowly she recovers, but it is like recovering from a long and debilitating illness.

MOLONEY: Is there a connection between the rape and Laura's madness?

JOHNSTON: Definitely. Partially because the rape, all rape really, is about power and control. Her father is the New Ireland of the 1930s and '40s. He is a De Valera man. He is going to take whatever he wants. She is his daughter and he wants her to know that he controls her and her future completely. If he wants her sexually, he can just take her. The fact that she is not allowed to acknowledge the rape, to talk about it, also contributes to her depression. She comes out of it when she can talk about it to the ex-priest, Dominic.

MOLONEY: Could you talk about Laura and Maurice's marriage? In the novel, you write that "Silence was like the splint that held a broken limb tight, she thought—prevented pain, prevented truth, prevented dislocation, falling apart. Long live silence!" Is this positive?

JOHNSTON: It's mature. In the real world, people have to compromise. Life is a series of complex negotiations.

MOLONEY: In *The Invisible Worm,* Laura's father is drawn to the Anglo-Irish culture, but you say that he becomes a part of it through his daughter, not through his wife. Could you explain that?

JOHNSTON: His wife did not conform. He could not control her. She did not become a Roman Catholic; she took up sailing; she stayed outside his world. She also mocked him in her own way. He could not use her.

MOLONEY: How did you decide on the ending?

JOHNSTON: I had planned a different ending, but the book stopped before it got to that ending. Some people have said they would have liked a different ending. A happy ending of some sort. Personally I think that the ending is as happy as you can get with a book like this. My brother wanted her to go off with Dominic. That was impossible.

MOLONEY: Because of her house?

JOHNSTON: Absolutely. That was very important to her. To keep her house. And of course her own integrity and little bit of new-found courage. It is impossible for the snail to leave the shell.

MOLONEY: *Shadows on Our Skins* seems less optimistic about Catholics and Protestants getting along.

JOHNSTON: That's not a very good book. It was short-listed for the Booker Prize, which is a completely political thing. That's the kind of

"Irishness" that people in England like. When I wrote it I was living in Derry; I just hadn't got the Derry idiom in my ear. People in Derry don't speak like that at all. The accents are all wrong. Since then I've published *Three Monologues* and here I have come to grips with the rhythms and patterns of Northern speech. You must read "High Noon" and "Christine" first because they go together, and then "Twinkletoes" later.

MOLONEY: In *Shadows on Our Skins,* Brendan and Mrs. Logan have a troubled mother-son relationship, as do Mrs. Cuffe and Jack in *The Railway Station Man.* Is that a particularly Irish phenomenon?

JOHNSTON: No, I think sons always have trouble seeing their mothers as anything other than mothers. A lot of sons, and husbands for that matter, expect constant service from their wives and mothers.

MOLONEY: Why do you think *How Many Miles to Babylon* has become a school text?

JOHNSTON: It's a school text in the North, not in the Republic. I don't know why it became a school text. But it's been very good for one's book sales. I think it suits teachers' purposes for a number of reasons. It is a well-written book. It talks about World War I. That period gets forgotten in Ireland. That four years has been successfully airbrushed from history in the Republic. In the North it is different. It has become an iconic part of the Protestant history and culture. Frank McGuinness in *Observe the Sons of Ulster Marching towards the Somme* was one of the first people to give us back that important part of our history.

MOLONEY: What do you think of your critics?

JOHNSTON: Reviewers are a necessary evil. So many of them take my books apart and analyze them and get them wrong. Julia O'Faolain just wrote a good review of *The Illusionist* in the *Times Literary Supplement.* She got it exactly right and she gets me exactly right.

MOLONEY: A number of critics have praised you for what they call your "art," but that art seems to be somewhat diminutive. You've been compared to Jane Austen.

JOHNSTON: I think some people are trying to be dismissive. Personally I think Jane Austen was a masterly observer of society and witty to boot. I should be so lucky!

MOLONEY: A number of critics have placed you in what is often called "the Big House tradition." In fact, you are discussed in several books about that so-called tradition. How do you feel about that tradition and being considered part of it?

JOHNSTON: I think it's a way of putting me in a box, of being dismissive. The Irish "big house tradition" goes from Maria Edgeworth's *Castle Rackrent,* through Somerville and Ross to Molly Keane. Supposedly Molly Keane couldn't write under her real name so she had to call herself M. J. Farrell because the "gentry" were so opposed to a woman writing. I don't believe that. My mother came from that class and she was an actress. She was virtually the only working woman among the parents of my school friends at that time. I'm very glad I was brought up by a working woman. That class tolerated eccentricity; there were always people who didn't conform, who were artists, actresses, writers. Nobody minded them. They were accepted to a certain degree.

MOLONEY: One writer has suggested that critics don't understand you very well; some of the images that seem to provoke various readings are birds, smoking women, and orphans. Could you comment on those?

JOHNSTON: I hate birds. I am absolutely terrified of birds. If a bird flew into this room this moment, I would have to go away and let it beat itself to death against the windowsill before I could come back in the room. I like watching birds out-of-doors, preferably through glass. Pretty little things in the trees. But if one ever comes near me, I am terrified. I don't smoke. I detest it. My mother chain-smoked and so does my daughter. I have always lived with smokers. I have seen their anguish in the early mornings when they don't have a cigarette to hand. I only created two orphans out of eleven and one-half books! If orphans had parents they would not be able to do so many interesting things. They would not be able to represent the conflicts of Irish identity as well.

MOLONEY: Are you a feminist writer?

JOHNSTON: No, not as such. I am a feminist in that I like women and I admire them and I understand the problems facing women and I try to explore them in my work. I think the militant feminists have made a terrible mistake. They have gone too far, and they want too much. They are responsible for many of the problems women have today.

MOLONEY: The backlash?

JOHNSTON: Yes. I am not a "feminist" as such; I feel it is most important that we all liberate each other.

MOLONEY: What do you think of the practice of including Irish literature in what is being called "postcolonial" literature?

JOHNSTON: I think it is an academic exercise that may have relatively short-lived duration. I don't like labels; I see them as an attempt to reduce the importance of the writer. I think that interesting and lively work is coming out of all the ex-colonies—Canada, Australia, India, and the Caribbean countries.

MOLONEY: Critics argue whether or not you are an "Irish" writer; is that a fair categorization?

JOHNSTON: I am an Irish writer. What else would I be? I am Irish. Everything I know is about Ireland. But I don't want the Irishness of my books and characters to limit them. All kinds of people can read my books and see themselves in them.

Liz McManus

Interviewed by

HELEN THOMPSON

Shane McCarthy

BORN: Montreal, 1947
EDUCATED: University College, Dublin
RESIDES: County Wicklow, Ireland
WORKS: Member of Parliament and Labor Party spokesperson on Health
GENRES: Fiction
AWARDS: Nominated for Aer Lingus/*Irish Times* First Book Award

---

Liz McManus was born outside Ireland only because her father was a diplomat working in Canada when she was born. At eighteen months, the family moved to France and then to Switzerland; her first language was French. McManus is an architect, writer, and politician. She is the author of one novel, Acts of Subversion, *and short stories published in various anthologies.*

McManus's political and architectural expertise find their way into her narratives. Gerry Smyth says that "many writers have sensed a need to challenge the received forms of 'Troubles' narrative, and to develop new languages and new perspectives as a contribution to the imagination of change" (1997, 116). As the title of McManus's novel, Acts of Subversion *(1991), suggests, she is concerned with undermining official narratives of not only the Troubles but also Irishness worlds away from Anglo-Irish privilege. The Troubles, according to McManus, stem from class rebellion against a system that offers one class nothing but manual labor and slum housing.*

Nor is terrorism the well-oiled machine of weapons, plans, secret rendezvous, and well-trained soldiers. It is young boys practicing with brooms instead of guns and hatching grandiose plans to kidnap the queen. The terrorists are like children acting out fantasies of their rage against privilege. Terrorism has more to do with poverty and class than a history of resistance.

While traditionally, the central focus of political narrative progress is masculine activity, Acts of Subversion *situates terrorism alongside domesticity, the traditional realm of women. Oran's mental picture of his mother is reminiscent of the Madonna and child, one that he describes as "domestic tranquility" (49). Even within the middle classes, women such as Jane O'Molloy are socialized to be reproducers of the nation, as she is told by the nuns, "You will become the mothers and wives of the leaders of the country" (54). Yet the novel also portrays the home as another site of political and economic struggle as working-class women barter sex for coal and middle-class women lament their loss of freedom within marriage.*

At present, Liz McManus is working on a collection of short stories. I met with her during the Irish Women Writers Conference in Dublin and conducted the interview via email.

◆   ◆   ◆

THOMPSON: Where were you born?

McMANUS: In Montreal, Canada. My father was an Irish civil servant who worked in various postings abroad. When I was about eighteen months old we moved from Canada to France via Switzerland and my first language was French.

THOMPSON: Can you tell me about your parents?

McMANUS: My father had a distinguished career in tourism, aviation, and industrial development, one of a number of pioneers within the modern Irish civil service. He came from solid Catholic middle-class stock in Cork.

THOMPSON: And your mother?

THOMPSON: My mother was a painter. Her parents were Northern Unitarian from Ballymoney, N. Ireland, of modest background but successful.

THOMPSON: Were there any objections to this "mixed" marriage?

McMANUS: My parents' marriage caused a rift. My Unitarian grandparents disagreed vehemently with Catholic teaching. Particularly, the Ne Temere papal decree outraged them. They had been supportive of independence, but the new Irish state, with its narrow Catholic confessional nature, was such a disappointment they left Ireland forever and moved to England. Because of the estrangement I had no contact with my maternal grandparents.

THOMPSON: What is the Ne Temere papal decree?

McMANUS: It forced a non-Catholic who married a Catholic to promise to raise the children as Catholics. Recently I was glad to see an Irish bishop actually apologize to Protestants for the damage done by Ne Temere.

THOMPSON: How did your mother feel about raising you Catholic?

McMANUS: It didn't bother her overmuch. We three sisters were convent educated. Catholicism was the dominant cultural force but neither my sisters nor I are Catholic now. Somehow it didn't stick.

THOMPSON: Can you explain your grandparents' disappointment in the new Irish state?

McMANUS: They were Republican in outlook and opposed to the bigotry of the Orange Order. My aunt remembers them refusing to stand for "God Save the Queen." My grandparents thought the new independent Irish state would be one of tolerance and acceptance of difference. Instead it became a theocratic state dominated by the Catholic Church. They left Ireland for Britain. Many Protestants did so at the same time for a variety of reasons.

THOMPSON: What was it like for you growing up in Ireland?

McMANUS: The fact that we had lived abroad was unusual for Irish people, and I suspect gave us a certain cachet among our peers. The fact that our mother was Protestant also set us apart. Ireland in the fifties was a place of censorship, simplicity, piety, emigration, and a high level of conformity. It didn't take much to be different.

THOMPSON: So the mixed marriage impacted you negatively?

McMANUS: My short story "Dwelling under the Skies" is the most autobiographical of all my work and describes what growing up as the daughter of a "mixed marriage" was like. My mother's not being Catholic was a strongly defining factor in my life. I was out of step with all the other children. Nowadays it seems ludicrous, but in Ireland in the

1950s, anyone who didn't fit the narrow confines of Catholicism was viewed with some suspicion.

THOMPSON: Did you always want to be a writer?

McMANUS: Actually, my mother was keen for me to study architecture. In those days you did what your mother told you to do, more or less. I was never suited to it, but I qualified as an architect from University College, Dublin, in 1969, and I worked for years as one until my children were born when I became a full-time mother. In 1981, when I found I had some time again, I went back to writing, which I loved as a child.

THOMPSON: Was it easier to write when your children grew older?

McMANUS: It is easier, but harder too, because like many women my age, I have a full-time job—I'm a member of Parliament—so I write less than ever before. Family, work, writing, something has to suffer. The writing suffers because I am an incredibly slow writer and writing is so damned hard anyway. The blank page and the blank mind. Writing is a crucifixion regardless of any political or personal context. In the end I cannot blame anything or anybody else if it isn't working out.

THOMPSON: How do you approach the writing process?

McMANUS: I have these blocks of images and thoughts scattered inside my head, and like an architect or a builder, I try to get those blocks assembled into a structure that has integrity. I am never very clear about the plan or purpose until the work is finished. I'm depending on my unconscious, rather than making many conscious decisions.

THOMPSON: So being a writer is like being an architect for you?

McMANUS: I was a bad architect. But even for me, some of the training took hold—form following function, less is more, the importance of structure—these are architectural principles which influence my writing. Although increasingly less, now that I am becoming more discursive in style. Still I have the sense of building an edifice, of a story taking on a shape, as I stack up the bricks and mortar.

THOMPSON: Did you feel any pressure to become a full-time mother when your children were born?

McMANUS: The early years put iron in my soul. Nothing in my life since was as hard as staying home with three small boys. By the time my daughter arrived, I was writing and breaking new ground. I also depended on other women in similar situations. We banded together and learned about feminism, another strongly defining influence in my life.

THOMPSON: Are you a feminist?

McMANUS: Yes, I am a feminist.

THOMPSON: What was it like going to University College, Dublin, in the late 1960s?

McMANUS: In university in 1968 I became politicized and socialist. I was very involved in the student unrest: sit-ins, student occupations, mass rallies. Radicalism was in the air. We were influenced by the anti-Vietnam movement, the French Marxists, the Black Panthers. We got involved in issues outside of the university: housing, early environmental issues, women's rights. The 1960s were exciting times.

THOMPSON: Did you remain politically active after you left UCD?

McMANUS: I embarked on a voyage of discovery within my own country. In 1969 I moved out of Dublin because my fiancé was doing his medical internship in Donegal, so I got a job in Derry in an architects' firm. I arrived the week of the Battle of the Bogside and spent the next eighteen months living with the smell of CS gas and the presence of British troops.

THOMPSON: What form did your political activity then take?

McMANUS: I was still very involved in radical politics. The Labor Party became too tame for me, so in Galway I joined what was then known as Official Sinn Fein, the left-wing socialist organization, not the break away Provisional Sinn Fein, which led the violent campaign in the North for the next thirty years. Now that the Provisionals have embraced peace the joke around Belfast goes: What's the difference between the Officials and the Provos?

THOMPSON: I don't know.

McMANUS: Thirty years.

THOMPSON: What did you think of Provisional Sinn Fein's violent politics?

McMANUS: I never supported their nationalist violence.

THOMPSON: You described your travels in Ireland as a voyage of discovery. What did you discover?

McMANUS: When you live in Dublin, as in any capital city, you consider it the center of the universe, and everywhere else is where the hicks live. That's why leaving Dublin was mind-expanding for me. I learned about country places as well as provincial towns and how people are shaped by them. I discovered Ireland and her many facets. Place is important. Possibly because I have lived in many places myself I have a heightened sense of its importance. Most of my contemporaries lived in the house they were born in, and didn't leave it until they were married. Dislocation was a strength for me but it also meant insecurity, and having to accommodate to a new environment.

THOMPSON: Did you ever consider leaving Ireland permanently?

McMANUS: I never wanted to live outside of Ireland. "Been there, done that." As a student I'd worked in Montreal during Expo '67 and traveled around the States, so I got that out of my system. It was wonderful to have so many strictures to kick against.

THOMPSON: I'm getting a picture of you as a nonconformist.

McMANUS: Certainly I came from nonconformist stock but actually, I went with the mood of the time among my peers but instead of "getting over it" I stayed with it, largely because of the influence of my husband, who was deeply politically engaged. It was, and is, a shared obsession. Being a woman meant I was the one who reared the babies, which wasn't always easy, but it was a good experience. Another woman with a similar background and political development—although she stayed with the Labor Party—was Mary Robinson and the Irish people made her president! Being female and political can be a plus.

THOMPSON: What in your background led to your political activism?

McMANUS: Middle-class guilt probably drove my politics but I also felt, as many of my generation did, suffocated by the strictures of church and state. I came from a well-off background at a time when Ireland was generally a poor country. The 1950s had been grim. In the 1960s there was an economic boom and we could afford the luxury of student rebellion. I suspect that the experience of being a Protestant's daughter made me feel an outsider. It was exciting to help break out of the old ways. As a young married woman I participated in campaigning for contraception, then banned; later for divorce, also banned; equal pay, etc.

THOMPSON: You have felt restricted being a Catholic woman?

McMANUS: Far from feeling restricted, I feel part of a generation blessed with good timing: a teenager in the sixties boom, a young woman in time to enjoy forming a challenge to male domination, in middle age in the era of the older woman and Mary Robinson, then ahead of me, into old age at a time when the elderly will be in a dominant position.

THOMPSON: Do you think your generation has been freer than women of the previous generation?

McMANUS: We had rock'n'roll, miniskirts, the Beatles, money, the pill, the freedom to travel and to come home knowing jobs were available, before and after marriage if you wanted it, unlike in our mothers' time.

THOMPSON: Do you think your nonconformity fuels your writing?

McMANUS: It does, although the subversive power of the writing of Joyce or McGahern or Flann O'Brien or Edna O'Brien is dependent on the context of an Irish society now unrecognizable and firmly in the past. Ireland has been radically transformed in one generation and my generation tracks the same course.

THOMPSON: Isn't it true, though, that Irish mothers have always held power within the family?

McMANUS: Mother, for the Irish male, has almost always been the defining influence, which is why the Catholic Church concentrated so much on educating women. In *Acts of Subversion,* Oran is breaking free of his class and his background, and his mother offers a way out both in terms of education but also of ideology.

THOMPSON: You create tensions related to class between your characters. How important is the class system in Ireland?

McMANUS: Class in Ireland is not like the British system. We are more parochial. The aristocracy was generally Anglo-Irish and therefore not "Irish" in the nationalist sense that we have perceived ourselves. Nationalism and independence meant that class division was blurred, not politicized as in other countries. But still the hegemony of the middle class is very real here. In terms of opportunities for the working-class male as opposed to the middle-class female, the first is still at a huge disadvantage today. In the seventies Oran would have been an exception to be going to third-level college at all, and while things have improved, the gap is actually worsening between the haves and the have-nots.

THOMPSON: Is it different in the North?

McMANUS: I was very struck by the fact that the first time I met working-class people with third-level college degrees—young graduates who had benefited from the British education system—was in the Bogside. It displayed a certain lack of gratitude on their part to be filling up the petrol bombs and firing rocks at the RUC, considering what they had got out of the hated British system, but be that as it may. It is history now.

THOMPSON: Your characters talk negatively about British imperialism. How do you feel about it?

McMANUS: I have no doubt that our colonized past means that the ruses and stratagems of the powerless and dispossessed are still part of the Irish psyche. Americans wonder why Irish people are not direct in their speech, why we embroider the truth. I suggest there are historical reasons. Also a religious aspect. Living with a faith that set impossible strictures and such a rigid code of behavior has meant that subterfuge has become a way of life.

THOMPSON: How useful do you find the view that Ireland's post-colonial?

McMANUS: Ireland is in its postcolonial phase. We no longer blame England for all our ills. We have grown up as a country; we're part of the EU; we're doing well, thank you very much. Now we don't particularly want the British government to relinquish its authority in Northern Ireland, certainly not if it means any bloodshed or indeed, any financial cost to ourselves. But in the early seventies, anti-British feeling ran high, the British Embassy in Dublin was burned to the ground after Bloody Sunday and a boy like Oran could easily be caught up in it.

THOMPSON: What are the residues of the historical struggle?

McMANUS: We tend to forget our history. Too much Provisional IRA violence has made us uncomfortable about the men of 1916. Ireland has changed so much it is hard to keep track. But nationalism still has its resonance. We are still dominated by the two political parties which emerged from the Civil War. There is no real difference between them now, yet they still have their hold on the people. We still have difficulty accommodating the fact that within Northern Ireland the largest community there wants and is entitled to be British. But overwhelmingly we voted for the Good Friday Agreement, which gives them that right.

THOMPSON: Has the new openness changed the historical record?

McMANUS: Interestingly enough, we are living at a time now when much that was hidden of the past is surfacing for the first time: the extent of political corruption, the widespread tax evasion, the hidden child abuse by religious orders. The dual standards of the past, the blind acceptance of authority is no longer in tune with the times. And a very good thing, too.

THOMPSON: The killing of the thirteen Irish by the British, a labor demonstration, and a robbery are all connected in *Acts of Subversion*. Is it because you think terrorism is criminal rather than political?

McMANUS: Yes, I think of terrorism as criminal. Many lives were destroyed by the paramilitary organizations of the last thirty years. And many young idealistic men were caught up and destroyed in a terrible, fruitless campaign. The potency of nationalism is frightening.

THOMPSON: Did the violence affect your own political decisions?

McMANUS: I became a socialist because I wanted to construct another way of viewing the world than as one nation against another. The internationalist outlook of my father, the impossibility of reconciling my mother's beliefs with the One Holy Roman Catholic and Apostolic Church, a background where privilege opened well-oiled doors, and an intellectual ferment that was University of Dublin in 1968 all lead me to reject nationalism in favor of the brotherhood of man. Until the Women's Liberation Movement challenged me again, and I had to learn to meld socialism and feminism together.

THOMPSON: How did you decide to run for office?

McMANUS: In politics I have always felt supported at home. My husband and I are partners in politics, at times obsessively so. He tried to become a TD and didn't make it. I tried and did. Luck, timing, that's the way this business goes. Being female in the 1992 election helped particularly. People thought I belonged to the Mary Robinson party. Later in government, I became a Minister for Housing and Urban Renewal. All those years of study at architecture were put to some use.

THOMPSON: Are your concerns as a politician and a writer separate or do they intersect?

McMANUS: I've always had different compartments in my life—political, literary, personal. Yes, of course they intersect and yet I could never, for example, set a novel or even a short story in Dail Eireann. It's too close, and yet it doesn't engage me in that deep sense required to write about a subject. But I've written about terrorism, about multiculturalism, about marginalization of people, I suppose which are issues that I do talk about in parliament.

THOMPSON: What are you working on now?

McMANUS: I am now working, very slowly, on a collection of short stories, but I am making progress. I am not too worried about publishing at this stage. The principal task is to get the work done. Time is so precious, and so it's hard to make time for myself that I feel I am losing the battle. At other times I am confident that every time I write I'm learning a bit more about writing in general and my writing in particular. Writing is not only a crucifixion. It is also an act of creation that is deeply satisfying.

THOMPSON: I know you belong to a writer's group. What's it like?

McMANUS: The writer's group is a great help. A discipline, a resource, a shoulder to cry on, a voice answering when you cry into the wilderness, a touchstone.

THOMPSON: How do you make space for writing?

McMANUS: I stay on occasion in the Tyrone Guthrie Centre at Annaghmakerrig in County Monaghan, an artist and writers' colony and my lifeline to my work. When the world crowds in I escape.

THOMPSON: Which writers do you admire?

McMANUS: Joyce (I live in one of his houses, as it happens), John Banville, Edna O'Brien, John McGahern, and American writers Grace Paley and Annie Proulx.

THOMPSON: Any other Irish women writers?

McMANUS: Mary Lavin. Elizabeth Bowen. Funny isn't it that at a time when women really were marginalized and excluded many really good Irish writers were women like those above and Kate O'Brien?

THOMPSON: Yes, but even now the gatekeepers are not acknowledging their importance to Irish literary history.

McMANUS: Yes, men make the agenda. We have to let more women into the canon but we also need more master (mistress?) pieces written by women.

THOMPSON: Do you think your book would have been banned under the era of censorship?

McMANUS: Yes, but I wouldn't have written it then. Different times. I would probably have lacked the courage to write as others did. The book, as I said, was well reviewed. It didn't sell in great quantities but I had not done it for the money anyway.

THOMPSON: You would not have had such varied roles either: writer, mother, feminist, activist, politician, government minister.

McMANUS: Born into the repression and the straightened circumstances of the forties and fifties and traveling through to the Celtic Tiger of the nineties. It is quite a trip!

Cláir Ní Aonghusa

Interviewed by

HELEN THOMPSON

Courtesy of Peter Heery

BORN: Dublin, 1953
EDUCATED: University College, Dublin (B.A. in English)
RESIDES: Dublin
WORKS: Teacher in the secondary system for many years
GENRES: Fiction, poetry

Cláir Ní Aonghusa began writing at twenty-three and, like many burgeoning writers, was first published by David Marcus in New Irish Writing. *Since then she has published short stories and one novel,* Four Houses and a Marriage *(1997).*

In a review, Djinn Gallagher says that Cláir Ní Aonghusa is "admirably unsentimental about her Irish roots" (1997, 27). Ní Aonghusa describes her own approach to fiction as one that bites back by offering a realistic but sometimes critical appraisal of the state of Irish culture, particularly as it affects women. Her writing does not provide simple answers to Ireland's complex social problems. She expresses conservative sentiments with regard to divorce and children, yet she is expressly outspoken about the historical rigidity of her culture and her desire to circumvent the official versions of history, sexuality, and religion.

These sentiments are echoed in her novel as the breakdown of Sinéad's marriage takes place within the context of a funeral. Within the close confines of family, Sinéad and Eoin put on the stereotypical brave face to hide their marital difficulties. While the reader might find fault with their decision because it reproduces dysfunctional coping mechanisms, Ní Aonghusa shows us the necessity for privacy in an environment where keeping a secret is nearly impossible.

While divorce is possible for Sinéad and Eoin in this postreferendum Ireland, it was not possible for her mother and May, who had children that they did not necessarily want but felt pressured into producing. The variety of women characters and responses to marriage in her novel suggests she does not see divorce as an easy or inevitable option, even now that it is available.

If women step out of the narrowly circumscribed space of domesticity, they are still in danger. We see the difference here between England and Ireland. While Sinéad walks in London at night, courting danger as a solitary woman, in rural Ireland, some English women are raped by locals for living together without men, for buying land, for not going to church, and for not behaving in ways that they think women should. So, an Irish woman is safe in London at night, but an English woman is not safe in Galway.

Ní Aonghusa has finished her second novel, which she describes as more elaborate and ambitious than her first. The plot follows three main characters in a family, including a heroine whom Cláir says is an adventuress. She is now at work on her third. I met with Cláir Ní Aonghusa during the Celebrating Irish Women Writers Conference and conducted the interview by email and phone.

◆   ◆   ◆

THOMPSON: Why did you publish with Poolbeg?

NÍ AONGHUSA: I went for Poolbeg because I didn't have an agent to get a London publisher for the book. I'd met Kate Cruise O'Brien and liked her, which was another reason for going with them.

THOMPSON: Where did you meet Kate Cruise O'Brien?

NÍ AONGHUSA: I met her at Writers' Week in Listowel because I had booked into her fiction workshop. She liked my work and invited me to submit the novel to her.

THOMPSON: What was it like working with her?

NÍ AONGHUSA: Kate was a complex person, great fun and highly amusing when in good form, imperious, bossy, and opinionated at other times, and extremely sensitive during personal crises. She was utterly wonderful to me when my father died, extremely supportive and kind. I could never forget that. There was that other side to her too, capable of extreme behavior.

THOMPSON: Was she a good editor?

NÍ AONGHUSA: What Poolbeg authors got from Kate was serious attention in the lead-up to publication. She had a wonderful eye for excess detail and she would tell you why a particular chapter or part of a chapter didn't work for her and ask you to find the remedy. It was a co-operative venture where we worked to achieve the best version of the novel. It was also great fun because, invariably, the bottle of wine came out, and the sessions were conducted in an atmosphere of high good humor. Occasionally, her husband [Joseph Kearney] and/or son [Alexander Kearney] would wander in. For me that was the highlight of the publication process.

THOMPSON: Did you have any problems with her?

NÍ AONGHUSA: We had a row about rights to the novel and were barely on speaking terms by the time the novel was launched. She wrote to me in January before her death in March 1998 looking for a second novel. I couldn't get back to her straight away. About a fortnight before she died I left her a message to say I had time to talk. The next thing I heard she had died. I remember Kate with great fondness. I'm sorry we fell out. I wish we could have done another book together. She was a great spirit.

THOMPSON: How much did the divorce referendum inspire you to write *Four Houses and a Marriage*?

NÍ AONGHUSA: Separation and divorce were part of the narrative. I wasn't making a point in favor of or against divorce; I merely pointed out the situation at the time. It was of more interest to write about a character who wasn't nice, who behaved badly and irritated others, but who changed during the course of the novel.

THOMPSON: How do you feel about the success of the 1995 divorce referendum?

NÍ AONGHUSA: Divorce is a necessary evil. It has to be there to give people an out in extremely difficult circumstances. However, when a couple has children, they should make every effort to make a go of the marriage. As a teacher, I've seen the psychological damage that separation and/or divorce, often involving a lot of acrimony between parents, inflicts on children. I don't advocate putting up with a dreadful situation for the sake of the children, but having children is a huge responsibility. I was once uncritically in favor of divorce. I now think we have to weigh up the social and personal consequences. Couples who don't have children are of course free to do as they wish.

THOMPSON: Your heroine, Sinéad, seems disengaged from the world because of her depression.

NÍ AONGHUSA: When she plunges into her depression in London, I make her speak in the second person to suggest her sense of displacement and alienation from the world, but she feels quite distanced from the world during most of the novel.

THOMPSON: Eoin, the husband, could be a heroic character, but in *Four Houses* his infidelity mars his goodness.

NÍ AONGHUSA: I saw Eoin as a sympathetic character, though not everyone agrees with this assessment. Some thought him absolutely horrible. Eoin would be liberal by comparison with many Irish husbands, even slightly liberated. He cooks, he isn't bad tempered, and he doesn't have hang-ups about masculinity. He isn't a domestic tyrant! I saw him as being utterly unlike Sinéad's father or Tom, two controlling men. I think younger men aren't under such pressure to be seen to control, dominate, and humiliate women. However, human nature being what it is, there are probably as many nasty men as there always were (likewise for women).

THOMPSON: Are conditions better for women in Ireland these days?

NÍ AONGHUSA: Conditions for women in Ireland are improving all the time, whereas in Northern Ireland society is still very patriarchal and women are disregarded. The advances in the Republic are due to the feminists in the 1960s and 1970s who fought for contraception, also the legal battles fought in Irish courts which allowed married women to be recognized as financially independent entities, and, to a huge extent, the European Union. It forced equality legislation on reluctant Irish governments. We have many reasons to be grateful to the EU.

THOMPSON: How is life different for women in the North?

NÍ AONGHUSA: Nationalists aren't famous for being wildly pro-women, but they are changing more quickly than unionists. Unionists are about thirty years behind the Republic. However, the advances in the Republic didn't happen because the politicians here were enlightened, but because the European Union forced them to make changes.

THOMPSON: How are women activists welcomed in the North?

NÍ AONGHUSA: A friend of mine, the co-coordinator of an educational program being run in conjunction with the North, went to Belfast for a meeting. She was the only woman in the room and she had to endure a dreadfully hostile atmosphere during the meeting. The next time she went with a male colleague; and they tried to ignore her and talk exclusively to him. He deferred to her all the time. In the South the older men have learned to hide their prejudices and to be civil to women. Nevertheless, in the Republic women are still not making it to the top of the civil service, and promotional opportunities for women in the legal system are not abundant, although women have been appointed as judges in the last few years. Again, when some of the old white males die off, this should change. There's still a long way to go in the Republic.

THOMPSON: What's your opinion of the so-called Celtic Tiger economy?

NÍ AONGHUSA: I'm sorry to see the move to a consumer society in Ireland. When people define themselves in terms of their spending power and lose sight of their values, I see huge dangers for society, in particular for the less well-off sectors. I would like to see a balance where people consider others and feel a sense of social and communal responsibility.

THOMPSON: Is this economic growth connected to Ireland's status as an ex-colony, redefining and reinventing itself?

NÍ AONGHUSA: I agree with people who say we're emerging from a postcolonial depression. When the British left Ireland the country was desperately poor; it took almost seventy years to shake off that poverty. The British occupation didn't enrich us in any way. It took our language and broke our culture. Modern Britain doesn't really appreciate or understand the Irish. If we were to join the Commonwealth I'd be most aggrieved. I see us as distinct and separate.

THOMPSON: Yet, wouldn't you say that this new economy has been accompanied by a more open climate that seems to benefit women writers?

NÍ AONGHUSA: The climate for women writers is more benign than in previous decades, although there are still difficulties. I think it must have been extraordinarily dispiriting to be a woman writer in the 1940s, 1950s, and 1960s. The poet Eavan Boland has spoken of the obstacles facing women writers and artists in the 1960s when there was incredible antagonism toward women. Women writers found it difficult to have their work accepted, published, and reviewed: it was a man's world. This all began to change in the 1970s. The battle is by no means over, but the terms of the exchange between men and women are improving.

THOMPSON: Have you ever thought of living outside of Ireland?

NÍ AONGHUSA: In my twenties I wanted to leave Ireland but my husband wouldn't consider leaving, so I stayed.

THOMPSON: How does England function for Irish immigrants today?

NÍ AONGHUSA: It offers opportunities and a quality lifestyle for our highly educated and skilled immigrants. Many of the previous generations of immigrants, with some exceptions, were uneducated people who worked in unskilled and poorly paid jobs, and with little opportunity for advancement. As a student I worked in London, and I'm particularly fond of it. An aunt, some cousins, and good friends of mine live there. For me, as a student, it offered anonymity, freedom of thought, and freedom to live as you pleased. It's a wonderfully cosmopolitan city, something that Dublin is only in the process of becoming.

THOMPSON: What does your novel say about Irish families?

NÍ AONGHUSA: The novel's family is typical of some Irish families—conservative and Catholic with rigid, almost Victorian attitudes. Some Irish families are very close-knit, more because of the strongly authoritarian and controlling nature of the parents than because of Catholicism. Sinéad's parents think the family is more important than anything else in the world, a world view informed by a strong traditionalism.

THOMPSON: In the novel women create domestic harmony. Even at the funeral, the women cook, clean, and create a comfortable space. Is this a problematic issue for you?

NÍ AONGHUSA: The women cook and clean at the funeral because that's the way things used to be in rural (and urban!) Ireland. In some places things haven't changed much. However, last year I attended my uncle's funeral in Tipperary and saw many developments in the allocation of gender roles. The men of my generation (and younger) were as likely to cook, clean, and wash up at the wake as the women. The men and women took turns to cook meals for the family, hand out food to visitors, and wash up dishes and saucepans. It's certainly something that's changing. I used to hate the way things were in Ireland because I hated the woman's domestic role, being uninterested in matters domestic.

THOMPSON: The scene where the locals express their hostility to a woman alone in the pub in Galway is unnerving. How typical is that behavior?

NÍ AONGHUSA: There is often antagonism toward strangers or lone women in rural communities, which is usually expressed through hostility or resentment, but occasionally it develops into something more threatening. The Irish are as capable of savagery as anybody.

THOMPSON: Most of the novel's women do have children, even though they may not want them. Are women who don't want to be mothers treated differently even now?

NÍ AONGHUSA: In Ireland it is generally thought that women should be interested in motherhood and children, and that women who aren't are somehow unnatural. That is changing.

THOMPSON: When I was first introduced to Maggie and Jean I assumed that they were lesbians. Even after Jean brings home a boyfriend, I'm not convinced that they are not in love with each other. Were they meant to be so ambivalent?

NÍ AONGHUSA: In all honesty, I never thought of Jean and Maggie as being lesbians. I've enjoyed very intense, nonsexual friendships with women so I didn't consider their friendship in that light. A friend pointed out the lesbian interpretation of their friendship before the novel went to print but I didn't change anything. However, now I wonder about them! Maybe there was something there. I don't know. It's a bit simplistic to reduce everything to sex, very tedious actually.

THOMPSON: Would you call yourself a feminist?

NÍ AONGHUSA: I'm a feminist and don't understand women who say they aren't. Women ought to be free to make the choices they want with regard to careers, children, and personal lives. However, it's much easier for a woman to lead a fulfilled and interesting life in today's Ireland. Men's attitudes toward women are changing. A lot of men now actively "like" women. I think that, in general, men of my father's generation neither respected nor liked women. The Catholic Church brainwashed them into a Pauline attitude toward them.

THOMPSON: What was your first published work?

NÍ AONGHUSA: When I was twenty-three I sat down and wrote my first short story. I stayed up all one night to write it. David Marcus of "New Irish Writing"—a weekly page devoted to poetry and fiction in one of the national daily newspapers—accepted it for publication. The following year he published a second story of mine. After the publication of this story some of my friends attacked me about it. I found this episode so disturbing and upsetting that I didn't write again for years.

THOMPSON: Why did they attack you?

NÍ AONGHUSA: They threatened to sue me for libel because they thought that I wrote about one of them. Libel laws in Ireland are very strict: a person only has to think they can identify themselves in a story, article, or novel to be able to sue. That accusation and threat devastated me. For years, if I even thought about them I was struck down by blinding headaches. Anything I tried to write I abandoned. Thirteen years later I hit a personal crisis—a really low point in my life—and, during the counseling that followed, I was able to let go of that episode and began to write again. Mind you, before the first novel was published, I suffered panic attacks and had nightmares in which people rose up and accused me of writing about them!

THOMPSON: Do you regret writing the story?

NÍ AONGHUSA: I regret the lost years but I'm glad to be alive, to have a family, and to be able to write again.

THOMPSON: Who encouraged you to write?

NÍ AONGHUSA: Mostly my teachers in secondary school. My family was unsure about my ambition to write, and so they didn't support me. I always thought that writing should have a "bite" in it, but my father and mother, conservative Catholics, were afraid that what I might write would reflect badly on the family. When my father saw my first published stories he advised me not to write about sexual matters because he thought people read fiction as autobiography and that I might get a bad reputation. He thought a woman should not be seen to know much about carnality and brutality. He would have hated my novel! He died in 1996 before it was published, but my mother has never read it.

THOMPSON: Why won't she read it?

NÍ AONGHUSA: She's afraid of what she'll find there.

THOMPSON: How did you learn to put a "bite" into your writing?

NÍ AONGHUSA: As a student in secondary school I had three or four wonderful teachers who weren't the slightest bit inhibited about speaking out in the classroom and questioning the "status quo" or perceived wisdom. They were wonderfully ingenious at getting their students to think. I was influenced by their probing of Irish society. They opened my mind. That's where the "bite" comes from.

THOMPSON: How did your teachers train you to question values?

NÍ AONGHUSA: One teacher used the poetry on the Anglo-Irish course to highlight the idiosyncratic nature of some of the accepted values in Irish society. She was very keen to point out that in Ireland unsanctioned sexual activities—fornication, adultery, masturbation, etc.—were treated as if they were graver crimes than murder. For example, women could be incarcerated in mental institutions if unmarried and pregnant. Sexuality was considered a sort of depravity. Please bear in mind that, while that is true of then, Ireland was in a state of flux and everything was changing. Nevertheless, when I returned to school to teach, one of the nuns discouraged girls from wearing patent shoes in case boys could see their underwear reflected in the shoes!

Our history teacher taught us to question the version of history we had been taught in primary school. She too was after the truth, rather than a glorified, sentimentalized version of the past. She taught us not to accept anything at face value. And our Irish teacher used historical exactness as a weapon against fuzzy nationalistic sentiments and religious intolerance. She gave us an appreciation of Wolfe Tone and other Protestant Irish patriots and told us about the 1913 lockout of strikers by the employers, and the riots during the first performance of Synge's drama *The Playboy of the Western World* in the Abbey Theatre. She told us about Beckett and Joyce and stimulated our interest in plays. Under her influence a friend and I used to attend cheap Monday night performances in the Abbey's Peacock Theatre while still at school. We saw, for example, performances of *The Tailor and Ansty* (once banned), *At Swim Two Birds*, *The Shadow of the Glen* amongst others in this way.

THOMPSON: Sounds like quite a liberal education

NÍ AONGHUSA: It was.

THOMPSON: Liz McManus talks of subterfuge as behavior by the Irish, who have learned not to speak openly. Do you think she is right?

NÍ AONGHUSA: I think so. When the British occupied this country, the Irish could not speak openly and so had to engage in a duplicity of expression: irony, equivocation, and playing the dumb fool were some of the weapons employed in the game. Our tendency to answer a question with a question stems from the need to be verbally dexterous while under interrogation. The Irish excel at circumlocution, and at not saying what they mean. However, TV and mass communications will end that. Already a certain blandness is creeping into the English language in Ireland.

THOMPSON: In your novel not only family but even friends such as Maggie, who appears to be a feminist, encourage Sinéad to return to Eoin. Why didn't they divorce, because the novel was set before 1995?

NÍ AONGHUSA: Technically they couldn't divorce then. I sent her back to him because I thought they had unfinished business to settle. Sinéad was depressed through most of her marriage, so she needed to see if the relationship would endure or collapse when she was recovering. They came together to try to salvage their marriage. She was as likely to succeed as to lapse into her former behavioral and thinking patterns. The original ending was more tenuous and ambiguous than the published version, and it wasn't clear if the relationship would survive.

THOMPSON: The resolution to the novel is not an easy one for me. It seems, in some respects, that the issue of infidelity is subsumed by Sinéad's depression. Were you trying to achieve a balance in terms of responsibility for the marital breakdown?

NÍ AONGHUSA: I think that the ending of the book is ambiguous. The relationship may or may not endure. I didn't see Eoin's infidelity as being the only factor in their break-up. Sinéad's extreme emotional states and physical coldness also contributed to their problems. Eoin had an affair because there was nothing for him at home—he's no saint. It's difficult for Sinéad to forgive him and let go of her sexual jealousy. She has to weigh his fall from grace against the benefits of staying with him. He's good-humored, considerate, interesting, liberated, domesticated, and interested in her!

THOMPSON: She's pregnant at the end of the novel, even though she had expressed a dislike of babies. Why?

NÍ AONGHUSA: I made her pregnant at the end of the novel to indicate that she was beginning to trust herself to be a good person, to be able to change from the way she had been. She was more open to life, more ready to take on challenges. The experience might not prove enriching. The challenge might be more than she was able for.

THOMPSON: How has *Four Houses and a Marriage* been received?

NÍ AONGHUSA: The novel received very favorable reviews and sold very well in the shops. However, a few reviewers didn't like the ending; some were unconvinced by her recovery at the end of the book and felt that her encounters with the psychiatrist should have formed part of the novel.

THOMPSON: I know that you're working on your second novel. Can you say what it's about?

NÍ AONGHUSA: The novel tells the stories of Sissie O'Sullivan, her gay brother, Donal, her repressed and unhappily married sister, Deirdre, their dying mother, Nora, and domineering father, Jeremiah [Miah]. Sissie, unlike her siblings, takes every opportunity to oppose and goad Jeremiah. After a terrible family occasion, a drunken Sissie begins a brief affair with her brother-in-law. The dying Nora imagines that her long-dead son, Joe, has come back to life. Sissie's unpredictable behavior upsets and antagonizes her siblings, but she finally realizes that she must live life on her own terms, and not simply by opposing her father in everything.

THOMPSON: Can you talk about the two working titles—*Roger Casement Is Not a Homosexual* and *The Old Pretender*?

NÍ AONGHUSA: The final title may be very different from the current draft versions. One comes from something Miah says in an exchange toward the end of the book, and the other obviously refers to him. I thought they illustrated the core moral dilemma in this novel, that is, Miah's refusal to accept life in all its manifestations. It's a feature of the brand of Catholicism he practices. He undergoes tortuous mental gymnastics to construct an alternative world, almost a virtual world, to avoid confronting certain truths about his family. It's a real dilemma for him when Sissie "outs" Donal's homosexuality.

THOMPSON: It sounds like you're attacking the fabric of Irish Catholicism.

NÍ AONGHUSA: There's an authoritarian Catholicism—once very prevalent here—that views people as sinful beings, and is uneasy about human sexuality. It detests fornication and the idea of physical pleasure, and values celibacy. It allows sexual intimacy only for the purpose of pro-creation. A lot of the book focuses on attitudes to sex.

THOMPSON: How does this fit into your general scheme for the book?

NÍ AONGHUSA: I wanted to get at the heart of how Ireland used to be, how it is now, and to study the struggles, hostilities, and estrangements that are exposed by a changing Ireland. Initially, I focused on the father [Jeremiah], but then the Sissie character became the main interest. I see her as the antithesis of the old value system—she's female, opinionated, stubborn, and confident—but she has designed a value system that is opposite to her father's simply to spite him. She discovers that she can't define herself by total repudiation of what her father stands for, and that she has to discover what she believes in herself, in order to live a meaningful life.

THOMPSON: Miah represents older Irish values and Sissie the new ones?

NÍ AONGHUSA: Miah's view of the world is not negotiable. It even necessitates the repudiation of two of his children. He won't listen to them or accept them because, to his mind, they are contaminants. Sissie openly, and Donal furtively, oppose him. His is a world without love, without tolerance, and without forgiveness. He thinks he's a Christian but he is deeply unchristian. Deirdre, possibly as the eldest, has been deeply influenced by her father. Her fear of sex and her inability to respond in a physical way to her husband destroys her marriage. At the end of the novel she faces a bleak future. Miah seems more accommodating at the end, but his apparent mellowing is a device to ensure that he's not left alone, that somebody will look after him. He hasn't changed.

THOMPSON: Why did Sissie emerge as the protagonist?

NÍ AONGHUSA: Sissie sets herself to oppose Miah's values because she believes that he is wrong. She tries to be the exact opposite of what Jeremiah wants her to be but realizes eventually that this lifestyle limits and demeans her in its own way, and she reconstitutes herself. She also learns that the family isn't necessarily a bad thing, that it can nourish, affirm, and sustain people. This is why she is the main character in the book.

THOMPSON: You call Sissie an adventuress. Can you explain what her adventures are all about?

NÍ AONGHUSA: She has physical, sexual, and emotional adventures. I call her an adventuress because she's fearless. She's content with her lifestyle until the crisis with Dante makes her pause to think about her values. She behaves deplorably when she starts the affair with Fintan, but decides she has to stop it. She doesn't feel any need to confess to Deirdre, but when Deirdre finds out, she's genuinely remorseful. She isn't initially enthusiastic about taking on the responsibility of Brian and his daughter, but she loves him and realizes that she has to accept him and the problematic daughter if she is to have any chance of happiness.

THOMPSON: Since Deirdre does not like sex yet her sister Sissie is promiscuous, should we read them as foils for each other?

NÍ AONGHUSA: I don't think that they're foils for each other, not like two sides to a coin. They react differently to the pressures put on them by Miah. Sissie rejects Miah's prohibitions on female self-expression in the area of sex, and Deirdre is inhibited completely as a result of his indoctrination of her as a child. Deep down she feels that sex is a nasty business, an unpleasant duty that is only justified on the grounds that it produces more human beings. Deirdre is one of the saddest characters in the book. She alienates Fintan but she's not a bad person. In her own way, she tries to do the right thing. She's jealous of Sissie's confidence and luck. She feels dumped on. It's possible that she and Sissie might find common ground at some stage in the future, after Jeremiah's death perhaps?

THOMPSON: I must ask you about Dante Bird. Is he a ghost or a dream?

NÍ AONGHUSA: Dante appears only to Sissie and she doesn't know if she dreams him or if he's a ghost. I leave the reader to make up his or her mind on this.

THOMPSON: He and his family are sinister presences. Can you explain their roles in the novel?

NÍ AONGHUSA: I agree that Dante is a sinister presence in the novel, but I don't think his mother and cousins are. His cousins, Tony and Giovanni, are hard-working, decent people. Dante rapes Camilla but her husband, although initially shaken by the revelation, is strengthened in his love for her. Camilla is strong, and eventually manages to come through the experience unscathed.

THOMPSON: But Tony and Giovanni are murderers.

NÍ AONGHUSA: Tony and Giovanni planned only to beat up Dante, not kill him. What they did was wrong in the eyes of the law. Perhaps they decide that their family has suffered enough from Dante, that they don't need to undergo additional suffering. They take on the task of looking after Mrs. Bird, Dante's mother, and take better care of her than Dante would.

THOMPSON: Why is the family Italian?

NÍ AONGHUSA: Remember that Dante is half Irish. He could be any man gone wrong, any nationality.

THOMPSON: But why did you give him some Italian blood?

NÍ AONGHUSA: The Italian community is part of the Dublin landscape, but my characters are fictional inventions and don't reflect at all on it. I think that, because I find Italy so fascinating, I worked an Italian element into the novel. Nowadays there's such a diversity of nationalities in Ireland that there's more scope to work aspects or fragments of other cultures into Irish novels.

THOMPSON: What do you like about Italian culture?

NÍ AONGHUSA: I've always been interested in Italy. I studied Latin and Roman history at school and loved it. Julius Caesar was a kind of hero to me when I was a girl. I'm just a great fan of Roman civilization and the Italian Renaissance. If I could ever design and build a house for myself, I would incorporate as many aspects of the Roman house into the design as were practical. I love the idea of an internal garden, for instance.

THOMPSON: None of the characters are particularly sympathetic, not even Nora, even though she has her reasons for being such a distant mother. I found my identifications shifting at times from one character to another, creating a decentered reading experience.

NÍ AONGHUSA: Well, I wanted the reader to feel for all the characters. I didn't intend that reading the book would be an unsettling, uncomfortable experience, if that's what you mean. The reality of family life for many people is that it's a mixed bag and parents don't always have the best interests of their children at heart. Jeremiah, for example, thinks that his children are there for him, and that they must live life according to his ways, values, wishes, and expectations. The love such a parent has for children is conditional, not total. Therefore, how can these characters—his children—be other than deeply flawed? It's such an effort for them, in the case of Sissie and Donal, to break free of him. Deirdre fails to break away and her life is very dark.

THOMPSON: What about Nora?

NÍ AONGHUSA: Nora married this man and found little comfort in the marriage. She reacted in her own fashion in order to protect herself.

THOMPSON: And Fintan?

NÍ AONGHUSA: Fintan probably had no idea, when marrying Deirdre, what he was letting himself in for with her family. He had recently left the seminary when he met her, was suffering severe guilt feelings, and repressed his sexuality. He finds, however, that he can't repress himself forever. All the characters are fighting separate battles in the book.

THOMPSON: Mary O'Donnell's book *Virgin and the Boy* was criticized for centering on a sexually active woman. I'm wondering if you anticipate similar responses to your novel.

NÍ AONGHUSA: Some people have difficulty with a strong woman character. I think that the old double standard is alive and kicking, in that a woman who engages in guilt-free sex with men is still ostracized by many people, while a man is significantly freer to satisfy his sexual appetites. I think this extraordinary myself. Critics should concentrate on the quality of the writing, plot, and characterization in a novel. It's hardly justifiable to condemn a book in its entirety because reviewers find it difficult to accept a character's behavior, although they may certainly state their reservations.

THOMPSON: What women writers do you like to read?

NÍ AONGHUSA: I only heard about people like Kate O'Brien, Elizabeth Bowen, and Barbara Fitzgerald later in life. In my late teens and early twenties I read Chekhov, Dostoyevsky, Turgenev, and Tolstoy, also a bit of Gorky. My favorite women writers were Jane Austen, Emily Brontë, Sylvia Plath, and George Eliot. Since then I've branched out and read people like Alice Munro, Pat Barker, Joan Brady, and have recently discovered the wonderful Annie Proulx.

THOMPSON: Why do you think you heard less about women writers?

NÍ AONGHUSA: Women writers don't get quite the same press or respect as men writers. Mediocre men writers still get more attention than good women writers.

THOMPSON: Like the situation with the *Field Day Anthology?*

NÍ AONGHUSA: A scandal in Ireland. The awful thing was that men like Seamus Heaney, Seamus Deane didn't disregard women writers—

they just never saw them or considered them. For them women writers don't exist. I comfort myself that they are men from the old school and those things are changing.

THOMPSON: Do you read any of the writers that the *Field Day* editors did include?

NÍ AONGHUSA: John Banville, John McGahern, and Myles na gCopaleen (Brian O'Nolan). I was absolutely besotted with Beckett's work once. I thought Seamus Deane's book *Reading in the Dark* really good. I've read James Joyce, although I've never managed *Finnegans Wake*—life's too short!

Éilís Ní Dhuibhne

Interviewed by

CAITRIONA MOLONEY

Courtesy of Photocraft, Bray

BORN: Dublin, 1954
EDUCATED: University College, Dublin, B.A. in English literature, Ph.D. in folklore
RESIDES: Bray, County Dublin, Ireland
WORKS: Manuscript librarian, National Library, Dublin
GENRES: Fiction, literary criticism
AWARDS: Shortlisted for the Orange Prize (2000) for *The Dancers Dancing*

Éilís Ní Dhuibhne is beginning to be recognized as one of Ireland's most talented writers. Ní Dhuibhne's intense interest in myth and history allows her fiction to embrace antiquity and modernity with versatility and authority. Her canon includes four collections of short stories—Blood and Water (1988), Eating Women Is Not Recommended (1991), Inland Ice (1997), and The Pale Gold of Alaska (2002)—a play, Dun na mBan Tri Thine (1994), and two novels—The Bray House (1990) and The Dancers Dancing (1999). She has also published children's literature and scholarly articles on folklore.

Ní Dhuibhne's fiction rewards critical attention as it uses history and myth to illustrate the multiple palimpsests underneath contemporary reality. Gerry Smyth recognizes that Ní Dhuibhne's use of "mythological

*tales and legends reveals a deep fascination with landscape and with hu-
mankind's role in nature" (1997, 166).*

*"Midwife to the Fairies," which has been frequently anthologized, is
Ní Dhuibhne's first use of an intertextual technique, juxtaposing a medieval tale to a contemporary legal case involving infanticide, the Joanna
Hayes Baby case. "Summer Pudding," a story in* Inland Ice, *also exemplifies Ní Dhuibhne's favorite themes, silence and collusion, which she
calls "turning a blind eye." "Summer Pudding," a story of famine
refugees in Wales, deconstructs famine history by interjecting factors of
race and gender: a nineteenth-century travel writer describes the famine
refugees as subhuman and apelike; the refugees themselves are confused
by the sexuality of Anglo-Irish aristocratic refugees, the ladies of Llan-
gollen. Traces of the ancient Deirdre story create a mythical resonance to
the story.*

*Using multiple perspectives comes to Ní Dhuibhne quite naturally, as
she says herself speaking of her Gaelic background, "ambiguity and dualism and bifurcation of identity started for me very early." Ní Dhuibhne
sees exile and migration as metaphors for an ambiguity and duality that
she considers typically Irish.*

*The Dancer's Dancing, short-listed for the Orange Prize, exemplifies
what Smyth calls the Irish "deep fascination with landscape" (1997,
166). The novel gives a luxuriously textured description of the landscape
of Donegal, in its geographical, historical, social, and spiritual aspects. In
the persona of Orla, a teenage girl at a Gaelic summer school, Ní Dhuibhne explores the contradictions of Irish identity that include urban/rural,
Gaelic/English speaking, Catholic/Protestant, North/South.* Dancers
Dancing *suggests some unusual conclusions about these familiar tropes,
makes an important contribution to the female bildungsroman tradition,
and successfully avoids both stereotype and sentimentality to capture
many of the voices of contemporary Ireland.*

Éilís Ní Dhuibhne was working on a collection of short stories called
The Pale Gold of Alaska *when I spoke with her during the Celebrating
Irish Women Writers Conference in Dublin.*

·   ·   ·

MOLONEY: I have a question about your Gaelic name. What is the significance of having an Irish name today?

NÍ DHUIBHNE: It does have political significance, and that's why I have kept it. I'm constantly tempted to change it because it's a real burden—nobody can pronounce it or spell it. It used to have an aura of shameful connotations for people in Dublin and English speakers in Ireland, which I have always been worried about. Even recently, my latest feeling that I would like to change it occurred because, as a result of this spurt of racism and nationalism in Ireland, the woman who has founded the society for trying to limit the number of immigrants to Ireland and who speaks in very racist terms is an Irish speaker and has an Irish name. I felt, "yes, of course," she would have; it does have that sort of connotation, which I find difficult to cope with. On the other hand, it's too late for me to change my name now; I would be betraying something. But, it's a very complicated issue. My family always had an English name which is Deeny; Deeny is the Anglicization for Dhuibhne, so that's what I was called when I was a child at home. But in school—and I think this ambiguity and dualism and bifurcation of identity started for me very early in that way—in school I was called one thing, at home another, and so I stayed with the name I had in school. Maybe because that was my literary name, and the name I wrote everything under as a child.

MOLONEY: What does your latest novel, *The Dancers Dancing*, say about the connection between the Gaeltacht and Irish culture?

NÍ DHUIBHNE: The novel explores the experience of young, urban, English-speaking children in the Gaeltacht, rather than the culture of the Gaeltacht people themselves. The perspective is of a teenage girl, Orla, who has family connections with both the city and the Gaeltacht. She has difficulty in reconciling these two aspects of her background, and is tempted to abandon both: she is ashamed of her parents, who live in the city, primarily because of class shame, and she is also ashamed of her Gaeltacht relations, for similar reasons. Her family in both camps is not sophisticated enough for her. In the novel, she moves toward a reconciliation and in particular finds that she can appreciate the value of the Gaeltacht and the rural culture more than she does at the start.

MOLONEY: It's interesting for me to hear you say "shameful connotations" in conjunction with Gaelic—I did take that impression away from a number of your stories. It seemed part of the relationship of rural Gaelic Ireland to the urban center.

NÍ DHUIBHNE: That probably emerges in the short stories in *Blood and Water,* especially the title story. There is another aspect of that apart from the rural-urban. My family had a rural background in an urban environment, so that adolescent feeling of being ashamed of your own parents was a huge factor in my development and consciousness which I'm still coming to terms with. That is not exclusively rural-urban; it's also a class thing. It affects people who move out of one social class into another. As a child, I was working class, with very socially upwardly mobile aspirations coming from my mother, so I was constantly pitched in with people who—it seemed to me at the time—were superior to me. That inculcates a huge feeling of inferiority and shame in the child. It takes a long time to come to terms with that, and to get over it.

MOLONEY: In *Dancers Dancing,* does Orla represent different kinds of Irishness?

NÍ DHUIBHNE: Orla represents the postcolonial Irish who are ashamed of their Irishness. Her view of her elderly aunt, whom she believes she has left for dead in a barn, symbolizes the attitude of such people—they are linked to the Irish and Gaelic past by ties of duty, but if the tie could somehow break, without their having to actively make the break, they would be pleased. Orla would not kill her aunt, but she would let her die. Later she repents, when she finds that other people, whom she looks up to, admire her aunt. What she is doing is what Irish people in general do to the Irish language—they let it die, although they would not take responsibility for killing it! And if an outsider, a foreigner, the European Union suggests that Irish is a valuable cultural commodity, they are liable to agree and think, "Oh yes! if they think so, then it must be!"

She also represents the Irish person who is straddling two cultures, city and country, and two periods, premodern and postmodern Ireland. But she is also just herself, a confused girl, and has other aspects apart from these cultural ones. Her closest relationship, in the novel, is with the river.

MOLONEY: You described your father as an immigrant, meaning that he was an immigrant to England. Did he feel inferior about his Donegal background?

NÍ DHUIBHNE: Yes. Oh, yes. My father would have had that sense of the inferiority that Irish immigrants to England and Scotland had as well. I can't say he transmitted that sense of inferiority to me, but I think

I re-experienced it as I was growing up. Some of those stories in *Blood and Water* and stories about childhood reflect that sense of conflict with the surrounding society.

MOLONEY: Between the rich and poor relations in "Kingston Ridge"?

NÍ DHUIBHNE: Exactly, that's the one I'm thinking of, yes.

MOLONEY: And, of course, the last line is ironic, that the poverty must be different now.

NÍ DHUIBHNE: Yes, it probably isn't different. Well, of course, everyone was poor. Everyone who grew up in the fifties and the sixties in Dublin says, "gosh, we were poor," but when I talk to people who came from more indigent backgrounds than I did, that they were protected by belonging to ghettos of like people. Whereas, I felt we were deprived within a very middle-class surrounding, thanks to the great ambition and hard work and energy of my mother, which I should appreciate, but it's difficult.

MOLONEY: To move you up a class.

NÍ DHUIBHNE: To move us up, yes. And now I don't feel we've moved. After a while, some kind of synthesis seems to occur and my mother seems to be very much the same as my friends or my husband, even though she's completely uneducated formally, and has had a totally different kind of experience. That whole class thing seems to evaporate, almost, as you move through life in Ireland. But as a child, I was terribly conscious of it. It was a real burden.

MOLONEY: Some of the stories express that sense of dislocation and unbelongingness.

NÍ DHUIBHNE: The collection of short stories I'm working on now called *The Pale Gold of Alaska* deals with that sense of dislocation and being an outsider, which has the advantage of making a writer of you, the experience of being on the margin. I always felt on a ridge, like "Kingston Ridge," in-between different societies, looking down at them. That's a painful place to be in a sense, but it also gives you a dual perspective. I'm increasingly interested in this duality and ambiguity of my own personality, which is very typically Irish.

MOLONEY: You're saying people can be exiles without leaving Ireland?

NÍ DHUIBHNE: Absolutely. The linguistic situation is the most clear-cut example; migration represents other dualities and conflicts and ambiguities in Irish society symbolically and metaphorically. My father moved from an Irish language-speaking region to an English-speaking region within the island. Language has a huge significance for Irish society.

MOLONEY: Does the mainstream, in a sense, view the Irish-speaking communities as primitives or exotics?

NÍ DHUIBHNE: It's difficult to sum up how the mainstream views the Irish-speaking communities; mostly nowadays they simply ignore them and forget they exist at all. They're not on people's minds in Dublin, which has its own momentum and is cut off from the rest of the country and especially from those little patches of Gaeltacht over on the edge. In the heyday of nationalism they were regarded as exotic and primitive, but in some way pure and desirable, and that has been turned around to just regarding them as unimportant and almost a nuisance.

MOLONEY: In 1990, you talked with Donna Perry about the publishing situation in Ireland, saying it was very hard for women writers to get published. Could you comment on how the publishing situation has changed since then, generally and for yourself?

NÍ DHUIBHNE: It isn't so hard to get published in general anymore; publishing seems to have become much more commercially viable. I've changed publishers because Attic Press, my old publisher, has disappeared, so I moved up to Blackstaff in Belfast. I've had two different editors on the two books—both excellent, I must say.

In 1990 I was talking about my own experience; I had published short stories in the newspapers. There was a great outlet for stories in the *Irish Press* where David Marcus, an amazing man, started me off by publishing a short story of mine every single week, but that's not there anymore. They do have the page in the *Sunday Tribune* once a month, but it's not really the same thing; I don't use it anymore. I've written three collections of short stories; for the first two, I would have published nearly all those stories in magazines and newspapers before I put the books together. The third one, more of the stories hadn't been published anywhere until they went into the book, and now, at this time, I am working on another collection of short stories, and it doesn't even occur to me to send them to magazines. I'm just assembling them, and I will publish them—all going well—for the first time as a collection. I mean, unless something wonderful happened. I've sent a few to the *New Yorker,* and they were interested. They didn't actually publish them, but I might try that again with some of the other ones. But otherwise, there aren't really many outlets for stories in Ireland one would bother with.

MOLONEY: Do you think it's getting easier now for women writers to publish?

NÍ DHUIBHNE: Oh, I think so; Lara Harte, who was with us the other day on the panel, had published her novel when she was about nineteen or twenty. That would have been unheard of when I was that age. Publishers would not have been willing to take a risk on a first book by somebody who hadn't published very much anywhere; you'd have to put in a long apprenticeship in the journals and the newspapers, and then when you're known as a writer, somebody would take you on and do your book. But everything in Ireland has opened up: people take risks; it's a more expansive, positive society, and that affects publishing as well.

MOLONEY: Do you think the current renaissance of women writers publishing can be explained completely in economic terms?

NÍ DHUIBHNE: No, not completely but economics, the terrible "Celtic Tiger," has a huge amount to do with it. It creates an environment where people are less cautious; they take a chance on things. There's this feeling: if you try something like publishing a young person and it fails, well, that's not the end of the world. You are allowed to do that. Whereas, in the past nobody could afford any losses. That's changed.

MOLONEY: Your writing combines folklore and myth "intertextually" with fiction. How did you get started writing that way?

NÍ DHUIBHNE: That's a good way of describing it. How did I get started? Folklore is what I did in college, and so I had an obvious interest in it and I began to write seriously only after I finished my Ph.D., for practical reasons. The Ph.D. is so time consuming and absorbing that I didn't have time for creative writing. I think the first story I wrote where I counterpoint a modern story with a traditional story is the one called "Midwife to the Fairies." I was motivated as much as a folklorist as a writer because I and other people had begun in Ireland, almost for the first time, to ask what the legends really meant. They seem to be about fairies and supernatural encounters and a world which has little to do with reality. In fact, people like Nuala Ní Dhomhnail and Angela Bourke—who's a folklore scholar and creative writer who recently published a collection of short stories—were beginning to analyze what these stories were really telling us about society. I wrote that first story to illuminate the real meaning of "Midwife to the Fairies"; I counterpointed it with a contemporary story in the news in Ireland, the Joanna Hayes Baby case, a story of infanticide which was very common in Ireland. I'm still interested in that whole phenomenon, given our political attitude toward abortion.

MOLONEY: In your work, there are several references to infanticide, and it seemed to me the narrative style is quite medieval in the sense of you don't make a big deal about it. It's just there. And your characters don't make a big deal about it, which seems to me to be very representative of a medieval attitude to infanticide, not using "medieval" in any pejorative sense.

NÍ DHUIBHNE: I know what you mean. It's taken as a given; it's probably a reflection of the sources of information. Infanticide is almost a given in the folktales, where it would never, of course, be referred to directly. "Midwife to the Fairies" is about turning a blind eye, being silent, which would have been the general attitude. These stories are commonplace in newspapers from the nineteenth century, which I look at in the National Library often; it's quite remarkable how often you find accounts of court cases about cases of child murder. It seems to have been a common feature of Irish life. But I do feel horrified at the implications of that.

MOLONEY: Well, your stories get that across. "Midwife to the Fairies" makes it more horrifying to the reader by communicating the character's attitude. There's a contrast.

NÍ DHUIBHNE: I would suspect it was simply taken for granted, not talked about, unless the unfortunate girl was unlucky enough to fall into the hands of the police. Otherwise, people just knew that this was going on and didn't do anything.

MOLONEY: I didn't really understand the last paragraph of "Midwife to the Fairies." What does the man in the story do to the hag figure?

NÍ DHUIBHNE: He puts out her eye. It's a very potent symbol of blindness and of not seeing. She has made a mistake after her visit to the fairy hill of recognizing the fairies who ought to be invisible, and so she is seeing and talking about what she should not see or talk about. It's a symbol for censorship, to see the secret thing. As a midwife, you must see all kinds of things, but you're not supposed to come back and blab about them in the marketplace. After she does that, he blinds her, so that she won't do it again.

MOLONEY: Is there a reference to infanticide in "Gweedore Girl"?

NÍ DHUIBHNE: There is, yes, and it's just a reference. It doesn't play a major part in the story; I found that story in a newspaper when I was doing research to get the feel of Derry during the period when the story is set, about 1890; there were little accounts of babies being found in brown paper bags.

MOLONEY: I see some connections between your story "Summer Pudding" and "The Exile of the Sons of Uisliu," the Medieral Deidre story.

NÍ DHUIBHNE: Well, it isn't a deliberate recension of that, because I do not think that was in my mind. "Summer Pudding" has got a folktale feel to it, hasn't it? It really was one of those stories—which doesn't happen to me very often—that seem to just come to me in a flash really; it arose out of the landscape.

MOLONEY: What is the time setting for "A Summer Pudding"?

NÍ DHUIBHNE: It's the last year of the famine. They're famine exiles. It had its origin not just in landscape, I should mention, but also in a book by George Borrow, *Wild Wales,* an account of his walking trip in Wales in 1850, a wonderful book. George Borrow was, among other things, a very good linguist and he could speak about fifty languages, including Irish. He had been born in Ireland in Clonmel at the Barracks where his father was in the army. In Holy Head, he came upon a group of people who were very wild looking and frightened. The Welsh were very hostile toward them because they were living off the land and robbing and marauding and so on, traveler-type people. They spoke Irish, so he talked to them, really to practice his Irish. He loved getting a chance to speak one of the many languages he knew. These people were waiting to catch a boat back to Ireland, but they wouldn't go on the boat until a priest blessed them. Because he spoke Gaelic and was dressed in a nice tweed suit, they insisted that he must be a priest. They knew there was a priest in Wales, a very Protestant country, who could speak Irish and who tended to the needs of the Irish community there. There's this interplay where both sides know a game is going on, but he pretends to be a priest and gives them a blessing in Latin, and then they catch the ferry, the mail boat, the packet, and come back to Ireland. What really struck me was that he was writing this in 1850. I read it at the height of the famine commemorations over here. It was immediately obvious that these people were famine refugees who had, like so many, gone over to Wales to try and escape, which he doesn't allude to at all. I found that so poignant and amazing; something which seemed so enormously important in history, he didn't even note or mention. I wrote this story arising out of that little incident. I might have been thinking of Deirdre and the "Sons of Usnach" and Diarmud and Grainne and the myths about great loves.

MOLONEY: Both stories have a character named Naoise, and Father Tobin seemed a Fergus figure, unreliable and a trickster. And in both stories, the young characters emigrate because of a catastrophe and then return to Ireland.

NÍ DHUIBHNE: I think there is something to that idea and what Liz McManus was saying this morning after the reading. A writer absorbs all kinds of plots and stories and archetypes in her mind when she comes to write, especially writing in an almost automatic way where my imagination is doing all the work. I'm always wondering about what we call the "imagination." Where did those images come from? They all come from somewhere, and I'm always aware as an addicted reader that I have read enormous quantities of material that I have no conscious memory of, but all that stuff is somewhere inside. I'm not quite sure of when it's going to start popping out: what Liz McManus was calling plagiarism even. I wouldn't call it that, but it is an aspect of the imagination and the imagination is the world's greatest thief. It takes in images from all over the place and rearranges them in another way. As a folklorist, I know that the stories are all the same. You have Cinderella told ten million times in all different places, and that's not because of an archetypal thing, or polygenesis; the stories actually traveled around an actual path of dissemination. One person tells the story to another person all around the world several times. On the other hand, in creative writing something else is going on—what we call intertextuality now. That's a nicer word than plagiarism.

MOLONEY: But it *is* different, like Stoppard putting James Joyce into his play *Travesties* as a character and having bits from Oscar Wilde's *The Importance of Being Earnest* transplanted in entirety; it's more deliberate.

NÍ DHUIBHNE: It's deliberate. It's postmodern. And it's great because it does acknowledge a relationship. As a medievalist I know that Chaucer never even thought he should have to write an original story; although his writing is terribly original, all the material is lifted from elsewhere. Shakespeare, too. It's a romantic myth that the writer is constantly inventing new stories. As Frank O'Connor said, "It is very hard to invent a new story." There aren't really all that many of them out there.

MOLONEY: Let me ask you about "The Search for the Lost Husband," the old Irish tale woven into *Inland Ice* as interchapters. This is a deliberate attempt to connect a folklore motif to the work as a whole. Why that particular story and how does it pull the collection together?

NÍ DHUIBHNE: Most of the stories in *The Search* and *Inland Ice* are about obsessive love, and "The Search for the Lost Husband"—a story I was editing and translating for the section on oral tradition in the infamous volume 4 of the *Field Day Anthology*—was about obsessive love and tells in a metaphorical way what the more realistic stories in my collection are telling. It's the same story told in a more poetic way. The real emotion is the woman's terribly compulsive obsession with the husband. She goes through everything, including losing her children, to keep him, which paralleled what the short stories were about. I don't want to be faux naïve. I suppose it's why Joyce used Homer as a kind of counterpoint to his story of Bloom and Stephen wandering about Dublin. It gives a depth and a universality to the individual experience. It places them in their context in the history of the world.

MOLONEY: It struck me that many of these obsessive relationships in the stories are not actually with husbands; they're with adulterous lovers.

NÍ DHUIBHNE: Right. There is that difference. The stories are parallel in the sense that the obsession is for an unobtainable man, who's married in the stories, and in the folktale, is very illusive.

MOLONEY: The men who are attractive to the women are unavailable, physically or emotionally.

NÍ DHUIBHNE: They are men who are illusive, who are cooperative and friendly and loving for a while, but then withdraw. I know that man very well. Part of that character is in every man; the goat in "The Search for the Lost Husband" is like that as well. Sometimes he's a man, sometimes he's a goat, sometimes he waits until the woman catches up with him, then he goes on again. I think it describes the chase of love or courtship. Of course, I changed the end of the story, the folktale, from the real one. In the real story, like all of the fairy tales, it ends with the union of the two people. I reversed that because I felt that wasn't an appropriate ending. I don't have a thesis about this kind of thing. In the book, I am exploring a destructive kind of sexual love, and having gone through all the trials and tribulations that the girl in the story goes through, and then to stay with the man, seems like the wrong conclusion. So I changed the folktale.

MOLONEY: It seems more liberating or emancipating if they don't stay together.

NÍ DHUIBHNE: It does, really; in the past, romantic novels always ended with a marriage, but now they don't; they usually end with surviving. Going on is a more typical ending now for the romance novel.

MOLONEY: Your stories remind me of the reversal of gender roles one sees in old Irish stories. "Bill's New Wife" especially seems to be about how one gets "gendered."

NÍ DHUIBHNE: How you get gendered belongs to that area of ordinary things which I think is crucial to the way people actually live their lives—the house, housework, looking after the children, and all the rest of it. That's where the ladders start, isn't it? The story is a humorous look at how life looks from the point of view of the other gender and of the confusion it caused. A children's writer, Anne Fine, has written a book called *Bill's New Frock*. Bill is a boy who gets up one morning and he's a girl. Fine does it beautifully. I was influenced by that story. Fine's quite critical of Bill's experience in school, the way he's treated; there are apparently studies showing that boys do get more attention—I know this because I go to school sometimes to talk to children. In a mixed group, the boys ask all the questions. They automatically get more attention from the speaker. You have to watch yourself.

MOLONEY: Oh, definitely.

NÍ DHUIBHNE: I love boys. I have two boys myself. But in that mixed group you wonder, why are the girls so reticent and reserved and shy? They won't put themselves forward. I know they're the ones who've read the books. The whole thing is fascinating. And frightening.

MOLONEY: A comparison can be made to women's literature. What do you think about the literary critical establishment now in Ireland? Do you think that has started to crack at all in terms of men reading women, paying attention to women?

NÍ DHUIBHNE: I think it has started to crack. It's a slow process, one step forward and two steps back. I read in the *Irish Times* a few of weeks ago that Nuala Ní Dhomhnaill is acknowledged as being possibly the most important poet in Ireland by an important male critic like Bernard O'Donoghue, another poet and an Oxford professor. I know Nuala is just one figure and other writers may think, "Oh, yes. That's fine, there's a figurehead." But even so, I think that represents a great change in attitudes, that even some women writers are taken seriously. Because my experience, as I was saying in that talk the other day, as a student of English literature in University College Dublin was that women simply were not acknowledged as having existed in the canon of Anglo-Irish literature. Although they were there. There was absolutely no attention paid to them in academia or in the more popular literary commentary.

MOLONEY: Your story "The Catechism Examination" has several related elements—the young student, the girl who probably has learning disabilities, the sadistic teacher, and the drill of 230 theology questions—then the priest arrives and doesn't even ask one of those questions.

NÍ DHUIBHNE: In the past couple of months, we've been having yet another terrible revelation of the sadism in our society in the past, through this television documentary *States of Fear*. About brutality of the worst kind in state institutions like orphanages. One of the phenomena which has been commented upon in these documentaries is the silent collusion of other people. I do think in my story "The Catechism Examination" the greatest hostility from the narrator—the girl at the center of the story, and my alter persona—is toward the priest, who keeps his hands clean, but he is the one. It's all for him: the teacher's frenetic violence and the catechism questions and this kind of horrendously crazy, frenetic activity coming up with the First Communion. He just comes in at the end and smiles, and doesn't get involved in any way. But he must know what's going on. He turns a blind eye. That's what the story is about. And I'm glad you mention that story because I remember, soon after I wrote it, before I had even published the collection, a man—English, my age, a literary agent—commented on the stories, "I like them all, except that one.

You know, that happened to everyone; it's not important." I know brutality to children wasn't exclusively Irish, thinking of English public schools. But, it is important, and I am more incensed retrospectively about the institutionalized violence to children which occurred in my childhood and was part of our society until recently. I think it's been hugely damaging to Irish people and is only now coming out into the open. In fact, the brutality in the ordinary schools, which was minor by comparison to what went on in the industrial schools and the orphanages, hasn't come out very much yet, because it's something you're supposed to take for granted and say it never did anyone any harm. But I feel there's something awful about it.

MOLONEY: Your story makes that clear, and it suggests that a lot of the kids who took the most abuse were probably what we would now call learning disabled.

NÍ DHUIBHNE: Dyslexic. Absolutely. Oh, yes. Everyone knows that. Well, what can you do about it now? I suppose just try and make sure the same thing doesn't ever happen again. We have a very dark history in Ireland. Geraldine Moane, who's at the conference here, has a really interesting letter to the *Irish Times* yesterday, referring to that *States of Fear* documentary. She links the psyche of the Irish, the problems and the violence, right back to the famine experience when people witnessed such terrible things. We're all the descendants of the ones who survived, who were probably involved and turned a blind eye to other people's suffering, probably colluding with all kinds of violence and maybe responsible for it. She says we haven't acknowledged the effect through the generations, not that long ago.

MOLONEY: What do you think about the American academic literary theory of postcolonialism as a way of looking at Irish culture and literature?

NÍ DHUIBHNE: It's very complicated, isn't it. I know our obsession with identity. I'm very interested in the question of national identity as an effect of our postcolonialism. I know that societies which aren't postcolonial (imperialistic, postimperialistic) societies don't seem to have that constant questioning, "Who Are We and What?" You don't really find Swedes, for instance, worrying about what it means to be Swedish. They're not so fascinated by this question. A self-loathing comes from it; I am interested in a duplicitousness, a split personality of the Irish psyche personality. My whole personality down to my names, my Irish name, my English name, even my job sharing—my ability to compromise. There's a tendency to always have two things running parallel. I do a job; I'm a writer. Two lives, two experiences. Always having your finger in both pies, which could be the result of the colonial experience, where you have to be two persons. You had to doff the cap to the colonizers: have one character for dealing with them and then another personality at home. Irishness is so dualistic: the duality of the North and South, Irish and English, Catholic and Protestant. And that is characteristic of other postcolonial societies.

MOLONEY: India is divided into Pakistan and India, Muslim and Hindu. The English partitioned India before they left. The Caribbean is not so neatly bifurcated. But, of course, in any colonial society you have a whole class of people who collaborate. Call that whatever you want, but nobody can run a colony without native colonial administrators.

NÍ DHUIBHNE: "Castle-hacks."

MOLONEY: Yes, they become a special class with a vested interest in colonialism: the Anglo-Indian, the Anglo-Irish, the "Westernized" Caribbeans who identify economically and politically with the colonizer. All those dynamics produce similar kinds of conflicted identities in people.

NÍ DHUIBHNE: Yes. What one would be aware of historically is that Irish nationalism constitutes a backlash against everything that's British, but has produced a terribly rigidly Catholic, censorial, punitive society which evolved after independence and which most people now would have enormous problems with. We have a legacy of a rigid, illiberal, punishing society which kept women and children down and was frightened of every sexual impulse and of writing. One of the legacies is constant reaction and constant change. Stability can't happen in any society, but it's impossible for a postcolonial society to have cultural stability. Many reactions have to occur before Ireland is a place where a constant, stable identity can be established.

Courtesy of James Delaney

Mary O'Donnell

Interviewed by

HELEN THOMPSON

BORN: Monaghan, Ireland, 1954
EDUCATED: Maynooth College (Degree in Philosophy and German)
RESIDES: County Kildare, Ireland
WORKS: Teacher of creative writing, writer for radio and other media
GENRES: Poetry, fiction
AWARDS: *Sunday Tribune* Best New Irish Novel for *The Light-Makers*

Mary O'Donnell was born and raised in Monaghan, a border town. O'Donnell claims that the residents, "border people," have a mindset quite different from those in the Republic or in the North. She has published several collections of poetry, a collection of short stories, and three novels.

O'Donnell says that she writes variations on life's three central themes: "birth, love or lust, and death." However, she also writes about the clash between traditional and contemporary paradigms in Ireland. Her canvas is contemporary Ireland, but she shows us that the old impulses of Catholic nationalism—narrow-mindedness, insularity, and the emphasis on guilt and shame—have not yet been eradicated. Her narratives are frequently nonlinear and woven together as diaries, research, and other texts, creating a multilayered effect. For example, Virgin and the Boy *(1996) reinvents the Catholic icon and interrogates the Blessed*

116

Mother's chastity, obedience, and purity within the new Virgin's per-
formance; she is herself an icon of modernity. The very thing that the
Blessed Virgin lacks—sexuality—is foregrounded in Virgin's existence.

Through the character of Hanna in The Light-Makers, *O'Donnell*
explores cultural constructions of femininity and compulsory mother-
hood by making her protagonist infertile. In Hanna's examination of
facts, myths, statistics, and cross-cultural connections, in a text that itself
becomes intertextual, we see her renegotiate her place in Irish society and
re-envision her own identity in light of this childlessness. Also, mother-
hood as a sanctified institution is interrogated through the character of
Nina in The Elysium Testament. *Instead of being a nurturing caregiver,*
she beats her son and because of her obsession with her work, neglects
her family, her husband becoming the primary caretaker.

Anne Fogarty describes The Elysium Testament *(1999) as gothic*
(2000). O'Donnell's third novel explores but does not resolve the scien-
tific and spiritual explanations for Roland's ability to levitate. His abili-
ties are complicated by his mother Nina's profession as a restorer of
grottoes. In her work, science and spirituality clash as her restorations
are grounded in concrete research rather than ethereal faith. Nina's vio-
lent response to Roland's levitations combined with the apparent blind-
ness of others to his situation suggest a regression, back to the old order
of intimidation, conformity, and belief in appearances.

Mary O'Donnell is at work on her next novel. We communicated via
email.

•   •   •

THOMPSON: Other writers I have talked to have another career aside
from writing. Are you in a similar position?

O'DONNELL: Ah, the vexed question of multiple careers! Yes, I suppose I am always running a couple of half careers. I say "half" because I
regard writing as my primary one, alongside the emotional commitment
of being mother to a seven-year-old daughter and my husband's partner.
I do occasional radio work, write scripts, write occasional journalism,
and when I'm asked, which isn't often enough because I do enjoy this, I
give lectures and write papers on various aspects of literature. The greatest gift/privilege a writer can achieve for herself is silence and time. On
the other hand, I don't want my daughter growing up slipping little notes

under the door of my study because "Mum can't be disturbed while Great Art is being made"! So the battle for balance goes on. Or imbalance, now that I think of it.

THOMPSON: Miriam Dunne said her son would put his fingers under her office door to try and distract her. Is it hard to put aside mothering to write?

O'DONNELL: To cut to the truth of it, I look forward to older age in some respects, because all things being equal, it is when creative women find the freedom to do what they need to do most. This mirrors perfectly one of the central unresolved problems of being female. Of course it varies from culture to culture—I'm not talking about Taliban issues here—but within the context of my own reality I need more silence than I actually have. Disruption impacts severely on most creative work.

THOMPSON: How would you describe the concerns of your fiction?

O'DONNELL: I'm interested in what certain experiences do to people, and how we redefine ourselves constantly through our preoccupations, disappointments, passions, and obsessions. In life there are a couple of themes: birth, love-lust, and death. Everything else is a variant. Apart from these central themes, we draw on primitive forces around us and within our own bodies and collective memories. Landscape and nature are elemental, primeval energies all around us, even in the cities; the rhythms of the body are very grounding forces too. I love these aspects of being human.

THOMPSON: Would you call yourself a feminist?

O'DONNELL: I am certainly a feminist, in that feminism informed my thinking and still does. I would have some questions about feminism in academia in Ireland, and in the arts as well, where a strongly held position or agenda can have constraining consequences for those who do not completely toe the party line. So, although I am a feminist, I am probably an unconventional one, in that I do not play the politics of feminism any more than I have played the politics of any other world view. I live as I wish; my ideology is my own. That may sound arrogant, but it's not intended to be. It's just that a writer needs to write, more than anything else, and must be prepared to move where the spirit of her art leads her. Unfortunately, the preoccupations and concerns of feminism are rarely discussed in a positive light now.

THOMPSON: What changes have you seen for women in Ireland?

O'DONNELL: The abolition of the status of illegitimacy marked a vital change in outlook in Ireland, sometime in the early 1980s as I recall; in fact, all the legislative changes brought about gradually through our EU membership—the coming of divorce, access to birth control, the ongoing debate about abortion, the decriminalization of homosexuality—have proven valuable to marginalized sectors of Irish society. It's funny because there was nothing to "decriminalize" about lesbian relationships. A Victorian assumption of vagueness about what women "did" seemingly prevailed! All these moves inevitably have improved the decision-making capacity of many people. None of these changes make the slightest difference to one's career as a writer. You write, regardless; as it happened, I found endless material in the labyrinthine territory of female oppression as I saw it active in Ireland.

THOMPSON: *The Light-Makers* and *Virgin and the Boy* take on perhaps the most contentious issues in Irish politics: divorce and sexuality. How were they received?

O'DONNELL: The revealing aspect about this experience for me—the one which spoke volumes about just how far we had *not* come—was in the critical reception which greeted *Virgin and the Boy*. The women who reviewed it, with the exception of Madeleine Keane, were mostly repelled by its depictions of sexuality. Indeed the *Irish Independent* reviewer Sophie Gorman went so far as to claim that it made her feel "dirty." Have we or have we not read James Joyce, Henry Miller, et al.? This was a revelation to me, that a novel published in 1996 could prove so distasteful to these reviewers. It proved to me, again, that men can write what they wish about their bodies or anybody's bodily functions and activities, and that this is accepted as the norm. When a woman does it, something seems not quite right. Perhaps had a younger woman written like this? I don't know. The point is, this response masked and occluded the issues I wanted to deal with in the book: the rather authoritarian backlash against women which I believed to be underway in the late 1990s, the dangerous hostility regarding pro-choice and anti-abortion groups which I have witnessed, and the loathing of women who are careless, irresponsible, or selfish.

THOMPSON: Did female reviewers respond as negatively to your first novel, *The Light-Makers*?

O'DONNELL: It was interesting for me to discover how many Irish men, of the few men who read it, described Hanna as a "bitch" and other various terms.

THOMPSON: Why do you think they responded in that way?

O'DONNELL: Men don't read fiction by women, by and large, unless they're particularly open and smart: they believe they have nothing to learn from us. We women, on the other hand, guzzle many of their works with zeal and real interest in both their preoccupations and technique.

THOMPSON: Is that why the editors of the *Field Day Anthology* left out so many women writers? Is it that we have nothing to teach them?

O'DONNELL: The *Field Day Anthology* most certainly omitted so many women writers due to a kind of self-induced myopia on the part of its editors. Also, they have been indifferent to our response to these omissions; it was a critically reprehensible act that cannot have been other than conscious. But this proves yet again that men believe they have nothing to learn from literature written by women. The very great sense of privilege which they acquire in the course of childhood and education, even an incomplete one, enables men to conduct much of their intellectual dialectic in this manner. Although I could be wrong about this, I do not think the idea of a fourth volume will ever be more than a whitewashing exercise.

THOMPSON: Edna O'Brien frequently recounts a grim experience of her first book, *The Country Girls,* being burned in her hometown. I have always hoped this is not a common reaction. How much support did you get from your local community?

O'DONNELL: Zilch, I would say. But if you remember that Monaghan had at that time only one published author—the poet Patrick Kavanagh—and held a slight, unstated suspicion of literary works anyway, in a country which was still in the throes of shedding its censorship laws, you'll understand that. It's not unusual in rural places to suspect art, whilst admiring it at the same time. It seems the artist is pulling themselves away from the collective. S/he makes a deliberate choice to "be away" from the group's concerns, and that in itself arouses subconscious collective doubts, in my view.

THOMPSON: You're from Monaghan?

O'DONNELL: I was brought up in rural Ireland, outside Monaghan town, which lies about five miles from the border with Northern Ireland.

THOMPSON: Are you Catholic?

O'DONNELL: I was raised as a Catholic, although my parents were not particularly rigid about this. The idea of unconditional forgiveness and mercy would have been part of my father's religious credo, something which I absorbed. The notion of a punitive godhead is alien to me, and always was, despite the diligence with which early school religious education attended to our little souls. The upside of being educated at an all-girls convent school was that the St. Louis nuns were very progressive: you gradually absorbed, by the time you were about fifteen, the idea that the world was your oyster. The sisters were empowering people, and contained most elements of life, from the oppressive to the artistic and managerial types of nuns. That was my experience of the education I received there. That being said, the nuns were so much into public self-expression etc. that it sometimes seemed they valued what was public and showy over what was quiet and restrained. Again, a personal view!

THOMPSON: Who do you read?

O'DONNELL: Margaret Atwood, Alison Lurie, Lorrie Moore, Ann Tracy (Canadian author), Dale Peck, David Leavit, William Kennedy, Annie Proulx, Tim O'Brien, Michael Cunningham, Dermot Healy, Colm Toibin, Éilís Ní Dhuibhne—an excellent Irish writer—Deirdre Madden, V. S. Naipaul, R. K. Narayan, the early Salman Rushdie, Michele Roberts, Marquez and Lorca, Christa Wolf, Willa Cather, Jennifer Johnston, John Banville's earlier work, Janet Frame, Louise Erdrich, Elias Canetti—one of my favorite authors—A. S. Byatt, John Cheever, George Eliot, Henry James, plus biographies, especially literary ones on the romantics.

THOMPSON: In *The Light-Makers*, Hanna and her family live in the Republic but are surrounded by the North; a character even calls them "Border People." What is it like living on the border?

O'DONNELL: I used the border as my setting, because I love it and it's what I come from. It's psychologically a kind of no-man's land in any Irish academic discussion. Those concerned with the nature of "Irishness" rarely look to the border regions, because they are, I suspect, uncertain of our allegiances. Many of the Irish-language traditions so highly valued in the 1960s and 1970s in other parts of Ireland were certainly not valued in the border areas. That has changed considerably with the incursion of people of a Northern nationalist outlook. Now, the question of Irishness is overzealous in the region.

THOMPSON: Did you feel you were in a no-man's land living so close to the North?

O'DONNELL: I never felt that I lived in a no-man's land, living so close to the North. That feeling, when I was a child, came from the condition of being Irish. Everything in our experience happened or had happened in relation to England. When I was growing up everything of interest was happening in London, preferably on Carnaby Street. In the late sixties and early seventies, Ireland didn't have a youth culture: the youth-oriented magazines that young people would want to buy, or the cool radio stations needed either, or indeed a television station with a contemporary feel. We who lived close to the border were able to receive BBC television, and I believe that it acculturated us to "English" ways of thinking, different from people who lived farther south. It was like being reared on a very high fence with a good view in both directions, something I have never regretted.

THOMPSON: Did the border make you more aware of English colonization?

O'DONNELL: I was examining the deeds to my parents' home recently and was struck by how the landlord system kept the country in considerable impoverishment. The home in which I grew up—an early Victorian house dating from the 1840s—was at that time part of the Dartry estate. The house's owners had to pay ground rent to absent landlords. Those who originally owned the land on which houses were built continued to gain from every property. The emergence of a postindependence country this century follows a fairly predictable pattern. Salman Rushdie outlined it very well in his novel *Midnight's Children*.

THOMPSON: Do you think of Ireland as an ex-colony?

O'DONNELL: Ireland was an ex-colony until the late 1990s when it suddenly became wealthy; economics is the underpinning to all national confidence, anywhere in the world. All the colonizers—Britain, France, Germany, Portugal, Spain—had at their disposal enormous wealth and a sense of supremacy, privilege, and right. Those whom they colonized inherited a sense of unworthiness, inadequacy, a lack of confidence which, in the case of Ireland, permeated this country until very recently.

THOMPSON: Would you say Ireland is postcolonial in chronology or in sensibility?

O'DONNELL: I don't suppose I regard Ireland as "postcolonial" at all: the term suggests the retention of all the characteristics of the former colonizer, if I understand it correctly. As an ex-colony, Ireland has tried to do other things. However, I do balk when I hear Irish people becoming fiercely assertive and saying things like "I'm proud to be Irish!" It's a defensive remark, really, which suggests they are uncertain of how they feel about Irishness. At base, nobody outside this country cares very much about the nature of Irishness, apart from intellectuals and academics. Nobody in another country lies awake thinking how great it must be to be PROUD to be Irish!!!!

THOMPSON: But questions of Irishness do inform your writing.

O'DONNELL: In my novel *The Light-Makers* I was conscious of the split inheritance—also in *The Elysium Testament*—of the divided Irish psyche which doesn't know which outside nation to support in time of war. Many Irish people supported the Germans during World War II.

THOMPSON: Do you think *The Light-Makers* might have been different had you written it after the 1995 divorce referendum?

O'DONNELL: The divorce referendum had no bearing on the writing of the book. Whether or not divorce existed in Ireland often had little bearing on a woman leaving her husband. People simply separated and lived apart, or set up home with someone else. Hanna is a fairly determined character. I was inspired to write the novel by the need to tell her story, by the need to write about betrayal on many levels. As it unfolded, I reacted to the Dublin/Ireland I was observing at the time, which often seemed to me to be full of tribal, insensitive rituals.

THOMPSON: By addressing infertility you also interrogate the nature of "woman," especially in Ireland, where motherhood is a constitutional mandate.

O'DONNELL: As everyone took a free hand in the interrogation of women's lives and how they chose to lead them, I thought I should follow up that interrogation on my own terms, which are not always easy or forgiving. I do not idealize women. But I had to lift the lid on the nonsensical insincerity which underpins so much that women were required to be. What Hanna wants most, I suspect, is to be free to be authentic. That's a huge undertaking for any human who lives close to other people. Those who live lives of total authenticity usually pay a high price for the contentment they believe to be theirs by right. Infertility was one of the greatest offences a woman could quietly commit in Ireland, if she was married.

I had heard so much over the years, and observed how harshly the infertile woman could be judged and pitied, not by outside friends, but within family circles.

THOMPSON: When you describe Sam's buildings you call them erections. There seems to be a connection between his work, his self-image, and his infertility. Why is Hanna so critical of Sam's environmental consciousness?

O'DONNELL: Hanna is scathing about the changes in Sam primarily because of her disgust at the disparity between his new love of the environment and of everything that is fertile, growing, and abundant, the nurturing side of him, if you like, and his denial of his own possible infertility.

THOMPSON: How typical is Hanna and Sam's marriage in that she wants to fix the infertility but he won't admit that there might be a problem with him?

O'DONNELL: The dynamic between Sam and Hanna is by no means typical. Most men are not as obtuse as Sam in this regard.

THOMPSON: Do male readers identify with Sam?

O'DONNELL: No, I don't see a parallel between Sam and other men regarding infertility. Nowadays, it's rare enough, according to medical accounts, for men to be so resistant. Some of the male readers of *The Light-Makers* typified the kind of man who loathes opinionated women. Hanna is opinionated, and some men hate that.

THOMPSON: Why does Hanna resent Rose?

O'DONNELL: Hanna's resentment of Rose stems from Rose's suicide attempt at the anniversary party in Clonfoy. Hanna is responsible, she gets on with it, but Rose is the opposite, although admired as bohemian and unconventional. Hanna herself is quite self-indulgent at times in this novel, but she is intolerant of what she sees as Rose's form of self-indulgence.

THOMPSON: In all three of your novels you focus on facades people create to maintain the appearance of normal relationships. In *The Light-Makers* Kate mentions that money helps to create the picture of a healthy, happy family, and even romance appears to be a sales gimmick to Hanna. Would you say that part of your work as a writer is to lift the facade or ridicule it?

O'DONNELL: Lifting facades has to be one of the joys of being a writer. All serious writers get a kick out of that. After all, we've set ourselves apart to say something we imagine to be "different," right? In general I don't set out to ridicule a facade—unless it is, clearly, ridiculous—but exposing it is always interesting.

THOMPSON: I'm interested in the way you show how the self is mediated by contemporary culture: film, advertisements, statistics, even mannequins. But self is also mediated by poetry, painting, architecture, photography.

O'DONNELL: Part of the facade-revealing process in the novel entailed looking at contemporary imagery and what it urges us to do. In *The Light-Makers*, Hanna is completely fascinated by this process, because it's so much at odds with what she feels and believes about herself and other people.

THOMPSON: Does Hanna use statistics as another form of this facade, reducing all to a countable amount to understand and control it?

O'DONNELL: Hanna herself is keen on information. It both fascinates and repels her, not unlike Nina in *The Elysium Testament*. She certainly uses it to try to make sense of the world. Nina is helped by all her facts. She needs them. She has a fierce logic and a great capacity to tease things out. She is a natural researcher who needs truth and who cannot rest until she finds one that satisfies her torment. I do not think she uses this to distance her experience, so much as to clarify, illuminate.

THOMPSON: The "stag party" that Hanna witnesses is sinister because the man may not be participating voluntarily. Were you aiming at ambiguity?

O'DONNELL: Ah, the stag party. Yes, the sinister stag party is observed by Hanna proceeding up and down a village street. I observed this myself the summer before I began writing the novel, and I was horrified. It happened exactly as described, shattering the peace of this beautiful country village, as a few of us sat around having a drink of cider in the sun. I found it primitive and frightening because of the way the man was forcibly bound up. There are startling variations on this Irish and British custom.

THOMPSON: Could you explain the symbolism of the enlarged black penis and the Kenyan woman who is stoned?

O'DONNELL: The penis fetishizes black sexuality and the mythical prowess of the black man. The reference to the Kenyan woman who was stoned for infertility, "caused" by promiscuity, came to me when I read it in a newspaper on holidays one year. Again, I was horrified! It aroused a sort of religious indignation in me, and I kept thinking how we literally crucify everything we do not understand. Naturally, I was drawing a connection between Hanna, an Irish woman, and the Kenyan woman. We also stone our women—and men—though differently. Those who abjure convention, no matter how beyond their control, often suffer shunning and avoidance.

THOMPSON: There is a reference in a 1930 Arensberg and Kimball study of a rural Irish community in the west which says that a husband would beat his wife if she didn't produce children.

O'DONNELL: Yes; I also refer to this in a short story of mine, called "Breath of the Living," in which the female character in the story imagines herself being crucified, hoisted, and stoned.

THOMPSON: *The Light-Makers* and *The Elysium Testament* make connections between Ireland and what we have called "Third World" countries. Are you suggesting Ireland has commonalties with these countries?

O'DONNELL: The parallel between the tearooms of Clonfoy and those in the village outside Alexandria is not intended to infer anything regarding Third World countries, so much as the similarity of local patterns one observes in country places worldwide. People want a place to rest in country towns; they want a cup of tea or coffee and a sweet cake, something restorative. It's the same in Turkey, right across North Africa, in parts of the U.S., and in Germany.

THOMPSON: In *The Elysium Testament* Arabs own the grotto rather than Irish people. Although they have no spiritual investment in the grotto, they are willing to restore it. Why?

O'DONNELL: My editor at Trident also focused on this question of the Arabs owning the grotto, but in the end, as she has a lot of dealings with the UAE countries, she came to the conclusion that one could, in fact, have an Arab family quite prepared to restore a grotto which represented things quite separate from their own domain of spiritual investment.

THOMPSON: *The Light-Makers* and *The Elysium Testament* are similar in they both shift back and forth in time. Why did you choose this structure for both novels?

O'DONNELL: I wanted to do something that was technically interesting. In *The Light-Makers* it was challenging to move back and forth in the novel between the distant past and Hanna's past and present, while handling this in the continuous present tense. I needed this to be a very intense novel, because it was my first and I was fired up with the urgency of getting things just right.

THOMPSON: The multiple interconnections within *The Elysium Testament* resemble the architecture of the grotto: Emily, the duke of Leinster and Nina, epilepsy and levitations, mental instability and mysticism, swimming and levitating, the grotto and the house. What was your goal in folding them into the weave of the narrative?

O'DONNELL: As the book developed, I realized that, as with *The Light-Makers,* I enjoyed the technical complexities of weaving and interweaving, of making connections between the past and the present, of uncovering the complex patterning at the heart of life. I was also fascinated by what the potential contemporary responses were to a phenomenon like levitation. How does a material society react to a levitating child? How would it react to a mother who thought she SAW a child levitating, a phenomenon which has been empirically proven to exist, apart from my fictional version of events? For me, the everyday is imbued with mystical properties. I don't know why, but I have always perceived the world this way. Brief moments of, for example, nature just "being," existing, communicate this feeling of self-transcendence. When writing is really working for me, I have felt a similar self-transcendence. I would rather transcend than reveal directly: it's better for books and it's better for people, too!

THOMPSON: How did you come to write *The Elysium Testament*?

O'DONNELL: I came to write it one summer, when what was thought to be rheumatoid arthritis was making my life a misery. I was living with an insistent and wearing level of pain, but was convinced I did not have r.a. I didn't: it turned out to be a very treatable form of lupus, but I was unable to convince anybody else of this. So death was on my mind all that summer. When you feel unwell enough, you start to think black thoughts, very black ones. This was my frame of mind. At the same time, I had been collecting random bits from newspapers that had begun to fascinate me about the restoration of grottos and follies. Furthermore, I heard a story about a woman whose child was accidentally impaled. I wondered how that woman could carry on and stay sane. Those are the book's origins.

THOMPSON: The protagonist says that "chroniclers have to be selective" (22). Does she tell the whole story?

O'DONNELL: The direct violence toward the child, as reported in Elinore's letters, is initially omitted. When I realized this vital element and response was missing, I decided to "report" it through Elinore. Her account reinforces what Nina herself admits at certain points—for example, when she finds the child levitating in the bedroom, and proceeds to beat him. Elinore makes it quite clear that none of this is imagined and that Nina is sane. Elinore is unafraid of blaming her, of telling her that she should be guilty, that she has failed in her responsibility. An older person might not have been so direct, or might have fudged the question of guilt, because the concept of guilt is so unacceptable to so many adults. But in a fraught or divided conscience, guilt is a useful indicator that something needs adjusting.

THOMPSON: The diary is not just about the child's death; Nina's grief seems to be centered on her inability to understand and treat him in a way that would have helped him.

O'DONNELL: Roland's death is part of the issue, but equally, Nina's attempt to understand her own failures in relation to him is the other major segment of this novel. I think she does understand her failures. The central problem for her in this novel is to find a route to some kind of reconciliation with herself, if such is possible. By the end, it is.

THOMPSON: How have readers responded to the character of Nina?

O'DONNELL: Most of the Irish readers who have commented on the novel have responded to Nina pretty much as I would have hoped. They have been amazingly able to sympathize with her and to understand her dilemma. I did not expect that. I had thought she might have been condemned much, much more. Even in the reviews I received, this sympathy prevails. People really responded to the novel's "gothic" qualities and its mysticism.

THOMPSON: The conclusion to the novel, with its cleansing and hopefulness, comes after a grueling emotional experience and a very calculated plan to end it all. Did you want to surprise the reader with Nina's redemption?

O'DONNELL: The novel's conclusion changed for me after three drafts. Initially, the book ended with the words "And yet" and there was no December 9th. But problems had sprung up. I realized during one of the rewrites that I wanted to develop John Holmes a little more and, for a change, to provide a likeable male character of some genuine use to Nina. And so, I allowed him a bit more space in which the issue of the halfway house for the hospital patients is touched on. My eventually allowing Nina to offer HER house to him for just that purpose is significant. I'm not suggesting that the halfway house patients belong to "the place of the blessed dead," to define "Elysium," so much as that she herself has been living in a demented zone for quite some time, and was in a way living in her own halfway house. Then, as John Holmes suggests that they take a holiday together, and a few other chummy gestures like that, it dawned on me—why not go for a symbolic rebirthing? The river, in both pagan and later Christian imagery, often signifies the return to a source, a moment of cleansing or healing. On a more mundane level I was plagued with publishers who turned down this novel on the grounds that it was "too bleak" for their readers! Perhaps I succumbed to a slight pressure to make it a little more palatable, although my instinct says "no." When the paperback appears, I am considering omitting the December 9th chapter.

THOMPSON: Are you troubled by the stories leaving Ireland that talk of abusive upbringings? You say quite late in the novel, "We have not been molested by our father, nor raped by our uncles, nor beaten, nor abused in the reported modern way" (141).

O'DONNELL: I was concerned to make the point that both sisters are still damaged anyway but that they have survived.

THOMPSON: Irish-Americans are ready consumers of these stories, for example, *Angela's Ashes*.

O'DONNELL: I read half of *Angela's Ashes* and decided not to finish it. This wasn't a criticism of the subject matter of the book so much as my realizing that it just didn't interest me. By the time the second or third child had fallen on its head, I'd had enough. I don't doubt the poverty, or the awfulness, or the validity of McCourt's story. And somebody needed to write up a story like this. It matters in the context of providing an angry, deliberately colored but challenging response to all the rose-tinted stuff about "old Ireland." It has social and historical significance, apart from creative value.

THOMPSON: Many writers have left Ireland to write and have

blamed their exile on the anti-intellectual, Catholic environment of Ireland. Is that your experience?

O'DONNELL: Many writers left Ireland for economic reasons. I know many claim that they left in order to write, but I suspect it was a random emigration, based on an artistic need to experience as much of the world as possible, and to survive economically at a time in the late 1970s and 1980s when it was very difficult to survive here. Excessively Catholic Ireland certainly was, our laws proved that, and their toll was very high for women. But anti-intellectual is not something I could call Ireland.

THOMPSON: Have you ever thought of living outside of Ireland?

O'DONNELL: Once or twice we thought of living outside Ireland. I have mostly lived in Germany for short periods, and I have traveled fairly widely, but I found Ireland an easier environment than many others. Despite the apparent rigidity of things here up to recently, there was also an anomalous flexibility, a sense of people quietly getting on with life and doing their own thing anyway.

Mobile Irish Identities

Introduction to Part Two

HELEN THOMPSON

VALERIE MINER was not born in Ireland. Kate O'Riordan was born in England to unmarried Irish parents. Catherine Brady was born in Illinois. When Maura Stanton visited Ireland she felt more like a foreigner than a native. Edna O'Brien left Ireland to escape its repression. Emma Donoghue left to get an education. Lia Mills returned to Ireland after living for periods in England and the United States. As a teenager, Ivy Bannister, with her German, French, Swedish, Norwegian, and Cherokee ancestry, moved to Ireland from New York. In this section, Irishness is not as simple as being born, raised, or living in Ireland. Instead, national identity intersects with other kinds of identities, residencies, and relationships to Ireland, thus reconfiguring what it means to be Irish.

As in the first section, these women consider themselves Irish. Yet, unlike the first section, where Irishness is defined primarily by the simple facts of birth and residency, the women have Irish identities that are frequently created or complicated by something other than birth or citizenship. With the exceptions of Donoghue and O'Brien, the writers in this section were not born in Ireland, and all but Mills and Bannister live outside Ireland. Indeed, it might be argued that these women have no place in a collection of Irish women writers because their links to Ireland are too tenuous; yet, we include them because we believe that identities have more fluidity than legal definitions. Our conversations with these women writers have endorsed our understanding of Irish identity being more than the sum of birth and residency. Irishness is a state of mind, an emotional relationship to place, people, and culture; and, most important, it is a self-perception based upon a myriad of subjective experiences of Ireland, the place and the concept.

The writers in this section define themselves as Irish, but the adjective is not static in meaning and during the interviews they reveal different ways of understanding Irishness. For example, O'Brien has lived outside Ireland for forty years, yet she still feels intimately connected to her homeland and claims herself to be unquestioningly Irish. Conversely, Bannister considers herself Irish because she's lived in Dublin for thirty years. Even though she was born in New York City, she feels more akin to her adopted home than her native one. For both of these writers, relationship to place and culture appear to be crucial factors in determining national identity. For writers such as O'Riordan, birth is not a useful indicator of identity, for while she is now living in London, the city where she was born, she considers herself Irish because she grew up in Ireland with Irish parents. O'Riordan's experience partially echoes that of Brady, who claims an Irish identity based upon her family culture. Yet Brady's Irishness clashes with the American culture into which she was born. She explains that her identity is bound up with conflict between public and private culture and shame in being different, in trying to quickly assimilate by taking on the values of the new culture while not forgetting the old. The further away from the "old" country a woman travels, the more dependent she becomes upon stories, myths, and the experiences of others for her Irishness. Stanton, for example, got an impression of Ireland as exotic and romantic after spending summers as a child with Irish relatives in Chicago. Instead of making her feel more Irish, the experience left her feeling inadequate because she didn't have the same lilting accent and she couldn't join in with their traditional songs.

It took Stanton years to discover the mundane behind the exoticism of Irish culture, and it is small wonder, given the marketing of Irishness as a commodity to consume. As Miner points out, it is hard to get beyond Ireland as a warm, lush, cheerful place, the image that many Irish-Americans seem to have. This Borde Failte (Irish Tourist Board) image has gained wide currency, and the fact that the Irish themselves subscribe to it suggests, according to O'Brien, a materialistic culture more interested in media bytes than historical and emotional truth. Indeed, the media clips are modifications of the old images of Ireland as a woman, which both O'Brien and Donoghue believe are still in circulation.

These icons of femininity—Mother Ireland and the Blessed Virgin—derive from the conflation of nationalism and Catholicism to shape Irish identity, particularly for its female citizens. So, when one is claiming a relationship to Ireland, it is virtually impossible not to address the issue of the Catholic Church, especially since approximately 95 percent of the country is Catholic, giving the church a monopoly on spirituality and politics. As Miner says, she was brought up believing that Irish-Catholic was a single word. With the exception of Bannister, who says that the Catholic Church has no hold over her because she was not raised within its confines, all the writers experienced a Catholic upbringing; however, few are still practicing. With the exception of Brady, none of the women writers claim to have maintained their Catholicism. Brady is still devout, acquiring her faith from her mother. In the interview she explains that the mysteries of faith have exhibited themselves in such circumstances as her mother's successful prayers, and she has translated these experiences in her writing, for example, in such stories as "The Lives of the Saints," where she equates motherhood with the process of canonization.

Many of the writers are critical of the church's practices. Like Miriam Dunne from the first section, Mills railed against a convent education by getting herself expelled from a series of boarding schools. O'Riordan points to the scars—both figurative and literal—inflicted on most people her age by priests and nuns. Miner points to the way the church has handled its nonheterosexual congregation. She says that in her church, gay and lesbian sexualities were never discussed except to suggest that such people are not quite human. Miner believes that the church is responsible for perpetuating hatred and prejudice within the Irish-Catholic community. While Donoghue blames the church for being more responsible for Ireland's colonization than England, O'Brien points to the loosening stranglehold the church has on Irish culture due to the recent stories of abuse emerging in the press.

The interviews also reveal reactions to a changing Ireland with its openness, revelations of clerical abuse, and increasingly global outlook. While the church has diminished power in Ireland, so has the Irish language. In the first section, writers such as Éilís Ní Dhuibhne discuss the language debate and their relationship to both English and Gaelic. In this section, few of the writers know Gaelic. Only O'Brien and O'Riordan were taught Gaelic in school, and O'Brien expresses an interest in the rhythm and sound of Irish rather than the meaning, something that influences her writing in English. Other writers, such as Brady and Stanton, define their relationship to American English, and they take opposite stances: Stanton does not feel constrained by the English language, believing that she can unambiguously embrace it as her own; however, Brady says she cannot own American English because Irish is her "mother-tongue," and this language constitutes a part of her identity. For Mills, language is the tool of her craft, and while she writes in English, she wants her work to have an Irish rather than "Anglo" slant.

Language and religion are important factors in Irish identities of all kinds, as are the concomitant nationalist concerns of history, struggle, and memory. In its contemporary form, the "Troubles" represent the residue of eight hundred years of occupation and revolt, causing Irishness, both inside and outside Ireland, to be associated with violent political struggle. In Ireland, just like almost every other nation, politics, war, and violence are the domains of men in terms of participation, discussion, and writing. Yet this is hardly the reason that few of the women in this section write about the North. Donoghue doesn't because she considers it a completely foreign environment; and while Miner writes about IRA violence in London in *Blood Sisters*, she does not write about the North as separate from the Republic.

O'Brien is one of the few to write about the Troubles in *House of Splendid Isolation*, and in doing so she transgresses a gendered boundary. Indeed, in her latest trilogy—*House of Splendid Isolation*, *Down by the River*, and *Wild Decembers*—she focuses on what she considers to be the three most political subjects in Ireland: the Troubles, sex, and land. In the interview O'Brien explains that critics have been particularly brutal to her because of her representation of Ireland and the North. She ascribes it to being a woman, yet also it is because she no longer lives in Ireland and is not from the North. Certainly, the identity politics of this region still demand that a writer must have the authority of living in Ireland and particularly in the North if he or she is going to write about it. O'Riordan confirms this attitude, saying that she has been castigated by BBC radio for writing about the North in *Involved* when, like O'Brien, she is from the Republic but living in London. O'Riordan's discussion suggests that literary as well as geographic territory are fraught with tensions that are sectarian as well as gendered.

For Irish writers in America, the Troubles are supplanted by the Vietnam War, a conflict that, like the Troubles, has revised an entire national identity. Similarly, it is a central event represented by a whole body of literature, mostly written by men. Even though Vietnam is distant from the Irish experience in Ireland, it is a part of the fabric of Irish-American identity and is, therefore, important to include in conjunction with the Troubles. While Brady writes about war veterans, Miner and Stanton reference the gender inequities in the draft, Miner discusses it via her novel *A Walking Fire,* and Stanton via her brother's being drafted in the lottery. Both women express their discomfort at their relative safety while their male compatriots went off to fight. Perhaps this explains why neither writer feels uncomfortable writing about war. Indeed, Miner explains that in *A Walking Fire,* Cora has multiple perspectives on the war because of her education, while her brother has only one and is blind to the war's hypocrisy. Stanton uses her experience of Vietnam to write about conflict in Paraguay in her novel *Molly Companion,* where she places her female protagonist, a journalist, at the center of the action, not safe on the periphery. Ironically, for both Cora and Molly, war provides them the opportunity to be mobile rather than traditionally static, keeping the home fires burning.

From the interviews, it is clear that each of these women's identities has been shaped by geographic movement from or to Ireland, either their own as in the cases of Bannister (America to Ireland), Donoghue (Ireland to England to Canada), Mills (Ireland to England to United States and back to Ireland), O'Brien (Ireland to England), and O'Riordan (England to Ireland to Canada to the United States and back to England); or that of their parents as in the case of Brady (both parents emigrated from Ireland to the United States) and Miner (whose mother emigrated from Scotland and father from Ireland to the United States), or grandparents for Stanton (from Ireland to the United States). These migrations are important because the story of one's leaving or arriving is a vital identity shaper, one that carves out one's relationship to old and new homelands. Breda Gray goes so far as to suggest that Irish identity is more readily characterized by mobility outside Ireland than within the country itself, that pure Irish identity is pure mobility (2000, 116). Certainly, migration is part of the Irish national myth, with America being "the next parish over" and the diaspora reaching Britain, Australia, and New Zealand.

The interviews reveal some interesting ways in which migration has influenced Irish identity. Indeed, these writers confirm what Edna Longley has said about Irish identities in the North and in the Republic, that interchanges and fluidity are far more productive than a limiting territorialism (Kirkpatrick 2000). The epigraph to Stanton's short story collection, for example, the old Irish blessing, "May the road rise to meet you. May the wind be always at your back," epitomizes movement as the quintessential Irish experience, suggesting that good luck from the Irish perspective is a trouble-free journey. However, she reconfigures its meaning by placing it alongside her title, borrowed from the Bob Dylan lyric, "the country I come from is called the Midwest." Stanton's version of Irish-Americanness is one that couples mobility of the migrant with Irishness and with American rootedness in place and land. Her revision of Irish-Americanness, perhaps, completes the migration story by giving it to first and second generations.

Bannister describes her identity as mid-Atlantic because, even though she feels more Irish than American, her migration from New York to Dublin has left her feeling outside both cultures. Her identity locates itself in a space in between the two countries, not fully residing in either. For Brady, her Irish-American identity is split between her parents: from her immigrant father she gained Americanness while her mother gave her a sense of belonging to Irish culture. While Mills experienced dislocation from moving to England, to the United States, and back to Ireland, her children have inherited some of that experience as Irish-Americans leaving their home in Texas. However, identity is a choice to them; as Mills explains, sometimes they call themselves Irish and sometimes American, depending on the circumstance. Hence, pragmatism becomes a criterion of identity, and Irishness can be worn like a garment for the right occasion.

Mobility also becomes useful to writers who want the fresh eye of an outsider on a new or an old place. Bannister, for example, sees mobility as essential to a writer's life because of the continuous stimuli travel provides. It gives her perspective on what she already knows. O'Riordan stays away from Ireland despite the financial incentives of returning. She fears that if she lived closer to her family, she would lose her artistic freedom and have impulses to censor herself. Stanton's traveling appears to be the exception because her mobility has further solidified her need to be home in the Midwest. In other parts of the United States where she has lived, she says she felt "exiled"; so mobility for Stanton is loss of and need for home.

Stanton points out that Irishness and Irish-Americanness are two different kinds of identity, proving that, when a migrant crosses a border, she becomes a foreigner, and national identity becomes a new experience defined by relationships with old and new homes. While certainly identity in Ireland is not a fixed category, when one's abode requires a passport, a traveler is more aware of her national identity and how others perceive it. In terms of external perceptions, both O'Riordan and Donoghue have referenced British racism toward the Irish, although they argue that the prejudices are usually reserved for the unskilled class and are no longer evident in British communities. They have not experienced racist slurs against themselves, although O'Riordan does cite a time when she was more aware of her Irish accent, during an IRA bombing spree in London. Mills says she experienced anti-Irish racism in England in the 1970s, so much so that she resorted to "passing" for British, which she could do as long as she did not speak. O'Riordan claims that it is almost fashionable to be Irish in Britain nowadays because an Irish person is not part of the British class system. Donoghue concurs and says that when she lived in England her lesbian identity marginalized her far more than her Irish one. In America, Miner takes the opposite stance and claims that it is her Irishness and not her lesbianism that represents her marginality.

As she talks about her childhood, Stanton references not the external issues of acculturation and prejudice, but her own self-perceptions of her Irish-American identity. Indeed, they represented two extremes of experience. While the Irish represented flamboyance, the American appeared mundane. As an adult she feels more Irish in America than when she visited Ireland for the first time. These experiences suggest that her dual identity always leaves a space where something is lacking, perhaps a fragmentation of identities that do not quite blend beyond the hyphen. Brady is uneasy as a representative Irish-American because as a child of immigrants, she is under pressure to become a successful American while not forgetting her Irish roots.

We expected that many of the Irish writers living abroad would say that they left Ireland for reasons of creative and intellectual freedom, yet just like in the first section, these writers do not conform to this expectation. Only O'Brien's migration resembles that of the expatriate writers from earlier in the century. However, unlike Joyce and Beckett who headed for Paris, she went to London in 1960 as an act of rebellion against the insular culture that Ireland was at that time. O'Riordan's migration resembles that of many working-class and rural people in the postfamine era who left for economic reasons. She left a small town in the rural west of Ireland for reasons of work. However, instead of looking for manual labor or domestic service, the occupations that have historically stereotyped the Irish immigrant, she moved to London to write for television. Donoghue's migrations were similarly pragmatic. She says that she went to England for a scholarship at Girton College, Cambridge, and instead of returning to Ireland upon receipt of her doctorate, went to Canada for love. Yet unlike O'Brien and O'Riordan, she does not find Ireland a particularly repressive culture and could comfortably live in Ireland if the need arose. Yet she does admit that her move to England helped her writing career because she found an agent who encouraged her to aim her work at international and sexually diverse audiences.

The reverse pattern of the Irish emigrant, returning to Ireland after leaving to live in Britain or further afield, is not a common phenomenon because even if the new country did not provide a better economic status, migrants were less willing to face the shame of returning, an act that would be tantamount to admitting failure. O'Brien's mother is one of the few who returned after working as a domestic in New York; Mills returned to Ireland so that her Irish-American children would get to know their roots. Also, she wanted to be close to family and to quell the loneliness she expected to feel when her husband went to work in Burma.

If it is uncommon for Irish emigrants to return home, it has been even less common historically for foreigners to immigrate to Ireland. Bannister is one of the few who reversed the pattern and migrated to Ireland in the 1960s, ironically at a time when literary censorship was at a peak. She says she thought Ireland would be a perfect place for a writer, citing the eloquence of her father's Irish workman as her experience of the Irish. Hence, she immigrated because of language.

Nowadays, in the age of the Celtic Tiger, Ireland is becoming a more global culture. O'Riordan discusses Ireland's membership in the European Union in terms of the economic boom and new openness in the culture. She points out that the new prosperity is putting computers in Irish classrooms. Also, immigration and multiculturalism are becoming facts of life for the Irish. However, as O'Riordan observes, while Ireland is benefiting from globalism, it is also importing some of the problems, one of which is racism. She says that for the first time, people of color are coming to live in Ireland, and the landscape of cities such as Dublin are becoming more ethnically diverse. O'Riordan suggests that not all Irish people welcome an influx of nonwhite immigrants, which means that Ireland is becoming more like other European nations—Britain, for example—which are working to assimilate a multitude of cultures, skin colors, and ethnicities.

Brady discusses a similar issue with regard to Irish America. In the new country, Irish immigrants, finding themselves in competition with other races of immigrants on the social and economic ladders, have resorted to racism. She explains that their prejudices bolster their own social standing by ensuring that they are not on the bottom rung. This condition of the immigrant is quite similar to what Ireland is beginning to face in its new international standing. So, while these new circumstances are largely positive, there remains a certain insularity within the Irish communities both at home and abroad, despite its active appearance on the world stage.

Geographic and cultural borders are becoming more permeable, which means that Ireland's global relationships, even those with Britain, are changing, perhaps putting its colonial status finally in the past. However, when we asked about Ireland's historically subject status and its possible postcolonial present, the responses we got were diverse and sometimes even vehement. They suggest that even though Ireland's identity is becoming distinct from its colonial past, the issues are still contentious because of different perspectives on the terms of debate—colonial and postcolonial—as well as the actual historical record.

Brady, Mills, and Stanton regard Ireland as a postcolonial nation, and this means to them that Ireland is in the process of sloughing its old identity as a colony and growing into a new, culturally distinct nation. Indeed, Miner is adamant that "becoming" be added to suggest that Ireland is not yet postcolonial, not yet free of its past. Both Brady and Miner also see connections between Ireland and other postcolonial nations such as India and Nigeria, while Mills believes that some Irish people resist the postcolonial labeling precisely because they do not see themselves akin to people of color. While Miner also recognizes global interconnections, she also suggests caution, pointing out that skin color makes people's experiences inherently different. Stanton compares Ireland's condition to that of Native Americans, citing similar disenfranchisement. Further, in a discussion of Seamus Heaney, she recognizes the difficulties of being an Irish writer writing in the language of the colonizer.

Donoghue and O'Riordan reject the idea of a postcolonial Ireland, neither believing that their nation's history is at all similar to African or Caribbean countries. While they do not dispute Ireland's subject status to Britain, they refute Ireland's continuing recovery from the effects of colonization. Furthermore, both agree that Ireland has had a strong identity despite its colonial past. The polarizing nature of these discussions of Ireland suggests that the identities of the writers are indeed dependent on their understanding of Ireland's past and present, even if they do not live there. It appears that only those writers who view Ireland in the process of redefining itself as something other than an ex-British colony find the term "postcolonial" useful in describing Ireland's history and sensibility.

Labels such as "postcolonial" and "feminist" are definitely problematic for some of the writers in this section, perhaps because meanings over time become more politically and ideologically loaded and subsequently less clear. Also, labels pigeonhole writers into specific categories that can marginalize their work on bookstore shelves and in reviewers' columns. Hence, responses to the question of their relationship to feminism produced results as varied as those to the postcolonial question. Mills, like Catherine Dunne in the first section, discusses some of the present problems with the feminist label by pointing out that the younger generation believes its political force is no longer necessary, and that the appearance of equality achieved in recent years has led women and men into a dangerous complacency. Certainly women who were raised in Ireland from the 1960s onward have benefited from the efforts of the second-wave feminist movement, which came later to Ireland than other Western countries, as Liz McManus attests to in the first section.

Brady and Stanton call themselves feminists, and both see this identification as being central to their work as writers. Stanton distinguishes her Irish-American from her feminist sensibility, however, and suggests that each one takes a different prominence in her work. Mills and Donoghue are also adamant about their feminisms. Interestingly,

Donoghue does not find her Irish, lesbian, and feminist identifications at all incompatible. Both Donoghue and Mills do qualify their identifications as feminist writers, however. Like many of the feminist-identified women in the collection, they say they do not write feminist fiction, because such an agenda hinders the creative process. For Miner feminism is a given since she has been active in the women's movement for many years and her writing centers upon women's issues. O'Riordan rejects the feminist label just as she did the postcolonial. Even though she holds faith with many tenets that are considered feminist—she's a supporter of female rights, for example—she finds the meaning of the term "feminist" ambiguous.

All of the writers in this section focus their work to a greater or lesser degree on the lives of women. In some cases the work becomes a conversation with contemporary and historical representations of women, thus adding intertextual layers to narratives that are also cultural critiques. For example, O'Brien's *Down by the River* is based on the infamous X case, the 1992 case of the young girl pregnant from a rape, seeking an abortion in Britain. In the interview O'Brien explains she wrote into the novel a variety of viewpoints on abortion to represent the complexity of such a charged debate as well as to add life to the narrative. Similarly, Mills explains that when she was writing her novel *Another Alice,* she experimented with different points of view and eventually decided on a structure that mirrors Alice's process of remembering her abuse. The distant narrative becomes increasingly intense and immediate as Alice's memories begin to flood her mind. Mills also makes Alice's coping mechanism during the abuse a fantasy world dominated by Irish myth; thus Alice's survival paradigms are connected to those of the Irish nation because, as she explains, Irish people tap into these stories for their own identities.

Mills is not the only writer in this section to blend contemporary and historical narrative. Many of the women see palimpsests as important because they challenge received knowledge and even redefine myth. Donoghue is interested in the patterns of folk and fairy tales, for example, and like Ní Dhuibhne in the first section, she blends traditional stories and structures with the more contemporary. She admits that her interest is in subverting these narratives by endowing traditionally passive female characters with agency. However, she is less interested in narrative experimentation, saying that sexual fluidity cannot become a subversive trope for the lesbian narrative because many lesbian writers, such as her, prefer conventional narrative.

Perhaps one of the most innovative methods of rewriting history to make it more inclusive is that of reclaiming lost women's voices, either real or imagined, and in Stanton's words, to play with history and make it new. Several of the writers in this section practice this kind of literary archeology by unearthing and representing these historical gaps in their fiction. Bannister's novel-in-progress on a popular writer and contemporary of Joyce, Beatrice Grimshaw, is a case in point, as is Stanton's *Molly Companion,* which recovers the story of Elisa Lynch, the Irish mistress of a Paraguayan dictator. Donoghue, in *Slammerkin,* imagines the life of Mary Saunders, a young girl who was hanged in Monmouth, Wales, in the eighteenth century. While all she uncovers of the real Mary Saunders is a broadsheet announcing her execution, Donoghue gives her life by imagining how this young girl ended up a murderer. O'Riordan's *Boy in the Moon* deviates slightly from this pattern in that it does not record the life of a historical figure; instead Margaret's diary gives voice to rural women such as O'Riordan's grandmother, who had little power to define her life, but who nevertheless recorded its intricate and mundane details. Also, while no one case stood out for Mills, she found inspiration for her novel in the myriad of abuse stories emerging from Ireland in recent years. She wanted to give voice to the victim, a voice she felt was silenced in the barrage of contemporary debate.

One of the unexpected trajectories that several of the interviews took regarded our questions about male and female characters. We foregrounded questions about creating female protagonists and the issue of agency. It is true that the women write predominantly about female protagonists, and certainly writers such as Donoghue and O'Brien are interested in creating female characters with agency but not necessarily feminist role models. Yet we got more varied responses to questions about male characters. Donoghue says that she wants to create new male role models, and characters such as Daffy in *Slammerkin* and Mr. Wall in *Hood* are men who are not unrealistically gallant nor excessively brutal; instead they are merely more tolerant of others. O'Riordan discusses her exploration of male patterns of fear in *The Boy in the Moon,* explaining that the tragedy of the boy's death occurs because of the common male impulse to teach their sons to overcome fear. She explains that in the novel, the gendered conflict that emerges out of this crisis centers around Julia's ability to forgive her husband for the loss of their son. Brady discusses her efforts to complicate the stereotypes of the typical Irish father in Irish literature through characters such as Mr. Daley in "Daley's Girls." She says she wants to show the vulnerabilities behind his patriarchal attitude by emphasizing that at work he is constantly reminded of the failure of his immigrant desires for a new and better life. O'Brien has become more comfortable creating male characters. She says that the male characters in her latest trilogy are more fully rounded than those in her first trilogy.

In the first section, Mary O'Donnell suggests that male writers are not interested in reading works by women. Indeed, one of the central concerns of women writers' canonical marginality in Ireland focuses on their exclusion from the original *Field Day Anthology*, the three volumes representing what Irish writers and academics consider Ireland's canon. Furthermore, the writers in the first section have almost unanimously criticized the fourth and fifth volumes devoted to women's writing. In this section, *Field Day* is not at the forefront of the canonical debate, although the concomitant concerns of women's publishing opportunities, critical reviews, and canonical inclusion are discussed by all the women writers. Indeed, O'Riordan's corollary to *Field Day* is *Finbar's Hotel*, a collection of short stories set in the hotel and written by predominantly male writers. Indeed, the same solution—a separate volume called *Ladies' Night at Finbar's Hotel*—was offered to redress the grievance. While O'Riordan is critical of what she describes as the "cliquish" impulses of the male literary establishment that result in women's exclusion from anthologies and collections, she did contribute, along with Donoghue and Ní Dhuibhne from this collection, to the supplementary volume.

While male Irish writers such as Joyce have literary reputations that obscure those of their female counterparts, Anne Enright points to an exception: Edna O'Brien. She calls O'Brien a "wonderful mistake" because this Irish woman writer has received some of the privilege usually reserved for men. Indeed, she is published internationally by top publishing houses and has a reputation that matches many of her male contemporaries. She is also regularly reviewed by critics, although O'Brien herself is a little more skeptical because she says that both male and female critics, especially those in Britain, are highly critical of her work partly because of her gender. Despite critical responses, O'Brien continues to enjoy a wide readership all over the globe.

In her contribution to the canonical debate, Stanton says she spent part of her youth with the blissfully misguided view that writing was predominantly a woman's profession, a belief garnered from her reading list of mostly women writers; the illusion was shattered in her college poetry textbook, where out of hundreds of writers only three were women. Both Stanton and Mills agree that canon reformation is helping literature to become more inclusive not just for women. Mills, however, is also cautious about being too complacent because of what she calls the ebbs and flows of opinion. She suggests that a backlash could easily begin to exclude women again; hence the need for constant vigilance. Miner concurs when she says that complacency is the most damaging attitude to women's equality in all arenas.

The interviews in this section represent Ireland as myth, mobility, romance, history, family, location, stories, accents, and political and academic paradigms. O'Brien describes Ireland as a story she is always searching for, and while she goes back there to plumb its depths, she feels more at ease with her Irishness living at a distance. Brady suggests that her Irishness resides in homesickness for a place she has never visited, an ability to hold grudges, and a certain sense of humor. More important, she finds the state of being conflicted about one's country to be a characteristic of Irishness, and we might add, particularly an Irish woman writer.

Ivy Bannister

Interviewed by

CAITRIONA MOLONEY

BORN: New York City, 1951
RESIDES: County Dublin, Ireland
EDUCATED: Smith College (B.A. in English); Trinity College, Dublin (Ph.D. in English)
WORKS: Children's chauffeur and writer
GENRES: Drama, fiction, nonfiction
AWARDS FOR DRAMA: Whitehead (1986), Listowel (1987), O'Connor (1991), Mobil Ireland Playwriting (1993)
AWARDS FOR FICTION: Hennessy (1988)

Ivy Bannister immigrated to Ireland when she was nineteen, not because of any Irish heritage or Irish roots. She has none. Instead, she said she wanted to live in a place where even the most mundane conversations are lyrical.

Bannister is a playwright and fiction writer. Her plays have been performed on radio and television; her short fiction has appeared in various venues, including London Magazine, Virgins and Hyacinths, *the* Irish Press, *and* The Salmon; *and she has published one collection of short stories,* Magician and Other Stories *(1996a), and edited another,* The Adultery and Other Stories and Poems *(1982). She is the author of* The

Shavian Woman: A Study of Women in the Life and Work of George Bernard Shaw *(1986).*

Ivy Bannister's fiction has been complemented for its understanding of difficult relationships (Sweeney 1997, 16). Indeed, Bannister herself characterizes her work as influenced by her optimistic view of life. She writes about the choices people make at the most challenging times in their lives and the moments of hope that emerge out of life's awful tragedies.

Stylistically Bannister has a light and eloquent touch. Her fiction is characterized by its theatricality, gained from writing plays for stage and radio. Bannister says that she likes her stories to gain the life given to them by performance, something that is lacking in print. Her collection, Magician and Other Stories, *demonstrates elements of magical realism and gentle humor when dealing with serious themes such as adultery, death, revenge, and abuse. The title story, "Magician," uses language so vividly colorful that it conjures mythology and sorcery through gourmet cooking imagery.*

She has currently finished Blunt Trauma, *a nonfiction account of the Swiss Air crash, and is at work on a novel about Irish writer Beatrice Grimshaw. I interviewed Ivy Bannister in her home office in County Dublin.*

♦   ♦   ♦

MOLONEY: Ivy, do you consider yourself American or Irish?

BANNISTER: I am half German, and French, Swedish, Norwegian, and a little bit of Cherokee in there. And so I have absolutely no Irish blood, although I have lived and worked in Ireland for thirty years, which is a lot longer than I lived and worked in America. Sometimes when I hear myself on the radio I get such a terrible shock because I think that is an American woman speaking—my god, it's me! It comes as a great surprise to me that I don't sound like everyone around me.

If I am anything, I mostly feel Irish. But I realize I'm not Irish because there are some very significant areas of experience that I have not shared with my Irish contemporaries, but when I'm in America I don't feel right either. You know I'm sort of a mid-Atlantic. At first, coming here was moving backward in time to a more gracious world. Now there is very little difference between New York and Dublin, although there is still a huge difference between New York City and the countryside of Ireland. Thirty years ago when I was nineteen, it was very different; it was an immense change for a girl who had grown up in a place like New York City.

MOLONEY: What caused you to make that move?

BANNISTER: I was passionately interested in writing literature, and when I was a child my father had a workman from Cork, and he was the most interesting person I had ever met in my life. He could speak so beautifully that I could listen to him all day. The way he put words together was different than anything I had ever heard; he was fascinating. When I got a little bit older I was interested in literature and writing and I thought if this is a country where the workmen understand the use of language so instinctively, so vibrantly, then what must the intelligentsia be like? I came specifically because I was interested in words.

MOLONEY: You reversed the emigration pattern of many Irish writers. You came to Ireland in order to write whereas they left in order to write, feeling constrained here. Have you felt fettered by Joyce's "nets of church and state" that Irish writers often complain about?

BANNISTER: No. Of course, church and state were never going to have much of an impact on me, or fetter me in anyway, because I was an outsider. I wasn't even a Catholic so I had none of that particular baggage. It struck me that the Irish state, even thirty years ago, was a hypocritical place where contraceptives were called cycle regulators. Illegal as contraceptives but not as cycle regulators.

Writers like to move around because when you come from one world into another, you have this huge colorful influence of all that is new hitting you, constantly assaulting you, exciting you, thrilling you. But you also have the distance on what you grew up in. So you have the double encouragement of perspective—you see what you came from in a totally different way because you are looking at it from a distance, and you are stepping outside it and all these new things are coming in. A lot of writers, certainly myself, like to sit around in corners looking and observing, and moving on your own from one community to another is very helpful.

MOLONEY: What writers are you particularly interested in?

BANNISTER: I've only started in my advanced years to read people like Edith Wharton and Henry James. I was educated in America, I went to a good private school in New York City and I went to Smith, where I always specialized in English literature. Today, I'm a great fan of Anne

Enright, also Mary Morrissey, some of the best people writing in Ireland today in my opinion.

MOLONEY: As well as being a writer, you are a wife and mother of two sons. Do you find a conflict between writing and motherhood?

BANNISTER: Certainly, with my older child, I felt frustrated because I had very little money and no help whatsoever. I did very little writing while he was small. The second one wasn't so bad. There's a huge gap, nearly nine years, between my two sons. The younger one is now eleven, and he still occupies immense amounts of my time, but each year I have a little more space and little more freedom. Having children has so profoundly enriched my life. It's just brought me many places I wouldn't have been and made me understand things so much more. So what if I'd written five books by now or been more successful as a playwright, which is where I started? I would rather have those children because what I write the rest of my life will be shaped by those overwhelming experiences. You don't get away from your responsibilities as a parent. I don't dispute for a minute that it has held me back in certain ways, but at the same time I strongly believe there are the most immense compensations in my understanding of the way things work.

MOLONEY: Can you talk a little bit about your career in playwriting?

BANNISTER: Well, it went nowhere. That's an exaggeration. From the very early stage I wanted to write plays more than anything else. I had a passionate interest in plays. Over a period of about ten years I wrote about ten plays. They won various awards—the Abbey bought the rights to one of them and paid me a lot of money for it—but when it didn't go any further, the frustration was very damaging. That's probably what made me turn elsewhere. I had them performed in the North of Ireland properly, and in Germany I had a wonderful performance. But here it was always readings, and rehearsed readings and all the prizes in the world. Unless you actually have a decent professional production of a play, in the end you're writing for the wrong reasons, not for actors.

Now during the same period I was also writing radio plays which were performed. I was under pressure at the time to make more money, so I started to write fiction. I came away from playwriting because I wasn't getting production. For nonperformed plays they were very successful, which is a terrible irony.

MOLONEY: How would you characterize your plays?

BANNISTER: They were definitely a young woman's plays. They were full of chance taking and risks. I know in one script, for example, I had a character who was a baby, being played by a young male in his early twenties. Some of the work had a link to Irish history but was also very much about contemporary things. I would throw the historical idea up in the air and catch the bits that I liked, really writing a modern play. I'm not currently interested in writing plays because of two big projects that I really want to complete.

MOLONEY: Can you talk about these projects?

BANNISTER: Yes, one is a novel about an Irish author named Beatrice Grimshaw who was a contemporary of Joyce, infinitely more successful during her lifetime than he was and for whom I have a massive interest. The subject matter is not all that much different than my own life, going off to a new world, changing where you are, and finding a new way of living.

MOLONEY: When Grimshaw left Ireland, where did she go?

BANNISTER: She went to Papau, New Guinea, which was really extreme. She moved against a strong family background; she changed her religion at a time when women did not change their religion. She had been a northern Protestant and she became a Catholic, which is extraordinary since the people she was involved with in Dublin were Protestants. She wrote a great deal. I'm taking the bits that interest me and writing something reasonably modern.

MOLONEY: Would you say there is an element of recovering women's history in your Grimshaw book?

BANNISTER: Absolutely. I feel a great pity that most Irish people have never heard of Beatrice Grimshaw. All her wild and wonderful tales of adventure stories were well received critically at the time. They were all pretty successful, although some of them were terrible. She was writing to make money. I'm particularly interested in female historical figures because they have more relevance to me. The men don't need to be done. What do I need to say about James Joyce that someone else has not said eighty million times. I'm much more interested in what's disappeared. And I certainly accept that in the education I received there were an inordinate number of fellows that you had to study and a rather small number of women.

MOLONEY: You noticed that too?

BANNISTER: I didn't at the time except only in the slightest way. I assumed that there wasn't anybody else. Now I realize this is simply not the case. I have come across other women writers while I've been looking into Beatrice Grimshaw. It was a very prolific and busy time for women; an awful lot of bright women were writing reasonably good books that have just been forgotten. What I'm doing with this lady could be done with many other writers.

Now in the interval I stopped and I'm writing this book of nonfiction called Blunt Trauma, an autobiography. "Blunt trauma" is the listed cause of death on my sister's death certificate. My sister's death at fifty-one is the triggering factor but it is a good title for the book, which is much broader.

MOLONEY: What was the blunt trauma?

BANNISTER: She died in the Swiss Air crash, September 2, 1998. It was a very public event. I found out about it when I turned my radio on in the morning; it had a major impact on my life and on my mother's life. It's the sort of thing you never expect to be caught up in. The air crash is only part of the book. There are vast amounts about my mother and her subsequent accident, but the air crash is the beginning and end of it. It plunges you into this most extraordinary world. It was a particularly high-profile event because it was Swiss Air, which is supposedly a very safe airline. The crash was mechanically induced by wiring, and the people on the airplane were very successful and well-known people.

MOLONEY: Did you find yourself involved in the investigations?

BANNISTER: Partially, and all the stuff that goes with it. For example, just to give you an idea, there are three of these notebooks. Just look there—just open it. That's something I got last summer. I got three books like that. [The "notebooks" are three large binders containing color print photographs of each item recovered from the crash, meticulously labeled.]

MOLONEY: There is something horribly flagrant about these personal possessions. These teddy bears, Barbie dolls, shoes, bags. Did they send these to everybody?

BANNISTER: The airplane was broken into over a million pieces so most of them were around the size of my hand. You could decline it if you wanted to. This is just a tiny bit; a certain amount of my book takes you through what happens after an air crash, stuff you've never thought about which has a creepy fascination. I met so many people with their own agendas. All these companies specialize in disaster management; lawyers move in like vultures. It's just extraordinary, and all the while you're coping with this immense sense of bereavement. I had to go to New York to bury her. You don't get a body. My mother didn't want to go, but I wanted to go. I was able to experience some of that in the autumn of this year when we went and scattered her ashes and then Swiss Air had two-and-one-half days of commemorative events.

MOLONEY: So this book is partially an autobiography?

BANNISTER: Yes, it's how we all ended up where we were. My mother subsequently had a serious accident at Christmas time last year, and I had to go and look after her for three months. I kept quite extensive diaries. That period of three months was highly traumatic. I made one extraordinary discovery about our family which was completely news to me. It's almost novelistic.

The book began because of plain old therapy because I just couldn't think about anything else. I couldn't work on the other book. I began it in October of last year. It's turned into something immense and massive. It's in four parts. I have parts one, two, and four done in draft form, and the third part I'm working on, which is the most painful in a lot of ways because it's the one that goes into the past. It is therapy but I will look to publish.

MOLONEY: Can we talk about your collection of short stories, *Magician?* Is the title story related to your autobiography?

BANNISTER: I think that particular story was saying good-bye to youth in a lot of ways. It's a story that takes chances and amuses and has fun and in the end it might work or it might not work. I suppose what's important about the title story was that I was moving in a different direction.

MOLONEY: The cooking metaphor communicates a substantial change; ingredients go through a process and they come out totally different. These stories are optimistic about the possibility of people living together.

BANNISTER: I think it is quite important to write books that are fun to read. I'm not saying you have to be necessarily stupid, but I don't want people sitting down to read my books to improve themselves. Life just has an awful lot of appalling things to dish out to all of us. No one escapes disappointments and frustrations and sorrows and the most hor-

rendous tragedies that just arrive out of nowhere. But success and contentment and happiness come out of the way you cope with the bad
things that happen. Living with anyone is very difficult—anybody—children, husband, best friend, mother, father, but I believe it is possible to
have good relationships and that is a better way to go through life.

I would have an inherently optimistic attitude toward life. Time does
heal. It doesn't get rid of things though. My sister's horrendous death is
very vivid to me today, but I don't want to write books that are depress-
ing. They may be about horrible things but I want people in the end to
find for themselves a way that works. So I don't want to fill them with a
sense of hopelessness, because I think life is a matter mostly of choice.
You can choose to focus on the horrendous things or you can choose to
put them in a box and respond to the little joys that are all around us. No
matter how awful things are, those little joys are still there all the time.

MOLONEY: Are you still writing short stories?

BANNISTER: I wrote two short stories last year that went out on
radio. They were written for something called Francis McManaford,
which is a radio award for which there were about seven hundred to
eight hundred entries this year. I've done a lot for BBC in short stories.
Radio stories suit me very well because I am a very intense craftsman; I
have never written a story where I haven't thought about every word.
Every story has gone through several drafts. Writing for radio is a particular knack and I understand it because I've done a lot of it.

MOLONEY: Do you like the idea that you will be heard, that you'll
have an audience?

BANNISTER: That's what I'm saying. You publish something between covers and you immediately limit the audience immensely. You
write a radio story for BBC radio and you have an audience of one million people. It goes back to my interest in drama, for the connection between the voice of the actor and their interpretation of it and the sole
listener.

MOLONEY: What is your relationship to the community of Irish
women writers?

BANNISTER: There are very powerful connections between many of
the women who are writing today. We meet regularly; we see each other
by chance and things. Not all my friends are writers but a great number
of them are and they are women. I don't have any close friends who are

men writers. I don't have any sort of division between the men that I read and the women that I read, but I like people to be open and guys never talk about what they're writing. It's just a different way of working. A lot of women don't talk about what they're writing but you can relate to them. I just have so much fun with my women writers. We just have a great time. I can't be working and always looking over my shoulder to see what's going on. I also don't have much time for the backbiting. It's too chilling. I don't want to get involved in all that. (A) I don't want to look behind my back, and (B) I don't want to stick a knife in anybody else's back.

Courtesy of Expressly Portraits

Catherine Brady

Interviewed by

HELEN THOMPSON

BORN: Evanston, Illinois, 1955

EDUCATED: Northwestern University (B.A.), Hollins College, University of Massachusetts at Amherst (M.F.A.)

RESIDES: San Francisco

WORKS: Teacher of creative writing at the University of San Francisco and the College of Notre Dame

GENRES: Fiction, nonfiction

AWARDS: Flannery O'Connor Award (2002), Zoetrope All Short Story Fiction Contest (2001), Brenda Ueland Prose Prize (2000), finalist in the Western States Book Award in Fiction (1999), finalist in the GSU Review Fiction Prize (1999), Redbook Young Writers' Contest (1983), nominated for Pushcart Prize (1981).

Catherine Brady is a first-generation American. Her parents emigrated from Ireland in the 1950s. Her fiction interrogates Irishness both in Ireland and America from the perspectives of gender and class. Brady's stories exemplify the burdens of remembering her past as well as forging a new, bifurcated identity. She says that her fiction, influenced by Chekhov, frames questions rather than answers. She has published short stories in a variety of journals, including The Missouri Review, The Greensboro Review, Nua, GSU Review, Kenyon Review, *and two anthologies,* I

Know Some Things: Stories about Childhood by Contemporary Writers *and* The Next Parish over: A Collection of Irish American Writing. *She has published one collection of short stories,* The End of the Class War *(1999).*

As well as investigating Irish-American identities, Brady is also interested in interrogating the new stories that have emerged in American culture and how they affect the Irish community. She focuses on the effects of war, disability, and hospitalization and explores racism in the Irish-American community and the larger culture.

Brady's stories are finely crafted with language that is both precise and lyrical. She connects external realities with the psychology of her characters as well as to the moral and ethical choices they must make. For example, "The Lives of the Saints" is structured according to the church's process for canonization, therefore complicating our understanding of the abuse the protagonist suffers at the hands of a disturbed child.

Catherine Brady's second collection of short stories, Curled in the Bed of Love *is being published by the University of Georgia Press. She is currently working on a novel. We conducted the interview via phone and email.*

◆   ◆   ◆

THOMPSON: How did you start writing?

BRADY: I've always written: the act of writing in many ways is utterly separate from the business of writing. Writing is not about keeping a record or writing autobiography, but about chasing this elusive idea of meaning, and I can't separate the effort from the goal. Writing, trying to make something beautiful, is the same thing for me as loving the world, having faith in its riches.

THOMPSON: How do you approach fiction?

BRADY: The point of any story is to ask the question, not answer it. This means it's my job to plumb the moral complexity of a situation as fully as I can, to be as perplexed by the dilemma as I'd like the reader to be. To get a reader to refrain from quick judgment, even momentarily, is a big achievement, I think.

THOMPSON: Did your family support your writing?

BRADY: I was encouraged by my family in many ways, but because both of my parents were working class, the world of writing and ideas was alien to them. My mother could encourage me to write, but I don't think she saw it as a profession (she was right!) and she worried that I should train for a respectable, ladylike job like teaching. Writing is not something that most communities encourage, in my experience, since it involves both a retreat from other obligations and an intense "paying attention" to the world, which too often results in a truthfulness that doesn't please the crowd.

THOMPSON: You are a writer who also teaches; what has that been like for you?

BRADY: Teaching has been meaningful to me as a writer for two reasons: contrary to popular illusion, teachers are out there in the world, engaged with their students in exploring the social reality we live in and facing its tensions in the classroom; studying great writers in order to discuss them with my students teaches me a great deal as a writer. Besides, in what other job could I sit under a tree on a beautiful afternoon reading Chekhov and be able to boast, "I'm working"?

THOMPSON: Could you tell me a little about your parents?

BRADY: My parents came to the United States from Ireland in the fifties. My father grew up on a farm in Kildare, and my mother grew up in Dublin. My father worked in a wire-and-cable warehouse and did yard work on evenings and weekends. Like so many immigrants, he worked hard to get ahead. Though my mother also worked to support the family, her primary work was her children, and this is a job that made her more open to life's pleasures.

THOMPSON: Are you Catholic?

BRADY: I was raised a Catholic. My mother, in particular, is very devout. I respect her faith and in many ways share it.

THOMPSON: Are you defining your faith in "The Lives of the Saints"?

BRADY: I wanted to write about an ordinary contemporary woman in the grandiloquent language of religion—the mysteries of faith, the sacrifices required of saints, and so on. The church has its own mythology of the saints, its heroes, and I wanted most of all to portray the heroism and poetry of this mother's everyday life. And the holiness. I understand holiness as a compound of attentiveness—deep regard for each moment—and the effort to love generously. In many ways this story expresses my own sense of Catholicism.

THOMPSON: How did the miraculous manifest itself to you in your life?

BRADY: My mother has an excellent batting average when it comes to praying for her children, and she always seems to know which saint is wanted to intercede; when my book was accepted for publication, she informed me she'd been praying for me—to St. Jude, the patron saint of lost causes.

THOMPSON: How has your short story collection been received?

BRADY: I've been pleased with the reviews. Most of them have been positive; for a while, I just thought people were being nice to me because it was my first time out. I couldn't quite accept or trust praise; when I saw a woman reading my book on a bus, my first assumption was that she must work for my publisher. I still have a hard time believing I've "gone public." I've been irritated at times that a few reviewers have made me responsible for their stereotypes of the Irish; for example, several reviews referred to the "standard" Irish drunks in the book and even misidentified a major character as an alcoholic, when he did not even drink alcohol. I've also wished that reviewers might pay more attention to the collection's focus on working-class issues—after all, the title includes the words "class war." Recently I learned that my book was a finalist for the Western States Book Award, and that made me happy, because a group of strangers chose to recognize the book for reasons that possibly didn't have to do with kindness and mercy.

THOMPSON: What's your experience of being an Irish-American?

BRADY: I only know my own experience, and for a long time, I didn't recognize how truly Irish it was. My father in particular became an "everything's-bigger-in-Texas" immigrant, enamored of all things American. My mother remained very attached to Ireland. She still calls it "home," and when I was a child, she would often remark on American customs by saying, "That's not the way they do things at home." At times not knowing how to be American made me feel inadequate or ignorant. This is a universal predicament for the children of immigrants, who often feel that shame attaches to their origins and that their duty is to endeavor energetically to adapt to the new culture as rapidly as possible, suffering a kind of amnesia in the process.

THOMPSON: Would you say that the Irish half weighs more heavily on you?

BRADY: My childhood was very Irish, and I know this every time I meet another Irish-American and we joke about Irish cooking. I know I'm Irish when I miss my mother tongue, which is not American English and which can arouse the greatest homesickness in me. I didn't know that everyone in the world didn't find misery hilarious, or hold mysterious grudges (my mother still curses Oliver Cromwell), or conduct family life as a wild melodrama. It's not something so definite as a set of cultural characteristics; it's imprecise and more conflicted—and being conflicted, about love of country or love of God, is a quintessentially Irish trait.

THOMPSON: Do you go to Ireland?

BRADY: I've visited Ireland two times. I have a lot of relatives living in Dublin, Naas, Kildare, and Mullingar.

THOMPSON: What was it like for you?

BRADY: When I first visited, I was sixteen, and the experience made me realize how American I was. It was not always a pleasant realization. I visited again in my mid-twenties. I didn't go as a tourist so much as to visit my family; I love Irish conversation and in Ireland itself it's the best—everywhere you go you hear poetry in the rhythm of the speech and the Elizabethan turns of phrase. I was also very struck by the ways in which Ireland still suffered from being a colony; the economy was poor on both visits (though better now) and I have a vivid memory of driving past ruins and being told, "Oliver Cromwell did that."

THOMPSON: Can you explain the title of your collection?

BRADY: I wanted to call the collection *The End of the Class War* because I felt that the lives of working-class women formed the essential subject matter of the book. The reference to the end of the class war is meant ironically; in America the question of class difference has nearly always been swept under the rug. Class still matters in this country; it is deeply embedded in discussions of race, for example.

THOMPSON: C. L. Innes recently said that in America some Irish people adopted racial prejudices because of their low social standing. You approach this issue in your stories.

BRADY: Yes, in some ways low social standing influences prejudice, but that comes dangerously close to assuming a working-class person is by definition likelier to be a racist. In "Don't Run," Nora sympathizes with the civil rights movement of the time—she needs one herself. The men feel threatened by it for complicated reasons—not just because they're laborers out there fighting for the scraps while the women stay home, but also because they may not want to see any flaws in the great American dream they hope to posses AND they're dealing with a multi-ethnic society for the first time. It's not always true, but because women are also, often, treated as "the other," they might hesitate more before imposing that condition on another person.

THOMPSON: In "Don't Run," America doesn't seem to be a land of opportunity.

BRADY: The protagonist Nora has immigrated because she has already failed at making a life for herself in Ireland, and her family believes that America will somehow magically cure what ails her. Being an immigrant is a uniquely tantalizing experience, because on the one hand, one arrives with the hope of many possibilities for change—there certainly are opportunities—but on the other hand, those hopes are nearly always out of line with reality, and unforeseen obstacles bar the way to the great American dream. She is an intellectual whose interests and experiences are foreign to her working-class family, and the difficulties of this are compounded by the fact that no one in her immediate family can imagine she would want anything other than to marry and make babies. When she was in Ireland she had already lost the person she was—she was forced to interrupt her studies to care for her sick father and was unable to overcome the claustrophobic closeness of her parents' home. Whether in Ireland or America, she can't reconcile the expectations of her family and class with her own interests and desires, and as an Irish-Catholic woman, she has been well-schooled to mistrust her own desires and regard them as selfish.

THOMPSON: Do working-class women lack power?

BRADY: Power is easy to identify and classify along economic lines: the poorest have the least, period. And we all pretty much understand that women have less economic power than men, all other things being equal; plenty of statistics support this notion. So the ladder of economic power is pretty easy to draw, with poor, unemployed women at the very bottom and working-class women a rung above poor, unemployed men. But I also would question what power is. Is it purely economic and political? How do we measure the social consequences or value of moral or spiritual power? Part of what interested me in writing the story "Daley's Girls" was this question of different kinds of power: the girl's mother has the power of genuine self-respect and compassion, where her father has the power of male privilege and his paycheck. Too often, working-class people are seen as lacking the power of awareness of their class predicament only because they lack earning power.

THOMPSON: You have said that one of your primary concerns is class conflict; would you also call yourself a feminist?

BRADY: Yes, I am a feminist and I feel militant about not having to apologize for that or how it might influence my writing. Joyce Carol Oates once commented on her frustration with the expectations placed on a woman writer: "Your writing departs from traditional feminist subjects, the [woman] writer is asked repeatedly—why is this? And the answer is, 'since I am a feminist, whatever I write about is in fact a 'traditional feminist subject.' "

THOMPSON: In the title story, "The End of Class Warfare," I like the tension you create between the mother and the daughter; is their conflict characteristic of immigrants?

BRADY: The mother clings both to old-country ways and to old-fashioned ideas of loyalty and duty, but her daughter is just as obstinately committed to the materialist values of the upwardly mobile. For me, the mother's belief that it's her duty as a wife to sacrifice herself for the sake of her senile husband clashes with the daughter's idea that the problem of the frail old man should be solved by putting him in a nursing home—that is such a materialist understanding of personal relationships, so connected to this immigrant child's embracing of the ambitious, get-ahead values of the new country. Peggy, the daughter, as a successful businesswoman, feels absolutely oppressed by her mother's lace-curtain Irish mentality and her passive acceptance of suffering. She experiences a war between the competitive values of her workplace and her mother's values, putting one's own desires last.

THOMPSON: I was dubious about Peggy's reason for hiring Shanelle. Wanting a lunch buddy seems superficial.

BRADY: Personally, I think that Peggy's decision to hire Shanelle because she'd make a good lunch buddy is a sound reason to hire someone—Peggy is looking for someone with vitality and force, and Shanelle has demonstrated at the interview that she isn't prissy or obsequious. You'll have to forgive me if I sound defensive—once I hear these characters, once they've let me in on how the world looks to them, I can't help being on their side, at least a little.

THOMPSON: Do you think that Peggy and her African-American protégé Shanelle have much in common?

BRADY: Peggy identifies with Shanelle because Shanelle is struggling to climb the ladder the hard way, just as Peggy did. I can't tell you if their class identification, or their identification with each other as women, is stronger than differences in race or any other barrier. I mean, I could tell you what I hope personally (which is yes, sisterhood is powerful!), but I can't tell you in terms of fact. The way I'm thinking in writing this story goes like this: Peggy identifies with Shanelle, but should she or can she? What are the ways in which fellow feeling flows over any of the obstacles—those tired old barricades of race, class, and gender—that presumably separate us, where and how is it blocked? What class does Peggy belong to now? In encouraging Shanelle to be ambitious, is Peggy helping her or perhaps forcing her to fit the mold that Peggy has tried to cram herself into?

THOMPSON: As you said earlier, you're interested in questions not answers?

BRADY: I couldn't write the story if I was sure of the answer to any of these questions, and it would be a boring story if I did. I have to pay enough attention so that the reader understands more than just the surface and can see what might be underneath. And I have to find a way to ask a real question if I'm going to make a story out of it. I have to question my own feminist certainties so that I don't write a moralistic fairy tale.

THOMPSON: Most of your women characters are connected to children and motherhood; is that the central experience women must come to terms with as part of their femininity?

BRADY: I don't think women have to come to terms with motherhood as part of their femininity, since some women may not want to become mothers. But I do feel strongly that as a feminist I want to honor women's traditional work, motherhood, and value its importance. Some feminists adapt a male attitude toward "domestic work" and raising children—saying it's unimportant, uninteresting work you should escape for better if you can. Raising a child is a miraculous, provoking, soul-defining experience, and it seems to me literature ought to pay attention to such spiritual fireworks. Sue Miller once remarked that when she wrote about parent-child relationships, her fiction was termed "domestic," but when Richard Ford wrote about a parent-child relationship, he was just writing serious fiction.

THOMPSON: Irish fathers in literature can be a stereotype, like Malachy McCourt in *Angela's Ashes,* the drunken lout who won't take responsibility for his family.

BRADY: I loved the portrait of the father in *Angela's Ashes,* because despite the fact that he abandons his family, his son Frank loves him, and he is a tender father at many times. We may want to judge him, but McCourt throws a wrench in the works if we try to make a snap judgment about this man.

THOMPSON: I feel the same about your Mr. Daley in "Daley's Girls."

BRADY: I very much wanted to consider the relationship between Joe Daley's work life, where he is relatively powerless, and his home life, where he, like most traditional, older Irish fathers, has dictatorial sway. On the other hand, I wanted to show a great deal more about this man and his relationship with his family.

THOMPSON: His transformation at the Knowles's house is quite interesting. Is this his fantasy of another life he could have had?

BRADY: Joe Daley's contentment when he stands in Mr. Knowles's house resonates on several levels: he believes that these people are worth more than he is and feels privileged to have access to their fancy home; he envies them the ease of their life and is proprietary about his pitifully small share in this luxury. He accepts his inferior status; he is jealous of his daughter's presence, fearful that she, who belongs to him, isn't fit to enter here. He doesn't want his daughter in the house to witness his envy and feeling of inadequacy, and he is expressing, with a great deal of innocence, aesthetic admiration for a place unlike any he knows, expensively arranged and reeking of yet another kind of privilege. If I've written a complex, convincing character, a reader might see all of these things.

THOMPSON: Some of his insensitivities are class based: shame at not being able to enjoy what others take for granted.

BRADY: Joe Daley is so tangled up by shame, as you say, and it is transferred onto his wife and children in hurtful ways.

THOMPSON: It seems that "Wild, Wild Horses" examines another side of the patriarchal family structure from the perspective of a generation in which patriarchy is most threatened. Is this the logical conclusion of this traditional family structure in an economy that won't support a solitary breadwinner?

BRADY: Certainly, the husband feels ashamed at his inability to earn money, and his young wife has grown up with the notion that men have a right to take things out on women. But mostly, they're crushed by the stresses of marrying too young, of perceiving (accurately) that not many choices are open to them in life. The narrator's husband is only a boy who doesn't know how to fight his problems except by using his fists on his wife. Yet the narrator, in spite of being a teen mother, poorly educated, and poorly loved by her own parents, has managed to go back to school so she can get a better job and to strive to do what's best for her own daughter. Unlike her husband, she has insight into her dilemma, but that insight can hobble her as much as it helps.

THOMPSON: Do "The Custom of the Country" and "Wild, Wild Horses" suggest that Irish women fear their fathers?

BRADY: I don't think of the father in "The Custom of the Country" as someone to be feared. Okay, so he drinks—but he's funny, playful with his children, etc. Irish fathers are, as a rule, a pretty tough bunch—autocratic with their wives and kids—but that might make their daughters angry, rebellious women rather than fearful ones.

THOMPSON: "The Custom of the Country" concerns immigration and distinctly mentions a memory of life in Ireland. How important are memories of Ireland to these characters?

BRADY: I wanted the father in this story to be a storyteller. The stereotype is that all the Irish are storytellers, witty drunks, but I don't think that's true across the board. In particular, I think rural Irish people tend to be much more silent, at least at home with their families. They may have to charm their companions at the pub, but there's no need to waste their breath on their own families. And among immigrants, it's not unusual to be fairly silent about home—it's a place you left, with a sense of failure or defeat, and America is the place where you are going to make yourself anew. At the time these immigrants came to America in the 1950s, Ireland was still very poor and backward, and something of shame attached to their homeland, where simple technology like a refrigerator was a rarity and where a young man might not find work even if he was persistent and intelligent. People don't like to remember failure. My own father never told me anything about his own childhood, which was desperately hard, until I was over thirty years old.

THOMPSON: Are family memories different for the women in the story?

BRADY: Memory is an uneasy mix of process (the imaginative re-creation of the past) and content (the report of what actually happened). The two sisters in this story don't remember their childhood in exactly the same way, and it's an enormous source of tension, precisely because memory is so untrustworthy and yet is what we use to create history. A lot is at stake in one version of events or another, for the sisters and for their father. His stories of Ireland emphasize quaintness on the surface but betray underlying cruelty, and this tension is at work in the narrator's memories as well.

THOMPSON: These questions of history and identity are political and pertain to nations as well as to people. Certainly, Ireland has struggled with its identity after independence.

BRADY: I think the Irish are struggling, like the people of many other postcolonial countries, to reclaim their sense of themselves and to begin to redefine themselves on their own terms, not in terms of their relationship to their colonizers. I see clear and absolute parallels to the experience of other postcolonial nations. In Nigeria as in Ireland today, there's a new generation of writers who are tired of casting their country's dilemmas in terms of resistance to the colonizers—that was a necessary step in creating a literature and reconnecting to their own past, but these young writers are seeking to expand the means and ends of self-definition and self-examination.

THOMPSON: What are you working on at present?

BRADY: I just finished another collection of stories loosely organized around the theme of romantic love and also connected by a focus on people who have struggled with their class identity. What's wonderful and dismaying about writing is that you can't run away from yourself—I set out to write love stories and found that more and more often, the main characters, all northern Californians, were people who had drifted from their origins and upbringing and in many cases fallen through the cracks of conventional middle-class life. Questions of class crop up of their own free will, so I live with it. Now I'm at the beginning of a novel, and it's really too soon to say anything about that.

THOMPSON: How would you like your stories to be read?

BRADY: There are many paradigms that we can apply to stories when we read them—we can look at them along a feminist axis, a class or social axis, a psychological axis, a moral axis, a historical or cultural axis, etc. All those perspectives can help us dig out meaning in a story, but it seems to me the purpose of a story is to defeat any single one of those "takes" on its meaning—as soon as we have tried to explain a story purely in class terms, or feminist terms, the story ought to turn around and defeat us by offering contradictions or complications the theory can't account for. In other words, stories should be as irreducible as real experience. Most of all, though, I'd like readers of my stories to be moved by the lives of the characters—stories belong first and foremost to the realm of feeling, not the realm of theory.

THOMPSON: Who do you like to read?

BRADY: I love Toni Morrison, William Faulkner, Ralph Ellison, Gabriel Garcia Marquez, and a host of other writers who are in love with embellishing language, also an instinct of mine. I love the ornate beauty of Shakespeare, yet I also love the simple transparency of Anton Chekhov or J. M. Coetzee. I tend to be enamored of both ends of the spectrum. Anton Chekhov, George Eliot, and Alice Munro are the writers I'd most like to emulate for their beautiful, refined precision and compassionate humanity. Among contemporary short story writers, I really like Grace Paley, Raymond Carver, Milan Kundera, Bharati Mukherjee, Gina Berriault, Ha Jin, Nadine Gordimer, Melanie Rae Thon, Junot Diaz.

THOMPSON: What about Irish writers?

BRADY: I've certainly been influenced by Joyce and Synge, but I have never been able to connect with Beckett. I admire and appreciate other Irish writers, such as John McGahern, Edna O'Brien, William Trevor, and Mary Lavin, but the writers who matter the most to me haven't been Irish.

THOMPSON: How has Joyce influenced you?

BRADY: His sense of language and his ability to portray experience as a kind of translucent envelope on some essential radiance have greatly influenced me. His world feels like home to me. When I was nineteen, my aunt returned to college to become a teacher, and she would relate to my mother the stories in Joyce's *Dubliners;* they would sit at the kitchen table laughing hysterically, recognizing in Joyce's characters the drinkers, the pious snobs, the lace-curtain respectable folks who were their neighbors in Dublin. They recognized themselves, in many ways, and that sense of recognition is how I know I'm Irish too.

Emma Donoghue

Interviewed by

HELEN THOMPSON

Courtesy of Claire McNamee

BORN: Dublin, 1969

EDUCATED: University College, Dublin (B.A.), Girton College, Cambridge (Ph.D.)

RESIDES: Ontario, Canada

GENRES: Fiction, drama, literary criticism, nonfiction

Emma Donoghue is an expatriate because of circumstance rather than design, and she has less ambivalence about her Irishness than other writers who leave. Donoghue is prolific. She writes for theater and radio, and she has published in a variety of genres, including essays of literary criticism, one literary biography, three novels, and two collections of short stories.

Donoghue's work is an alternative narrative to the marriage plot. But while her fiction might "interrogate and expose the received narratives of the dominant culture" (Smyth 1997, 22), her novels are still conventionally structured. For example, Stir-fry *(1994) is a bildungsroman. However, instead of the more traditional coming-of-age convention where a young woman realizes her end goal of marriage, Maria discovers not that she's a lesbian even, but that her love for Jael is misplaced and that she actually loves Ruth.*

Donoghue is also concerned with how historical narrative might sup-

press the telling of certain stories of women who were disenfranchised because they did not marry or were otherwise deprived of male protection, and who took on professions either not suited to women or were unrespectable. So, while Kissing the Witch *(1997) rewrites myth by lesbianizing popular fairy tales,* We Are Michael Field *(1998) examines the unconventional relationship between aunt and niece Katherine Bradley and Edith Cooper.* Slammerkin *(2000) combines historical archaeology with creative vision to examine the possible life and motivations of Mary Saunders, a real girl who was hanged in 1764 in Monmouth for killing her employer. Both Mary and her friend, Doll Higgins, follow the narrative pattern established for girls who do not conform: they die, Mary at the gallows and Doll from starvation and cold. Yet in the world of Donoghue's novel, even the conforming woman, Mrs. Jones, who marries and tries to reproduce, does not survive on her goodness.*

Emma Donoghue's latest collection of short stories, The Woman Who Gave Birth to Rabbits, *was published in 2002. Emma Donoghue is presently at work on a theatrical adaptation of* Kissing the Witch. *She is also writing a radio play for the BBC called* Don't Die Wondering, *a study of lesbian narrative motifs in Western literature. Her next novel will be a contemporary romance about long-distance relationships and immigration called* Time-Zone Tango. *I interviewed Emma Donoghue via email.*

• • •

THOMPSON: When did you start to write?

DONOGHUE: I started writing ghastly rhymes about fairies, nature, and the Holy Spirit at about six. I wrote poetry continuously through my teens, mostly melodramatic closeted love poetry to girls. I published a few and won some competitions both at school and national levels, which caused my head to swell even further.

THOMPSON: Your family has been supportive?

DONOGHUE: Since my father is a literary critic [Dennis Donoghue] who has published scores of books, and my mother is an even more passionate reader and has worked as an English teacher and now writes documentary pieces for Irish radio, my family was the ideal environment for a young writer.

THOMPSON: When did you start writing fiction?

DONOGHUE: At University College, Dublin, I got an idea for my first novel, *Stir-fry*, and made the switch to prose. I've written prose in a variety of genres (including plays) and I've never gone back to poetry in any serious way.

THOMPSON: What was it like doing your Ph.D. at Cambridge, one of the bastions of English elitism? What was it like for you, an Irish lesbian woman?

DONOGHUE: I know that many Irish people have experienced hostility in England, but I think it's often associated with job competition at the unskilled level. Cambridge is a special case; to me it felt like a rather cozy town full of liberals with Ph.D.s. As a graduate student and a writer, I attracted no resentment for being Irish; the only thing I ever noticed was a slight tendency on the part of English people to assume that I would be witty and eloquent because of my national origin! I was a student at Girton (historically a women's college and now with equal numbers of male and female students) so I didn't have to endure the patriarchal atmosphere that a friend of mine did in Trinity College, Cambridge.

THOMPSON: Did you spend most of your time at Cambridge with women?

DONOGHUE: My supervisor was a feminist woman and I was immersed in women's/les/bi/gay groups from the start of my time in Cambridge. Probably the only way I felt like an outsider was being a lesbian. But given that I'd never met so many lesbians in my life before—and I moved into a mostly lesbian women's housing co-op—the "outside" felt like a comfortable and generally hilarious place to be.

THOMPSON: Was it different from University College, Dublin?

DONOGHUE: Compared with Dublin, Cambridge seemed like lesbian heaven; most dykes I met were out of the closet and there was a lot of activism and socializing going on.

THOMPSON: Some women in ex-colonies find more freedom in the colonizing country. Was this your experience?

DONOGHUE: I'm very dubious about this line of argument. I was born into a republic that had shaken off British influence long ago. If we still have a special relationship to Britain, it hardly compares to that of the developing nations struggling to recover from more recent colonial regimes.

THOMPSON: You don't think that Ireland is still recovering from colonization?

DONOGHUE: As a privileged and highly educated Dubliner, I absorbed an immense confidence about the business of writing, and I can't claim I came to it as any kind of disenfranchised, colonized outsider. (If it wasn't for my sexuality, I must admit I probably would never have realized what it's like to be an underdog, or developed any empathy for those who live on the margins.)

THOMPSON: What about the North, the Catholic Church, cultural isolation as a consequence of colonization?

DONOGHUE: The nation I grew up in, from the 1970s on—meaning the Republic of Ireland (to be honest, the North is a foreign place to me)—felt like a country with a strong identity of its own despite its colonial past. It wasn't lacking culture, education, skills, or politics of its own; for instance, I always felt proud of the antiwar, antinuclear position we took. It still had a bit of an inferiority complex and a grudge vis-à-vis Britain; you could call that a colonial leftover. Our culture has certainly been influenced by having been colonized in the past, just as British culture was influenced by sending colonists and bureaucrats all over the world. But it's history; we should be able to take history seriously without lamenting our postcolonial status every time we go to buy a pint of milk! The fact that British navvies are now building Irish roads shows how rapidly the page can turn.

THOMPSON: What about the control the church has had on Irish culture?

DONOGHUE: The things I resented in Ireland while I was growing up, the things I still resent—the Catholic Church and general conservatism—I wouldn't blame on Britain. The church has been a powerful colonizer on its own; its strength in other countries proves that. So yes, perhaps we got caught between two powerful systems—British rule and the church—but the church's power was hardly a product of British rule. And in the twentieth century I'd say the church has done a lot more harm to Ireland than Britain has. Think of censorship, the Mother and Child Bill, the antiabortion amendments, institutional child abuse, homophobia.

THOMPSON: Did you leave Ireland because of homophobia?

DONOGHUE: I didn't leave Ireland for reasons of sexuality; I just wanted to do a Ph.D. in English literature and there was more funding available in England. But in the event, I think it did me good to get away from Ireland and my family for a while, and Cambridge was a great setting. Knowing no one when I arrived, I was able to be absolutely "out" as a lesbian from the start, and learn to live alone and then in a co-operative. I became much more extroverted, for one thing.

THOMPSON: How did the move to England affect your writing?

DONOGHUE: I got an English literary agent who questioned my timid assumptions that I should aim my novel at an Irish or feminist readership only; she encouraged me to write for the widest possible audience.

THOMPSON: Did she suggest changes in content?

DONOGHUE: She suggested that when I redrafted *Stir-fry* I should bear in mind that readers would not necessarily be Irish and so couldn't be assumed to know about arcane Catholic concepts like transubstantiation! I will always be grateful to her for broadening my horizons; I think it was sheer timidity that made me expect that only an Irish publisher would be interested in my work.

THOMPSON: Did you see *Stir-fry* as an opportunity to educate non-lesbian audiences or did you want to offer lesbians validation?

DONOGHUE: *Stir-fry* was aimed first at Irish lesbians and then was rewritten to find a more general worldwide audience as well. (This included putting in the American boy.) Rereading it now, it has rather too many of those let-me-explain speeches for my taste—but they seemed more necessary (for both straight and lesbian readers) in 1994 when it was published, when questions like "why do you hate men?" had more currency. I suspect those sections are the reason why lesbians often tell me they've given the book to their mothers!

THOMPSON: Do you have an audience in mind as you write?

DONOGHUE: From my own perspective, I am very aware that some of my books will end up with a broad literary-fiction audience and others will be sold to a target audience of lesbians (for instance, my *Mammoth Book of Lesbian Short Stories*), but I can't say I feel constrained by this knowledge. I'm certainly troubled by the fact that I've met several straight women who read *Hood* and were appalled by the oral-sex-during-a-period scene!

THOMPSON: Why did you opt for an English publisher?

DONOGHUE: The epicenters of the publishing world are London and New York. London-based publishers take the Irish market very seriously and hire Irish publicists, so I've probably sold just as many books in Ireland as if I'd gone for an Irish publisher. I don't feel disloyal; my loyalty would be to readers, not publishers.

THOMPSON: Does the critical writing you do conflict in any way with your creative work?

DONOGHUE: I find academic work easier and creative work more thrilling. This means that they balance very well. On the days when I don't seem to have an original thought in my head, I can always go off to the library and do the mundane slog of looking things up!

THOMPSON: Do you find that your critical prose looks and sounds like your creative prose?

DONOGHUE: A certain healthy cross-fertilization occurs: when I'm writing critical prose I am concerned to make sense and tell a story, as it were, and when I'm planning creative work I research and plan it in a pretty organized manner, as a historian might. But I don't end up with texts which are half fish, half fowl. I find distinctions of genre very useful (even today!); I think someone sitting down with a novel is looking for very different pleasures from someone consulting a historical study. And the standard of truth differs in the two genres. When I'm writing history or biography, I do try to stick to what I know or can argue was true, whereas fiction/drama allows me to try and express the spirit of the truth rather than the letter.

THOMPSON: Does *Kissing the Witch* demonstrate this overlap, since it seems to demand of you both critical and creative skills?

DONOGHUE: No, I'd call *Kissing the Witch* pure fiction. Yes, it has an intertextual/allusive aspect, which is certainly based on a rethinking of a literary tradition, but the genre is clearly fiction.

THOMPSON: Was the fairy-tale allusion in the title of *Hood* an inspiration for *Kissing the Witch*?

DONOGHUE: My title/epigraph for *Hood* didn't inspire *Kissing the Witch*; it's more that both works reveal my permanent fascination with folk/fairy-tale patterns.

THOMPSON: It also follows in a tradition of subverting these traditional, patriarchal narratives.

DONOGHUE: Yes, I've read quite a lot in the genre of feminist rewritings of myth/fairy tale; Angela Carter is marvelous, as are Anne Sexton, Olga Broumas, Bryony Lavery, Jeanette Winterson, Jane Yolen. It was Attic Press who first asked me to consider writing a book of fairy tales, so though I didn't end up publishing it with them, the *Kissing the Witch* project could be said to be inspired by Attic's series of feminist fairy tales.

THOMPSON: Would you say they're also lesbian fairy tales?

DONOGHUE: I came under pressure from publishers to make it either "less lesbian" or "more lesbian," but what I wanted was a seamless mingling of varied women's stories, roughly half of which turned out to be overtly lesbian.

THOMPSON: Critics argue about whether the definition of lesbian narrative should focus on the writer, reader, or text. What do you think?

DONOGHUE: I'm a lesbian writer, but for a novel of mine to be a lesbian narrative, I think there has to be a central lesbian character or relationship. I'm old-fashioned that way.

THOMPSON: One line of argument suggests that lesbian texts offer us new and subversive narrative configurations of ways women can exist outside patriarchal linearity.

DONOGHUE: I think making "lesbian" a metaphor for narrative subversion, say, both weakens the specificity of the term and denigrates writers whose narratives aren't obviously subversive. My own experience is that "new" material—say, about contemporary lesbian relationships—is often best delivered to a wide readership in what seem like comfortingly old-fashioned forms. Apart from the odd dabble in postmodernist waters (e.g., the self-conscious rewriting of fairy tales in *Kissing the Witch*) I think I write fairly conventionally shaped realist novels.

THOMPSON: What about *Stir-fry*? Were you playing with the conventions of heterosexual romance plots in this case?

DONOGHUE: Yes, I might sometimes play with narrative conventions, but so do most writers these days; lesbians have no monopoly on it. In fact, these days (compared with the early 1970s, say) lesbian writing is not particularly known for its stylistic or structural experimentation; we're getting noticed for the new things we're saying, not for how we're saying them.

THOMPSON: Does sexual fluidity help to define lesbian narrative?

DONOGHUE: I'm interested in the fluidity and unpredictability of human sexuality, which is more and more obvious in the stories we're hearing these days. (Though we're not all multisexual; my own sexuality doesn't seem remotely fluid, funnily enough, as I'm 100 percent dyke so far.) My historical work has confirmed that women can't be herded into neat camps called "lesbian," "bisexual," and "heterosexual." *Stir-fry* is all about drifting into attraction, rather than discovering a crystal-clear sense of identity. I like fluid texts too.

THOMPSON: In *Hood,* you explore the consequences of living a closeted life. Do you think that is emotionally and psychologically damaging to lesbians?

DONOGHUE: Yes, the closet is a bastard, and in *Hood* (where the title image is all about secrecy) I wanted to analyze why it is so damaging, but also what are its particular comforts (privacy, hiding one's wounds, the status quo) which make it so hard to escape. By the time I wrote *Hood* I was long out of the closet myself, but I knew so many people (particularly in Ireland but also elsewhere) either fully or partly still in the closet, that I wanted a character who would be more representative than me. I still think the number of "out" lesbians and gays is just the tip of the iceberg of queer life; for instance, I know a small English village where the PTA is full of closeted housewives having affairs with each other. I wanted to show that some of Pen's fears are self-deluded. For instance, she doesn't realize that Mr. Wall knows and accepts her relationship with his daughter Cara and that there are other ways of life, for example, the kind of community on offer in the Amazon Attic, which may not appeal to her but suggests that there is warm, loving friendship out there for her to find.

THOMPSON: So you think women should risk all and come out?

DONOGHUE: These days I have very little tolerance for other people's closets, having wasted too many grim teenage years there myself. I've lost my knack of Irish discretion and euphemism on these matters! Unless someone has a very concrete reason to lie—a serious risk of losing child custody, for instance—I have little sympathy. The closet is not a personal matter; it's more like a spreadable virus of fear. The Jodie Fosters of this world could do so much good by coming out, if they had the guts; they could make a difference especially to the lesbian and gay teenagers whose suicide rates are so appallingly high. Excuse the rant. I'm subtler in fiction!

THOMPSON: Liz McManus said that the cheerful exteriors that tourists see in Ireland actually hide unpleasantness because the Irish have circuitous ways of expressing their feelings. Does this indirectness facilitate the closet for gay people?

DONOGHUE: Yes indeed, the Irish are traditionally circuitous, which makes the outpouring of frank speech on the radio and in newspapers over the last ten years particularly strange. It's as if we reached a certain point where we had to "speak bitterness" or burst! But that clever, coy, or just timid habit of indirectness in speech in Ireland has certainly contributed to the high rates of closet clinging among Irish gays and lesbians I know. I've no patience for it myself.

THOMPSON: Could you talk about what it's like for you, being an out Irish lesbian?

DONOGHUE: In my panic-stricken teens it seemed to me that "Irish lesbian" had the ring of a contradiction in terms. But since then I've learned to define both terms rather more broadly, and I find them not at all incompatible. Besides, at this point I've met so many Irish dykes that I don't feel remotely unique. We have history, community, and a refreshing eclecticism, especially when it comes to religious matters. Some of the same women who conduct pagan rituals among the standing stones will go off to midnight mass in a Catholic church at Christmas.

THOMPSON: These contradictions of paganism and Catholicism bring to mind Pen in *Hood,* who is sexually aroused while mourning, which seems out of place yet is a normal response.

DONOGHUE: I'm glad you like that bit. I was struck by some discussion of sexual feelings in studies of the bereaved that I read; I had assumed they'd be numb to feel any desire, but not at all. Besides, I wanted the week described in *Hood* to stand as a sort of microcosmic version of Pen's post-Cara life, so I definitely wanted to include hints that her sexual feelings were alive and well. And hopefully, in the post-book future I fantasize for her, Pen will have the wit to pick a nicer girlfriend.

THOMPSON: Do you think that you are being subversive by placing these marginal characters within a central human experience?

DONOGHUE: Certainly *Hood* did get many reviews that mentioned the "universal human theme" of bereavement; those critics clearly felt they needed to make a case for a lesbian book's relevance to a straight readership. Looking back, I can now see that *Hood* is part of a small but interesting body of lesbian novels of loss and bereavement (by people like Sarah Schulman, Marion Douglas, Sarah Von Arsdale, Carol Anshaw) written in the 1990s. We were catching up with the boys, perhaps; gay men really took the lead in writing honest and beautiful books about mourning.

THOMPSON: How do you approach your female characters?

DONOGHUE: I am a lesbian and feminist writer. I'm writing stories, not utopian manifestoes. Besides, I think it's much more affirming to an

Irish lesbian to read a book which has the ring of the real, which features women in some sense like her going about their daily struggles and complications.

THOMPSON: Is it important to see the problems in relationships?

DONOGHUE: I tend to write about bad relationships because they make better stories, not because I don't believe in happy lesbians. And villains have their own glamor; in *Stir-fry*, say, Jael might seem to be set up as the "bad bisexual" character but she's given so much space in the novel, and so many of the witty lines, that readers have the freedom to get to know her, and many like her better than the more "positive" character Ruth. Satire is another wonderful tool; there's a strong tradition of feminist/lesbian writers affectionately taking the piss out of their own communities, which is what I was trying to do with the inclusion of the "Amazon Attic" sections in *Hood*.

THOMPSON: Do you see yourself as having a political voice?

DONOGHUE: We writers should never be trusted as the political "voices of the community" because our loyalties are generally to literature. We often have a taste for ambiguity, parody, conflict, and confusion.

THOMPSON: How difficult is it to create a female character who is real and has agency?

DONOGHUE: Ah yes, I like the idea of female characters with agency. I think my characters often start out rather passive or stuck but come into their own power by the end of the story. My main character in *Slammerkin*, Mary Saunders, is a teenage prostitute in London of the 1760s, and she's a much more dislikeable, bad-tempered heroine. I think she comes into her own power by about halfway through chapter 1!

THOMPSON: Do you have difficulty creating credible male characters?

DONOGHUE: I'm interested in creating new male role models— male characters who aren't the thug or the Prince Charming either. With Mr. Wall in *Hood* I wanted to create a father figure who had quite a lot to offer Pen despite not being related to her by blood or law. Then in *Slammerkin* I've included a character I rather like, a self-educated Welsh footman called Daffy who is meant to stand for Enlightenment values of tolerance and rationality.

THOMPSON: Elaborate on your move from Ireland to England. Where are you living now?

DONOGHUE: I've made a "second immigration" to Canada. Yes, I feel some nonsensical guilt for living away from my native land. Its persona is such a seductive one: the beautiful sad woman abandoned by her sons and daughters. But then I go back—every two months or so for a quick visit, and much of the summer—and realize it's becoming a rather brash, moneyed, modern country, and so full of returned emigrants that I'm not needed at all!

THOMPSON: You didn't consider moving back to Ireland?

DONOGHUE: Yes, I could definitely see myself living in Dublin if fate hadn't led me to Canada, and I will always think of myself as Irish and write about Irish matters (as well as others).

THOMPSON: Does the female image of Ireland still have currency?

DONOGHUE: I don't visualize Ireland as female myself, but the historical traditions are so strong—the wild crone, the wailing mother, the raped girl—I don't think they'll be forgotten any time soon.

THOMPSON: What led you to Canada?

DONOGHUE: Love.

THOMPSON: Do you get homesick?

DONOGHUE: If it wasn't for the love aforesaid, I might well have gone back to Dublin after my time studying in England was up. I do get homesick the odd time, or feel displaced, a sort of what-am-I-doing-here sensation.

THOMPSON: Is there something appealing about being a foreigner, perhaps as an exotic presence?

DONOGHUE: There are definite benefits to living "away." It's good for a writer to experience a subtly different culture, and a fresh angle on her own home culture; I've realized, from the point of view of North America, that Ireland and England are more similar than I thought. They share a lot of TV programs, for one thing, and a rainy climate! I'm not exactly exotic here—Canada has been full of the Irish for two centuries, and I'm a white English-speaker—but I am a little different, which I like. Though it should be said, most Canadians I meet are either immigrants or the children of immigrants, so the us/them distinction is much less firm than I found it to be in England; I wouldn't say anyone makes me feel like a foreigner, exactly.

THOMPSON: Tell me more about your new novel, *Slammerkin.*

DONOGHUE: *Slammerkin* is about a teenage prostitute in 1760s

London who ends up in a small town in the Welsh borders and commits a murder. I've taken great pleasure in shedding my usual time, place, and concerns for this one. It has a dark tone, no lesbian content, and is much more about class and ambition than sexuality. Lord knows what my regular readers will think of it.

THOMPSON: Have you enjoyed the Celebrating Irish Women Writers Conference?

DONOGHUE: I'm mildly curious whenever I'm placed by critics in a context of "Irish letters" but I doubt it affects my writing. I do like attending the odd academic/literary conference because it's a chance to hear new ideas and put faces to the names. And it is immensely flattering to have my work become the subject of literary criticism, which is so much more thoughtful and analytical than high-speed book reviews.

THOMPSON: Who do you read?

DONOGHUE: I like lots of writers, including some who haven't influenced me at all because they're in such different genres, such as Terry Pratchett. But my sense is that I've been most influenced by—or can be best placed within—a vague tradition of Anglo-American women novelists writing close-up emotional dramas, including Jane Austen, the Brontës, George Eliot, Ann Tyler, Carol Shields . . . they're just a few names.

THOMPSON: Do you think you have been influenced by writers such as Beckett, Joyce, Synge?

DONOGHUE: Much as I like the work of the famous Irish men you mention, I'm not aware of an influence.

THOMPSON: So you don't think that all Irish writers have to slay the dragon of Joyce in order to pursue the craft?

DONOGHUE: Women generally don't slay dragons; they avoid them and take shortcuts through the woods to the castle.

Lia Mills

Interviewed by

CAITRIONA MOLONEY

BORN: Dublin, 1957
RESIDES: Dublin
EDUCATED: B.A. and M.A. in women's studies
WORKS: Lecturer at University College, Dublin
GENRES: Fiction, literary criticism

Lia Mills returned to live in Ireland after spending ten years in London and Texas. While she is Irish, her children were born in the United States and consider themselves Americans. Mills is an academic, a feminist, and a writer and was one of the organizers of the Celebrating Irish Women Writers Conference in Dublin in May 1999. Mills has published short stories, literary criticism, and one novel, Another Alice.

Mills's first novel, Another Alice, *examines the relationship between a damaged daughter, an abusing father, and an apparently cold, complicitous, and uncaring mother. Mills brings considerable expertise to bear on the psychology of the abused child and woman, and the novel tells Alice's story through an innovative narrative strategy. The protagonist's storytelling parallels her psychological process in recovering memories of her past in psychotherapy and its manifestations in her life.*

Another Alice *is both bildungsroman and kunstleroman as it describes a girl's emergence as a person and as an artist. Although Alice's self-destruction and self-hate result in her pregnancy, the event turns her life around. She begins to take responsibility for her addictions and self-inflicted injuries as well as her psychological condition. Two women friends accompany Alice on this journey, Nell and Kate. Kate is supportive and she becomes more liberated and independent as Alice's story unfolds; Nell retreats from Alice's history into denial and alcoholism.*

Gerry Smyth writes about this novel in The Novel and the Nation, *pointing to its treatment of the changing paradigm of women's identity in Ireland, its use of Irish myth, and the cyclical nature of abuse that Alice only narrowly avoids in her role as Holly's mother. Smyth notes that the novel "represents the hidden underside of an Irish society in denial about abuses of all kinds" (1997, 96). Both the* Herald *(Glasgow) and the* Irish Times *acknowledge* Another Alice *as an important story that needed to be told, saying that Mills's narration is "one of extraordinary power and resilience" (Macdougall 1997, 14) that handles sensitive issues "with consummate care and understanding" (Corcorna 1996, 14).*

Mills has finished her second novel, tentatively called Aisling, *and has started working on a novel about immigration. I interviewed Lia Mills in her home in Dublin.*

• • •

MOLONEY: Can you tell me about your background and education?

MILLS: I was born in Dublin, the youngest of six children. I was sent to boarding school when I was six years old and I went to a succession of boarding schools after that. I was one of those kids who was constantly getting into trouble, and I was expelled from every school I ever went to. I left school when I was sixteen. I had an interrupted education. After I left school, I did go to college for a year, but then I dropped out, went to London, studied radiography over there, and started working. Then, later on, when we were living in Texas, I went back to college as a mature student on a distance learning program and got my B.A. in women's studies.

MOLONEY: What did you study in that program?

MILLS: Mostly women in fiction: I did a lot of reading in psychology, Carol Gilligan, Mary Daly, but my dissertation was about feminist fiction.

MOLONEY: Why did you go to America and why did you come back?

MILLS: We went because of my husband's job. We came back after ten years, because he was going to work in Burma, and it didn't really matter where we lived, because there was going to be a lot of separation involved. At that stage, the girls were growing up, and I had always had it in my mind to come back, so they could go to school here. I wanted them to know their grandparents and cousins. I wanted them to know where they were from.

MOLONEY: How did your children feel about living in Ireland?

MILLS: I think we have passed a sense of dislocation on to them. We left home to go to the States and I felt that was a huge disruption; by coming back, I have passed that disruption on to them; they all see themselves as Americans. They were all born in the States. I know that they will all go back there, at least to see what it is like.

MOLONEY: They see themselves as American not Irish?

MILLS: Yes. I think they see themselves as fractured. I think it depends on the circumstances. Sometimes, it suits them to see themselves as Americans, and sometimes it suits them not to.

MOLONEY: So they have a choice of identity. How about your identity: do you describe yourself primarily as a writer, teacher, or academic?

MILLS: Writer. Now I would. I would have had a lot of trouble with that before, but I have left academia. I am a full-time writer now. I was a Ph.D. candidate, but I have decided not to finish, because the things I had to take out in writing academic papers were the things that interested me most. I would get an idea and I would want to run with it, but I don't want anything as trivial as a fact to get in my way. Those two impulses, I do think, are opposed to each other in academia.

MOLONEY: How about the feminist question? Would it be fair to call you a feminist?

MILLS: Absolutely, but I love the way you even ask that question: the "feminist question," would it be "fair to say" . . .

MOLONEY: I am trying to develop a neutral way of asking that question that doesn't immediately reveal my position because I have encountered a surprising number of negative answers.

MILLS: In a way it is ludicrous to ask any woman whether or not she believes in her right to equality, and yet, the fact that the question needs to be asked recognizes the fact that a lot of people have problems with it. I see why.

MOLONEY: What do you think are currently the problems with being a feminist?

MILLS: The problem for feminism in Ireland is many women don't see feminism as especially relevant. They see feminism as actively hostile to the way they live their lives, which is a problem feminism needs to address.

MOLONEY: How much of a presence is feminism in your writing?

MILLS: I do see myself as fundamentally feminist; that informs the way that I think about a whole range of things and so, obviously, it is going to be in my writing: I don't however set out to write feminist fiction, because I think that is almost a contradiction in terms. If you have an ax to grid, I don't think that fiction is the place to do it; the fiction suffers as a result. The story doesn't come to life. The characters don't come to life.

MOLONEY: There is a relationship of fantasy and reality in your first novel, *Another Alice*. Where did that come from?

MILLS: Irish folklore is full of images of shape-shifting and extraordinary powers; the fantasy stuff for Alice is very much about myths of disappearance. For a child who is as disenfranchised as she is, that sort of fantasy life feeds her and keeps her going.

MOLONEY: Were you thinking about Irish mythology specifically?

MILLS: Oh, absolutely. In so much as she is an Irish child. Certainly, reading and knowing my own childhood myths and legends would have played a huge part. On a conscious level, I was very aware of Irish myth. For a lot of kids of my age, half of our reading would have been English fiction for children, when we were at boarding school, but it was all very "Anglo," so I wanted to put an Irish slant on this work perhaps because I had just come back to Ireland. If I had never gone away, maybe I wouldn't have felt it was important.

MOLONEY: How did you find the right voice and language for Alice?

MILLS: Language was a core issue. Language is the writer's medium: difficult and easy. The novel is about storytelling and how one arrives at a sense of oneself and self-definition. Alice learns to tell her own story, not to accept what other people say about her. I had to experiment with point of view, with whether to use first person, third person, past or present. In the end, the solution that I came to was to locate the story in the foreground and put the more present story in the past tense, to create a separation. Alice was very distant from herself at the beginning of the novel. But to collapse that distance, there are interruptions throughout the story of the first-person voice in the present tense, which is very immediate, very urgent, and very young. Then, in the end, that voice becomes more insistent, until Alice can recognize it as her voice, which collapses the distance completely. The psychotherapist Ruth mediates all that.

MOLONEY: Thinking about feminist theories of the body and hysteria, Alice's body seems to know about her abuse and to act it out before her conscious mind. Was that something that you were thinking about?

MILLS: I was aware of that; it's as if her body is her enemy, and they are competing for whose truth was going to get told. Alice treats her body like an enemy, because she was abused. As a child, she despised her body, because she was too small and she was too weak. She had no options so her body is her enemy.

MOLONEY: Her early adolescence, when she takes drugs and is sexually promiscuous, is a form of self-punishment. How common do you think Alice's story is?

MILLS: Judging by the responses that I have had, incredibly common. I have had a number of letters from total strangers who said X, Y, or Z happened to me. Not necessarily in its entirety, but some aspect of Alice is in everyone. The level of identification that people felt on reading the book was very deep and very strong. It was also the best thing about writing it—receiving all of those letters, from people just saying "thank you."

MOLONEY: Is there a relationship with eating also in the novel, between abuse and food? Alice is hungry when her mother dies. She is hungry for a child, but after she remembers the rape, she eats.

MILLS: Not eating is a classic way of withholding. I think she was withholding herself, punishing herself, wanting to stay small and not sustain herself. At that level, it was, yes, I was aware of it.

MOLONEY: Although the book is not didactic, it is instructive at the moment in Ireland because of all the abuse stories coming out.

MILLS: I did not set out to write a didactic book, but at the same time, *Another Alice* was written in response to a very specific set of events in Ireland, in 1992, which provoked the novel. That year we had a series of really horribly violent crimes against women and the whole area of abortion rights was revisited. A number of sexual abuse cases were reported in the press. Suddenly everywhere you turned, you had the story of a court case and comments by a judge or by a lawyer, redefining what happened for the women or girl who was at the center of the case, deciding whether or not it was significant. Under the current criminal law in Ireland, if a woman brings a case against a man for rape, she goes in and has to face a defense counsel whose job is to say she is a liar. Women, at the moment, do not have the right to their own legal representation. They go in as a witness against the man she accuses of raping her. His lawyer then brings all his legal experience to bear, so what chance does she have?

Every time you open the newspapers or turned on the radio, there was somebody giving the benefit of their opinion. Some people were saying that these things should never be spoken about. Other people were saying, "isn't it great, it is finally out in the open." But, what was really happening was a lot of white noise; the one thing that we never heard was the story of an individual speaking out and saying, "this was my experience, this is what happened to me," without any interruptions or anyone in a gown and a wig coming on any saying, "we don't believe you." I didn't particularly want to write this novel, but once I realized that, Alice came into my mind. She was real for me from the very beginning. I became obsessed by her. I wanted to let her tell her story. Fiction is the ideal medium for that because there are no interruptions. What I wanted to do was to set out with something that was apparently normal, apparently ordinary, and little by little draw a reader in. At the beginning, the story is relatively superficial. It has an emotional distance and the tone, so that by the time that the full force and weight of the story comes out, it is really shocking. Any reader who stayed with Alice long enough to get to that point is going to stay with her and go through it.

MOLONEY: Let me ask about the other women in the novel. Are they complicit in the crimes against Alice?

MILLS: It is a cloudy issue. Alice really can't get past feeling that her mother should have intervened on her behalf and didn't. I am completely sympathetic with this viewpoint. I really wanted to resist contributing to Alice's sense of herself as a victim. So, if Alice is not a complete victim, then I suppose by extension, nobody else is purely evil either. Her mother was a frightened woman; she is not as powerful in the situation as Alice imagines her to be.

MOLONEY: Was becoming a mother herself relevant to Alice's being able to remember?

MILLS: Oh yes, it is central. It is only when she has a baby herself that she sees how vulnerable and dependent her daughter, Holly, is. In recognizing that, she has to recognize her own vulnerability as well. When her therapist says to her, "If Holly was showing all those bruises and those marks, how would you react?" Alice is devastated. She has to recognize that if what happened to her were to happen to Holly, she would know what it was. But, because it was her, she didn't think it mattered. It helps her escape that victim position, because she learns that it is very hard to be a parent. She makes a lot of mistakes. She is far from being perfect as a mother, so she has to learn to accept that side of herself, as well.

MOLONEY: What are you working on now?

MILLS: I just started my third novel. I finished my second and it's gone off to my agent in London and she will send it out to publishers. It's working title is *Aisling*. It is set in contemporary Ireland, and the two main characters are female: Aisling works in an old people's home, and the other main character is a resident in the home. The novel is about the relationship between them and their stories outside of that environment. Aisling starts out essentially passive, not liking to make trouble. She has to learn to make trouble.

MOLONEY: So, what is the third novel going to be?

MILLS: The third one is my immigration novel. I'm not sure where the immigrants go; it could be anyplace, U.S.A. I am fond of Texas, although it is not the kind of place anyone would want to go.

There is something really funky about Texas that I learned to like. Besides, everybody knows California. Readers have a mindset about landscapes in California and New York, Boston, Chicago.

MOLONEY: Because Irish immigrants have always gone and written about those places?

MILLS: Yes. Nobody writes about Texas, however, except Molly Ivors.

MOLONEY: Let me ask you about postcolonialism. I have run into some opposition to the idea that Ireland was an English colony. Also, many Irish people do not see themselves having anything in common with other British colonies. They don't see any similarities between Ireland and India, the Caribbean, South Africa, and Nigeria.

MILLS: That amazes me. Although, I can see why. I lived in London for two years as a teenager. At that time, in the mid 1970s, there was a huge amount of anti-Irish racism over there. But I learned very quickly that because I was white, I could pass. It wasn't until I opened my mouth that I was identified. Given our own shameful record in regard to racism, people are slow to claim a level of oppression that we don't necessarily share by virtue of our color. I can understand that people would be reluctant to say that we are oppressed and have experienced racism, because patently we don't experience it to the same extent as other ethnicities. But we are just in denial. Those patterns are there and, to me, undeniable. I don't know why people would even want to deny them. This is an area of literature that has been overlooked, and as a result of that, whole areas of the concept of Irish identity haven't been properly explored. When you say, for example, "Well, the Irish were civil servants in India," that is true, but you have to ask yourself which Irish? There are the Anglo-Irish and there were the Irish and there are so many layers and levels.

MOLONEY: You have written an article on Irish literary history, haven't you?

MILLS: It is called "Forging History: Emily Lawless's *With Essex in Ireland.*" It is in a special issue on Irish writers in the eighteenth and nineteenth centuries that *Colby Quarterly* has just published. My focus is partly on the construction of history, because Lawless's *With Essex in Ireland* was written at a particular historical moment. It left a lot of room for maneuvering between who was constructing history, the unreliable writer Lawless who was taking liberties with actual history.

MOLONEY: Could you comment on the issue of gender within the Irish literary critical establishment? Are the traditional hierarchies changing there at all?

MILLS: My sense is that they are, but at the same time, because my area is really literary history, one of the things I have learned is a hundred years ago women were highly active in politics and writing; their popularity, or their exclusion, seems to come in waves of progress and regression. It doesn't do to be complacent.

Valerie Miner

Interviewed by
CAITRIONA MOLONEY

Tom Foley

BORN: New York City, 1947

RESIDES: Minneapolis, Minnesota

EDUCATED: University of California at Berkeley, B.A., M.J.

WORKS: Professor, Department of English, University of Minnesota, Minneapolis

GENRES: Fiction, nonfiction, literary criticism

AWARDS: Fellowships and awards from the Rockefeller Foundation, the McKnight Foundation, the NEA, the Heinz Foundation, the Australia Council Literary Arts Board, the Fulbright Commission, and many other sources

---

Valerie Miner is a major figure in Irish-American writing. Looking at the titles of Miner's seven novels, her short story collections, and her nonfiction essays, one can draw several conclusions: her topics are woman centered, she often works collaboratively with other women, she writes from a lesbian perspective, and her work is informed by social activism and a working-class sensibility. What might not be so immediately obvious is that she also comes out of a Scottish and Irish heritage and that many of her themes are informed by Irish literature and culture.

Miner has published numerous co-edited and co-authored works;

she credits a feminist writing group in London for helping her move from journalism, her first career, to fiction.

Miner's novels are often concerned with violence in the lives of women. In Blood Sisters, *Miner looks at the political beliefs of two cousins, one who is committed to the Provisional IRA and one who is very active in the women's movement. The novel illustrates the conflict between nationalism and feminism. In* A Walking Fire, *Miner explores the dynamics of an Irish-American working-class family; the novel's analysis emphasizes the subordinate role of women in Irish culture, on the one hand iconized as spiritual mothers, and on the other hand often oppressed as unpaid servants.* Range of Light *explores the consciousness of two college friends who have taken different paths through life.*

Miner's fiction also explores lesbian themes, such as the heterosexual community's response to same-sex couples in "Trespassing and Other Stories," family acceptance of a child's lesbian sexuality in Blood Sisters, *and friendship between heterosexual and lesbian women in* Range of Light. *Miner works to incite readers to social consciousness and political activism.* A Walking Fire *comes out of Miner's own experiences with the Vietnam War as a antiwar activist.*

Miner's characters are working class, or like Beth and Liz in Blood Sisters *and Cora in* A Walking Fire, *children of working-class parents who are the first generation to attend college. This is also Miner's history, the first person in her family to graduate from college. Class consciousness plays an important role in Miner's novels. Miner seeks to expose the myth that the U.S. is a classless society by illuminating the lives of working-class characters; she also advocates seeing writers as workers, a shift that would improve the working conditions of American artists.*

Miner has recently returned from six months in India, and she has recently completed and published a memoir-novel, The Low Road, *about her mother's Scottish roots. I interviewed Valerie Miner at her cabin in Mendocino, California, in December 1998 and by telephone in 2000.*

◆   ◆   ◆

MOLONEY: Tell me about your background: how you became a writer, an academic, and a feminist activist.

MINER: I started out my writing career in 1970 as a journalist, motivated largely by political concerns. I attended U.C. Berkeley during the

1960s where I become active in the antiwar movement, met the women's movement, and learned about social class. I worked as a journalist in Canada and England for about seven years altogether. I also did some reporting in southern Africa. As I was writing journalism, I decided I could go deeper politically, psychologically, spiritually, emotionally, stylistically if I moved into fiction. After having been in a writing group in Canada with a group of feminist nonfiction writers—in which we produced a book of essays about contemporary Canadian women, *Her Own Woman,*—I moved to London in 1974. I gathered together a group of fiction writers—two of us were journalists, one was a playwright, one was a short story writer, and one was a poet—and we worked together on a collection which we eventually titled *Tales I Tell My Mother.* I got courage and direction from that group, but I still carried with me many of the concerns expressed in my journalism. All of my fiction deals with the individual in the larger world, the individual in the historical moment.

My fiction involves research and often a political or moral dilemma with which I'm trying to engage.

MOLONEY: How does Irish-American identity impact your writing?

MINER: In several ways; the topics about which I write are sometimes Irish or Irish-American. A big part of my Irish-American identity has to do with Irish-American Catholicism, which is different from Irish Catholicism. I think my work is very Catholic in metaphor, as well as in some of my moral and cultural concerns. I think having come from an Irish-American and Scottish-American background, which in some ways are very different but in others very similar, I'm deeply aware of colonialism and I have been interested in writing about it my whole life. This background has given me an understanding for marginality of various sorts.

MOLONEY: Are there conflicts between a lesbian and gay community and the Irish-American community, specifically the Catholic Church?

MINER: I think that as I was growing up certainly in Catholic schools we never talked about lesbian, gay, bisexual, and transgender people. There are many of them within the church, within the hierarchy, some even teachers. My argument is with the institution of the church and how it says one cannot be fully human if one is a woman, a lesbian, etc. Lesbians and gay men and bisexual people have been excluded from things like the St. Patrick's Day marches. The church is primarily responsible for providing a rational and a conservative and very parochial backdrop from which people can draw those opinions and hatreds.

MOLONEY: Has the Irish construction of women had a role in your writing?

MINER: Could you define what you mean by the Irish construction of women?

MOLONEY: The idea of the woman in the Irish constitution: a mother who doesn't have to go out and work, or the Virgin Mary, all of those traditional constructions, some of which are obsolete but can still play a role in literature and society.

MINER: There is no unilateral construction, but if you look at the tradition of the Irish-Catholic patriarch who sees women as baby machines, as virgins or wives or daughters who have to be virgins, that is a restricted and restricting view of women. Yes, I was brought up with many of those constructions and expectations, and I think conservative Protestant Irish people have similar constructions. It has to do with institutional religion [rather] than with Irish Christianity. I write about women's lives, their struggles, their friendships, their successes, their reflections, partially out of resistance to being immersed in this Irish-Catholic culture for so long. But in recent years we have the wonderful Mary Robinson, we have divorce laws, which aren't perfect but are making some changes. We have a much more active lesbian population in Ireland and so the Irish construction of women is changing in some very positive ways. I am very encouraged by that, and I am not sure how that will affect my work but I am sure that it will.

MOLONEY: Many of the women I have been talking to are saying that they would probably not have written if they'd been born a generation earlier.

MINER: I think it depends on one's class background. As somebody who is the first person in her family to go through college, becoming a writer was a strange and unexpected thing in my family. My becoming a writer was surprising because I came from a conservative and unlettered background. Really unlettered—my mother didn't go past grade eight, my father didn't finish high school, there weren't books around the house, we didn't go to theater, we didn't listen to classical music, and so I think members of my family are still wondering how I got wherever I am.

MOLONEY: Is *Blood Sisters* a particularly Irish book, particularly in the mother-daughter relationships?

MINER: It concerns immigrant mothers and their first-generation daughters; the characters are Irish-Catholic so that is an influence as well. I think immigrant mothers, especially working-class immigrant mothers who were raised in Irish-Catholic families, are very concerned about limiting the independence of their daughters because they are fearful about what that independence would bring. Ironically, both these women were enormously brave and independent in the steps that they took. Polly married a Protestant and immigrated all the way to California, which in those years was very unusual. And Gerry herself immigrated to England, a more frequent occurrence among Irish women. Both mothers are heroes in that they had the courage to strike out and try to make better lives not only for their children, which is sort of a classic mandate for a mother, but for themselves.

MOLONEY: *A Walking Fire* is a novel about Irish-Americans. Is the main issue gender or class?

MINER: It's hard to separate them because, for instance, Cora was female so she wasn't liable to be drafted. She didn't have to make the same decisions about engaging in the Vietnam War that her brothers did. She was free to go to college where she started to become middle class. I don't think you can separate the two; as she was growing up she experienced gender discrimination within her family, but that gender discrimination also had a protectiveness attached to it; her father didn't beat her up. He wasn't as physically violent to her as he was to the brothers. On the other hand, that violence was an expression in a certain perverse way of affection and acknowledgment and she didn't have that. It is very complicated. I don't think one is primary. The war in Vietnam was for many working-class families in the United States a civil war which tore those families apart. Cora had the privilege of going to college and of being exposed to other ways of looking at that war, so she was able to see the hypocrisy in it. She traveled on Greyhound buses, but at least she developed a world of her own which her brothers really didn't; they were stuck in their social class and that was partially determined by their gender.

MOLONEY: *Range of Light* is your most recent novel. To what extent did you see this novel as kind of a meditation on feminism and the women's relationships?

MINER: I'm a feminist and I'm in the women's movement so that's just a given, which all my work reflects. I saw the book perhaps as a meditation on friendship and aging among women. I see it as a book that speaks to the divisions within women's everyday friendships and raises issues such as class, sexuality, lifestyle, career. In *Blood Sisters* I was dealing with people's direct political engagement in feminist and nationalist movements. Here I see the tension in the way these people have lived their lives, because these women are older than the women in *Blood Sisters*. They have perhaps more nuanced layers in their lives. They are both politically active. Kath is involved in working with inner-city children and Adele is a feminist academic, but I see the book as primarily about their friendship rather than their engagement in, or conflict between, those activities.

MOLONEY: Do you think a commodity called Irishness is marketed to Americans?

MINER: That is quite true. One of the things that Irish-Americans see is Ireland as a happy country, a green and sunny land full of cheerful people. Well, if you spend any time in Ireland, you know it certainly isn't sunny most of the time, either metaphorically or literally. What Catholic Irish-Americans forget is the way the church has imprisoned people for two thousand years.

MOLONEY: Speaking of the difference between the Irish and the Americans, do you find that they respond differently to your fiction?

MINER: At the beginning of my fiction writing, most of my books came out first in Great Britain and were read by Irish women in the British editions. I had wonderful reviews and wonderful responses from people in both Britain and Ireland. Subsequently, the books were published here and I got wonderful reviews but it took a while. There was a lag. Partially because of the changes in feminist publishing in Britain, my most recent books haven't even been published over there, so I've had virtually no response to them. *A Walking Fire,* which has a very strong Irish theme, *Range of Light,* and *Rumors from the Cauldron* are actually not available there unless people import the American edition.

MOLONEY: Why do you think that your writing and other women's writing in Ireland has not been sufficiently acknowledged?

MINER: Is this a rhetorical question? I mean, what changes? Although there are a few more women represented here and there, for the most part publishing in this country as well as in Ireland and Britain is a very male pursuit. It is really very sad about the vanishing of feminist publishing houses. Some people think women have made our point and things will move upward and outward from here, but I don't believe that is true. I think in some ways we're in more danger than we were in the early 1970s.

MOLONEY: Why do you think that is?

MINER: Because there is a smugness among some men and women that we are enlightened and inclusive and we are neither. We don't think we need feminist publishing houses or feminist journals; feminist bookstores are going under in this country. Firebrand Books and the *Feminist Bookstore News* just went under. In the 1970s we had this momentum; we were aware of possibilities and dangers. The most dangerous situation is when we're not aware of the dangers.

MOLONEY: What do you think about the postcolonial paradigm for Irish literature?

MINER: I think it is really important we distinguish between imperialism and genocide, and between ethnic bias and racism. Contemporary Irish literature is often postcolonial, but I do see a difference between the bias that Irish people have faced and the bias that people of color have faced. For a while in Great Britain some people held an attitude that if you were from Ireland you were black; but I am not comfortable with that. Ireland is becoming more and more a postcolonial country. I see Ireland, North and South, as one country, that's my perspective, and the North is colonized. One of the things that does join Nigerian writing and Indian writing and Jamaican writing with Irish writing is an understanding about what colonial powers can do to the individual, to the nation, to the language. Irish writing is infused with that kind of understanding. Most Indians don't use the term "postcolonial writing" at all. They use the term "new literatures," which they see as a more positive term, less defined by former ties to the past or the residual ties to the past. They include in these "new literature" courses literature from Canada, Australia, Ireland, Africa.

MOLONEY: I know you just came back from a Fulbright in India. What effect do you think it will have on your writing?

MINER: It was an enormous opportunity and great privilege and complicated, enriching experience. It renewed my commitment to social fiction. I didn't go to India with the idea of writing an Indian novel; that would be a very impertinent approach. I really went to read Indian writing in India and to have the experience of working with Indian students and colleagues. I have brought back books which I would like to teach in my classes. I am even more aware of American consumption devastating the rest of the world. I will be doing some reviews of contemporary Indian writing to make those books more visible here; I am going to approach publishers and try to get that work published.

MOLONEY: What writers are they?

MINER: One of the writers who impressed me the most is Ambai. Her other name is C. S. Lakshmi, and she writes fiction and nonfiction but I particularly like *A Purple Sea,* a collection of stories.

MOLONEY: What projects are you working on right now?

MINER: A family memoir, *The Low Road,* has just been published. I'm currently working on a collection of stories and a novel, *After Eden,* which is, in part, a postcolonial revision of *Paradise Lost.*

Edna O'Brien

Interviewed by

HELEN THOMPSON

BORN: County Clare, Ireland, 1936
EDUCATED: Pharmaceutical College, Dublin
RESIDES: London
GENRES: Fiction, nonfiction, poetry, drama, screenplays
AWARDS: Kingsley Amis Award for *The Country Girls, Yorkshire Post* Book of the Year Award for *A Pagan Place*, the *Los Angeles Times* Book Prize for *Lantern Slides*, the Writer's Guild Prize for Fiction for *Time and Tide*

Edna O'Brien is one of the first women writers to come from the rural west, to write outside the "big house" tradition, and to openly write of female desire. She is the author of fifteen novels, six collections of short stories, various plays and screenplays, one collection of poetry, and a variety of periodical articles. She published her first novel, The Country Girls, *in 1960. Her early work was banned by the Irish government and vilified by her local community. Since then she has earned an international reputation for her fiction.*

O'Brien's fiction consistently interrogates the cultural and political imperatives that reproduce femininity in Ireland by showing the ideals—celibacy in the convent and heterosexuality and motherhood in marriage—and the impossibilities of actually living up to them. To free women's sexuality from the confines of the heterosexual family, O'Brien

197

undermines the sanctity of the family by exposing its dysfunctions, high-lighting its subsequent disintegration, and showing its repressive and, therefore, debilitating effects on women's psyches. In short, O'Brien attacks the foundations of Irish culture—state control of women's reproduction, and the nationalist and religious mythologies, Virgin Mary and Mother Ireland—that have framed and, therefore, limited Irish women.

In The Country Girls *trilogy (1960–67), O'Brien contextualizes the lives of her female characters in newly independent Ireland to demonstrate the social and psychological effects of nationalism and the founding of the Irish state on Irish women, particularly those in the rural west. Three texts in the 1980s demonstrate O'Brien's interrogations of compulsory heterosexuality. "Sister Imelda" (1984),* Virginia *(1985), and* The High Road *(1988) explore lesbian sexuality as either an explicit refusal of motherhood and marriage or as a way of maintaining emotional health.*

*In her latest trilogy—*House of Splendid Isolation, Down by the River, *and* Wild Decembers—*the same attitudes toward women prevail in the rural west of which O'Brien writes. However, in her investigations of politics, sexuality, and land, we see that her female characters—Josie, Mary, and Breege—are all active in their own survival.*

O'Brien's language is both rich and precise. At times her prose is closer to poetry with its lyricism. She also experiments with narrative points of view in her fiction as well as with form. While A Pagan Place *has a second-person narrator,* House of Splendid Isolation *has multiple perspectives, and* Night *is a stream of consciousness monologue.*

Edna O'Brien's fifteenth novel, In the Forest, *was published in 2002. I conducted the interview by phone and fax.*

◆ ◆ ◆

THOMPSON: Do you speak Gaelic?

O'BRIEN: Yes I do, a bit.

THOMPSON: Was it something that you learned in school?

O'BRIEN: Oh sure. I learned all the subjects actually, except English, you'll be pleased to hear. I learned everything else through Irish: science, sums, algebra, history, geography. I remember all the poems I learned in Irish and so on.

THOMPSON: Was it a difficult language?

O'BRIEN: Learning everything through Irish was a wonderful experience, not because it gave me a rational education, but because the rhythm of the language was so rich and intoxicating. I learned, for instance, the principle of Archimedes through Irish and loved it more for its sound than its sense.

THOMPSON: Your language has been described as "lush." Do you think that your knowledge of Gaelic has influenced your prose?

O'BRIEN: I do not regard my own language as "lush." The word was used in a nice review in the *New York Times* and has been appropriated by others. I consider language very carefully. Sometimes when necessary it is a torrent of words and sometimes it is pared back to the bone. All is in the service of the emotion and the narrative that is getting told.

THOMPSON: Are you happier with critical response in Ireland in recent years?

O'BRIEN: My books are not banned now, and my recent trilogy was well received. But, English critics give me a hard time.

THOMPSON: Why do you think that is?

O'BRIEN: Some of it is political; I've been fairly vociferous about what I feel about Ireland and being Irish. Some of it is, actually, I think, a genuine fear or passionate repugnance at writing.

THOMPSON: Do you think it has anything to do with the fact that you're a female writer?

O'BRIEN: Oh definitely. Sorry, I should have said that first. Yes, of course it does. But one has to soldier on.

THOMPSON: Why do women writers have more difficulty establishing their credentials?

O'BRIEN: I think it is no secret that men in an age-old solidarity stand by each other. Women do not always show the same consideration or admiration for the woman artist. Women writers have a harder time with critics both male and female, unfortunately.

THOMPSON: Yet, the title of your latest novel, *Wild Decembers,* comes from the Emily Brontë epigraph, suggesting solidarity with another woman artist.

O'BRIEN: Yes, it is homage to Emily Brontë. I was shocked upon rereading a preface to *Wuthering Heights* to learn of the odium, cruelty, and ignorance that were meted out to that book. I thought not for the first time that a woman artist has a far tougher climb than her male counterpart.

THOMPSON: You said reviewers have critiqued the politics in your work. Do think of your work as political?

O'BRIEN: Well, everything is political: one's upbringing, the culture in which one grows up, even religion is political, whether we like it or not. Religion is supposed to be spiritual but we all know it isn't. My later books—*Down by the River, House of Splendid Isolation,* and *Wild Decembers*—are more openly and overtly political. *The Country Girls,* although it is, I hope, a tale of girls growing up in Ireland, has its own inherent or latent sense of politics. The novel is about what the society was culturally, historically, and emotionally.

THOMPSON: Do you think that fiction is inherently political?

O'BRIEN: A polemic or political work wouldn't in my book of life be acceptable. Fiction is fiction and hopefully imagination and the power of language always stirs the reader. It would be absurd and it actually would be banal to simply have a political agenda and put it down. Story is imperative.

THOMPSON: You mentioned that your later novels tackle overtly political issues.

O'BRIEN: A trilogy of three themes important to Ireland and to me: politics, sex, and land.

THOMPSON: In *Down by the River* the court decision in the novel doesn't seem as important as in the real X case. Why?

O'BRIEN: It is as important. In the real case you only got a journalistic version. I was trying to imagine what the judges, the girl herself, and the pro-life people would feel like. It's the novelist's prerogative. Seven chords of music instead of one. It is ironic because by the time they've given her the decision to go to England for an abortion, she doesn't need to go out because she has lost her child.

THOMPSON: Yes.

O'BRIEN: In fact, if you read of the actual X case, that also happened. The girl got the permission to go out and have the abortion, but she lost the baby. It's like fate or the gods have their own strict agendas.

THOMPSON: Your latest novels offer us multiple perspectives. Why did you decide to pursue a variety of points of view rather than just one?

O'BRIEN: To make a story both more alive and more suspenseful one has to think of altering the point of view of each chapter. In doing that one changes styles because each person thinks differently. I find it stimulating though a little daunting, but as reader and writer I am not interested in anything less.

THOMPSON: This trilogy is different from *The Country Girls* trilogy. Is there a connecting link?

O'BRIEN: The connecting link in the two trilogies is Ireland and in particular that corner of the southwest to which I have given the fictional name of Cloontha in imitation of and homage to my hero, William Faulkner, although his fictional name is harder to pronounce!

THOMPSON: I see the connection of land and the female body in *Down by the River* and *Wild Decembers*. Both elicit emotional reactions and yet both refuse to be bound by history and law: Breege's pregnancy, Mary's miscarriage, and Joseph's loss of land.

O'BRIEN: Land and the longing for possession is central to those two books. The female body in *Down by the River* is something that others, her father and the pro-life zealots, wish to possess. Birth pervades the stories because birth is how we all arrive in this world; a novel necessitates the same long, painful gestation.

THOMPSON: You also tackle political strife over territory and women in *House of Splendid Isolation.* Can you explain your approach to these myths in your writing?

O'BRIEN: I don't know about myths except that I have always thought of Ireland as being a woman and have written in the first lines of *Mother Ireland,* "Ireland has always been a woman, a womb, a cave, a cow, a Rosaleen, a sow, a bride, a harlot, and, of course, the gaunt Hag of Beare."

THOMPSON: What images of women were you familiar with as you grew up in County Clare?

O'BRIEN: The Blessed Virgin and Caithleen Ní Houlihan were probably the two most dominant female icons in my thinking—the one being religious and the other poetic and romantic.

THOMPSON: Does Mary in *Down by the River* resemble the Blessed Virgin?

O'BRIEN: No. Another Mary. My two sisters were older than me and there had been a sister born two years before I was born, called

Mary. She died. I miss this sister; she would have been my little comrade. So I called the little girl Mary in *Down by the River.*

THOMPSON: Critics have suggested that your early female protagonists are passive. Yet, it seems that the later characters, Josie, Mary, and Breege, address that criticism because they are definitely active in their own survival.

O'BRIEN: I can only assume that critics misconstrue fate with character. You could as easily say that characters in Homer are passive when misfortune befalls them. They are not. A story is a story is a story.

THOMPSON: Critics also say that your male characters are unsympathetic. In this trilogy you seem to be addressing this criticism by offering men who are bound by their own desires and their histories. They are less domineering and less fearful.

O'BRIEN: I may have been more ill at ease when writing about men in my early novels. I do not think that is any longer the case and as you suggest, Bugler, Joseph, and McGreevy are fully rounded characters. If those books were to be filmed, an actor would have to find a way to play them. By that I mean, they are realized. Writing of any experience, male or female, is difficult. One has to keep one's eyes and ears open and then delve into the imagination.

THOMPSON: You focus a lot on women's relationships with each other. I'm thinking of *The High Road* and the relationship between Anna and Catalina, which reviewers had difficulty explaining.

O'BRIEN: Well, it is my least realized novel to tell you the truth, but I'm not going to rewrite it. I hadn't written for a long time. I had a kind of paralysis or writer's block or fear or I don't know what. I went away to an island off Spain and I was inspired by that landscape. But, that's the obvious explanation; the inner reasons are always more complicated and usually one doesn't know them. I think the place, which of course had nothing to do with Ireland, was surprisingly beautiful to me. And I felt that within this beauty is the sexuality and the secrecy both between men and women and between women and women. The landscape, though not the weather, reminded me of Ireland. We always compare places to our roots. *The High Road* didn't really work, and I feel bad about that, but I wouldn't be able to go back to it and write it again. I couldn't.

THOMPSON: Friendships between women seem to be important to your writing.

O'BRIEN: I think friendship is one of the vitals of life. There's a wonderful poem of Yeats that says, "friendship never ends." It's a poem called "All Soul's Night" in which he imagines the ghosts of friends coming in to the college in Oxford where there are two brimming glasses of muscatel. And at first when I read that poem—it's a beautiful poem—it made me think that my friendships do end and they end for the wrong reasons, often, or for half wrong reasons.

THOMPSON: Do you mean friendships with women?

O'BRIEN: I am wary of women, especially calculating and controlling women. Probably I want women and I want men to be artists. I value the friendship of a few women that I trust. But, I don't have that many friends, either men or women.

THOMPSON: Why do you think that is?

O'BRIEN: One of the things that I most seek in another person is a meeting of minds. There's an excitement in it. I don't just mean a sexual excitement; I mean a creative stimulation. Women often want to know, to pry into one's secrets, and I am a very secretive person. I'm also an intolerant person, and I resent intrusion into my private life.

THOMPSON: Do you have to cultivate a distance between you and your friends to have space to write?

O'BRIEN: Yes. One must live the inner life to the utmost. Samuel Beckett wrote a preface to a book of Jack Yeats's paintings, and he said: "the artist who stakes his being comes from nowhere. And he has no brothers." Well, of course, he does come from somewhere and that somewhere informs and permeates the work as it did for Samuel Beckett and it did for Jack Yeats, but solitary is how an artist has to be. It's crucial to the work. And painful for the life!

THOMPSON: Was it the merging of minds that drew you to the friendship between Vita Sackville-West and Virginia Woolf?

O'BRIEN: Not really. I think their friendship was erotic. There was plenty of artistic buzz flying around Bloomsbury anyway, too much of it. The blazing genius to come out of Bloomsbury is Virginia Woolf, but not because she was in Bloomsbury. She could have been in Lancashire or Wandsworth. Her madness, her inner conflict was the whetstone of her work, not some literary coterie.

THOMPSON: How did Nigel Nicolson, Vita's son, like your play *Virginia*?

O'BRIEN: In his memoirs he refers to it. I was staying at Sissinghurst and I gave him the play to read and he read it all night and deemed it "magic." I thought that was generous of him.

THOMPSON: The work is dedicated to Nigel Nicolson. Was it he who asked you to write it?

O'BRIEN: The producer Arthur Cantor asked me. I had to get permission from Quentin Bell and also talk with Nigel Nicolson and others. Her letters and diaries were, however, the greatest inspiration to me.

THOMPSON: How did you revise the play?

O'BRIEN: I saw from the original production that act 2 was weaker, that it had to be fleshed out.

THOMPSON: How much do you think Ireland has changed since you wrote *The Country Girls*?

O'BRIEN: A lot. The world has changed and Ireland has changed with it. The changes are fairly obvious—television, advertising, magazines, and tourism.

THOMPSON: Much more materialistic?

O'BRIEN: You know, ironically the Ireland in which I wrote *The Country Girls,* and *The Country Girls* was subsequently banned along with some of my other books, had more feeling for literature, more fervor. But that is true throughout the world. Literature has only a marginal place in people's minds. Rock, pop, image, these are sovereign now.

THOMPSON: Do you see any positive changes in Ireland over the last thirty years or so?

O'BRIEN: Ireland has become more open as a society. Tourism is Ireland's most lucrative income, as you know. It is a more open society and not in the clutches of the church. A plethora of scandals in the Catholic Church have caused both dismay and disillusion. Yet people continue to feel the need for God and salvation.

THOMPSON: Would you say that these changes have been comfortable for the Irish? What about those in the rural west, the area that you grew up in?

O'BRIEN: In very isolated country parts, very backward parts, like where I'm from, there is still a very strong sense of guilt, shame, and sin. Between country and cities there is a vast divide.

THOMPSON: Has the west remained untouched by change?

O'BRIEN: There are changes, but you know deep change is a very slow thing. It doesn't happen in twenty or thirty years. Rural Ireland is now probably like two-headed Janus in that it looks back and inevitably looks forward for its financial boom. One does not cancel the other. Moreover, the great wealth we hear of only arrives in the pockets of a few.

THOMPSON: Do you ever think of returning to Ireland to live now that it is becoming a more open society?

O'BRIEN: It is not a question of ever returning to Ireland, since I go there all the time. I could not have written my last trilogy without endless journeying, researching, and talking with people there. County Clare inhabits my thoughts and my writing wherever I happen to be. Ireland is always speaking a story and I have to search for it.

THOMPSON: Is it always familiar territory?

O'BRIEN: Yes and no. With each book I hope to dig deeper. That is all I ask.

Kate O'Riordan

Interviewed by

CAITRIONA MOLONEY

Courtesy of Tony Davis

BORN: London
RESIDES: London
WORKS: Writer of fiction and screenplays
GENRES: Fiction, drama, screenwriting
AWARDS: *Irish Tribune* Hennessy "Best Emerging Writer" Award (1991)

Kate O'Riordan has written two plays, numerous film scripts, and four novels. Born in London of Irish parents, O'Riordan was raised on the west coast of Ireland and lived in Canada and the United States before settling in London. Her first two novels, Involved *and* The Boy in the Moon, *have met with considerable critical interest from reviewers. In-volved was shortlisted for the Dillons first fiction award;* Boy in the Moon *reached number two on the Irish bestseller list. They touch on such themes as exile, violence, lost and recovered history, and the international implications and gender dynamics of Ulster politics. Her third novel,* Angel in the House, *takes a detour from the world of tragedy and psychological realism into romantic comedy. Her fourth,* Memory Stones, *returns to history and trauma.*

Involved *juxtaposes two plots, a political thriller involving the main characters with stereotypically retrograde IRA types, and a politically doomed romance between an "Irish" woman and a "Northern" man.*

206

The novel problematizes both categories and employs a technique of emphasizing gaps and silences that will be even more fully developed in Boy in the Moon. *O'Riordan's novels' strained family relationships exemplify the Irish family romance, dominated by questions of nationality and politics.* Involved *also examines the complex role of women in Irish society.*

O'Riordan's second book, The Boy in the Moon, *intersperses a subplot about the death of the protagonist's twin, for which he feels guilt, with the contemporary story of his son's death, for which his wife holds him responsible. Two plots on dual historical levels suggest a duality to history itself. This novel also incorporates women's hidden history in the journal of the mother. However, as Louise East points out, the journal offers only "odd, censored glimpses of an unspoken history" (12).*

O'Riordan is currently working on a fourth novel, Memory Stones. *I spoke with her at her home in London.*

·   ·   ·

MOLONEY: Let me ask you about your background and how you got interested in writing.

O'RIORDAN: Well, I was born in London, strangely enough, and we were here, my parents, I'm the eldest, for two years, and then I got brought up on the west coast of Ireland in a little town called Bantry.

MOLONEY: How did that happen?

O'RIORDAN: I imagine they had to take a little boat trip to have me; that would have been the norm in those days. You don't know what I mean by that now?

MOLONEY: Your parents weren't married?

O'RIORDAN: Yeah, or she was pregnant. It was called "taking the boat" in those days; we haven't discussed it. Anyway, they went home and my father was an absolute bookaholic among other -holics; there were always books in the house, so we grew up reading nonstop.

MOLONEY: How long did you live on the west coast of Ireland?

O'RIORDAN: I left at the age of twenty-one and went to Canada. Then I lived in Los Angeles for a year, and then back to Ireland and ended up in London, where I have been for seventeen years.

MOLONEY: What writers have been an influence?

O'RIORDAN: I take something from every book I read. I like a lot of contemporary American stuff. You have two women writers that I just adore. Annie Proulx is one, she is a fabulous writer; the other is Anne Tyler—I love Anne Tyler. She is one of the few writers I will put in an order for the hardback as soon as I know it is coming into the shops rather than wait for the paperback. But growing up, it was the Russians I loved; I was a real book nerd. I just stayed in my room reading all the time. I didn't move on to modern stuff until I was in my twenties.

MOLONEY: Let me ask you a question about Ireland as a writing environment. Is England a better writing environment for you than Ireland?

O'RIORDAN: It wasn't a factor. I came here like so many Irish people looking for work; I used to be in the travel business. But I was always writing short stories. And now I choose to stay here. I say to myself—it's where I live now, and my kids are going to school here, and they consider themselves half Irish and half English. It is home. Also I do scripts as well, and London is where the work is. But it's more than that, because if I chose to go and live in Ireland, which we have thought about in the past, I would be tax-free. There is a huge incentive to move there, and yet, I still balk at it for some reason.

MOLONEY: A lot of Irish writers in Ireland complain about Ireland and say they think about leaving all the time. It's hard to pin them down as to exactly why though.

O'RIORDAN: Well, I suppose it's a small island, and I think the literary thing can be quite tricky in Dublin, and the smaller it is the more competitive. Whereas here it's such a huge, vast metropolis with so many writers. And also your family's there. It's one thing for me to sit here in front of my computer and stare out the window. I wonder if I was meeting my husband's family—he's from the same town as me—and my own family, on a day-to-day basis, would I censor myself? I think I would.

MOLONEY: How do you feel about being included in the category "Irish writer"?

O'RIORDAN: In some respects I'd rather not have it. I prefer "writer." But having said that, I know my publisher looks at me as a commercial proposition, and they want to sell books, so I get bracketed as Irish female writer. And, I live with that—it's fine.

MOLONEY: How do you feel about the category "woman" writer?

O'RIORDAN: I'd really rather not have that; Irish female writer unavoidably presumes a certain genre and certain subjects. Publishers are looking for attachment markets to buy the book for reviews, which is how they will sell the book, as well, so they will be sending it to other Irish women writers.

MOLONEY: How do you feel about feminism? Would you consider yourself a feminist?

O'RIORDAN: I think it's all up its own ass these days, to be honest. Very confusing messages are going out, and the women who were our cornerstone are contradicting what they said before. They are now saying that things have come so full circle that men have become emasculated. I do think men are in the same place we were some years back, not knowing for sure the way they used to, and part of me thinks, so what, good, face it and get on with it. In the same way, we used to have very definite paths as women—to get married and have kids—now we've had to face choices and different paths and everything being blurred at the edges. I never know how to answer "are you a feminist"? What does it mean nowadays? If it is pro-female and certainly pro-female rights, then yes, of course.

MOLONEY: Isn't there considerable inequity between men and women writers in publishing?

O'RIORDAN: That is very cliquey as well; the first batch of *Finbar's Hotel,* were mainly men, the same stable of male writers; whereas the women are considered, with a few exceptions, more sex and shopping sagas.

MOLONEY: In *The Boy in the Moon,* I see Julia's reading her mother-in-law Margaret's diary as a feminist activity as she is bringing her history to the light of day.

O'RIORDAN: When I saw that question first, my gut reaction was no, but then I thought, yes, there is an element of that. Margaret is a woman who didn't have a voice in rural Ireland, not too long ago. She was even in an arranged marriage, which my grandmother also was, and very often wouldn't even be able to read and write, so her young son was teaching his mother as he learned. Her husband didn't even know she could write, never mind keep a diary. I don't think she was unique there. She would probably have had between ten to fourteen kids, and running a farm, everything is centered around what you will eat next. It wouldn't have given a woman like her time to do anything except exist.

MOLONEY: But she kept a record.

O'RIORDAN: But she felt some compulsion, didn't she, to record just the most basic things. Most of the diary is just lists, lists of what they had that day.

MOLONEY: Did you discover any actual diary like this?

O'RIORDAN: No, I haven't found anything but it did come from observing my own grandmother. Everything she buys she writes down in a little book and the price beside it. There's no need for her to do that anymore, because she is comfortable now, she has enough money. But she's still doing that from the time she had nine kids and wasn't quite sure what was going to go on the table tomorrow.

MOLONEY: I want to ask you about your national identity; do you see yourself as Irish or English? And your children?

O'RIORDAN: I see myself as Irish, absolutely, but I like aspects of living here. But I would always say I'm Irish. My daughter wouldn't know what she is; she's just four. My son is eleven, but he is very definitely English; he wears his English football shirt and everything. We go to Ireland a lot; his grannies are there, and he is very conscious of his Irish heritage. We don't let him go home wearing a Union Jack; that's pushing it. I know lots of second-generation Irish kids here, and the parents were militant about being Irish. They gave the kids this dilemma: were they Irish or were they English? I'm not going to do that to Jack. I think it's time to move on from that.

MOLONEY: Do you experience problems associated with being an Irish person living in England?

O'RIORDAN: No, I never have. People have in the past; when my parents came in the 1960s they still had on doors, "no blacks, no Irish, no dogs." That's not that long ago. But in my era, it has completely changed. Now, in the days when the people had to come here to work, which they don't any more, a lot of rural young men would have come on the building sites, and there would have been a lot of "Paddy" jokes. They would have felt very ostracized and that people were looking down at them. Nowadays, a whole new breed of people choose to come here; they can stay in Dublin; they can go to the States. It is almost cool to be Irish. British society is a very class-ridden society but people are comfortable with the Irish accent, because it's not making judgments on them; whereas if someone comes out with a very defined, upper-middle English class accent, you can see hackles raising straight away. Irish are very successful in broadcasting here.

MOLONEY: Does that change at all when the political situation changes? Do you feel any ripples from events like the terrible Omagh bombing? Are British people particularly tuned into Northern Ireland?

O'RIORDAN: No, they're not at all. They look at the whole place and "just wish it would go away." They don't have any understanding of the Unionist. I think they find them embarrassing—that ranting image that they have. When the bombs went off in London, that's a different thing. Omagh, they don't care—to be honest with you, it's not their country. The people I know look at Northern Ireland as a strange place where they're all fighting each other. Even years ago when the bombs were going off regularly in London, nobody ever said any thing to me; they wouldn't say to you, "oh you Irish bastard," in the shop. I became conscious myself at times of my Irish accent and things that I was never conscious of before. For example, if I were in a café and left a bag somewhere for a second, I was conscious that people might think, "there's an Irish accent and she's just put down her bag." But that's a fair enough thing for people to be worried about.

MOLONEY: Let me ask you about postcolonialism. Does that resonate with you in terms of Irish literature? Do you see any connection to other British postcolonial literatures like Indian, Caribbean, South African, Nigerian?

O'RIORDAN: I don't think so actually. I can see it very clearly in Indian literature, but just even thinking of Ireland as a colony seems absurd. When I think of colony I think of India and Africa, but I never, ever think of Ireland that way. And I don't see it reflected in the literature. I think we have always had our very, very strong literary strand, which was quite independent. If you look at George Bernard Shaw, Oscar Wilde— there is a British influence, but the sense of humor is particularly Irish. We all learned Irish, at least in my era growing up, and one of the things we bring to English nowadays is not worrying about grammar, reversing sentences, and putting things back to front.

MOLONEY: Could you talk about your relationship to your current publisher?

O'RIORDAN: Well, I think the start of it was a short story which won the *Irish Tribune* Hennessy Prize, in 1991; I had a rough idea for a novel, when I met my current agent. I said to her, as I'm sure fifty people do a day, "oh, I have an idea for a book." She said, "why don't you write it and send it in." And I did luckily enough. If you don't get a good agent, your book can spend ages in the "slush pile," and you don't know who is reading it; whereas if it comes in from a good agent, it will get on the right desk. I was lucky she sent it to Harper-Collins, and I've been with them since.

MOLONEY: You've had the same publisher all along. So no real conflicts there?

O'RIORDAN: Oh, we've had conflicts, but I am pathologically loyal, Caitriona, and so I think I'll probably stay with them for the fourth as well.

MOLONEY: The fourth? I didn't know you had a third novel. So, what is it?

O'RIORDAN: The third one, *The Angel of the House,* is my romantic comedy. I had done a few scripts that were doom-and-gloom as well, so I wanted something light.

MOLONEY: Were you thinking of Virginia Woolf with that title— the angel in the house?

O'RIORDAN: No, she's got it from Coventry Patmore. It was the Victorian phrase for the woman—the angel in the house—and my characters meet in the Victoria and Albert Museum, and my main character loves Victoriana. The fourth novel, I'm still at notes stage, so hopefully I'll start on that in the autumn, but I know the title: it's called *Memory Stones,* and it's back to doom-and-gloom again. I'm happiest with that.

MOLONEY: Have you done any film scripts recently?

O'RIORDAN: I've done things for British TV, shows like *Casualty.* And I've done the script for *Involved,* which was commissioned by, of all people, Welsh TV; about the only place in the British Isles that isn't mentioned in the book is Wales. That's sitting on a desk somewhere in the HTV offices never to be seen or heard of again, which happens with scripts. As long as you get paid you don't care. Well, of course you care, but some times you care more than other times. I care about *The Boy in the Moon* because I feel that was a good script. It's not long gone in to BBC TV, so it is just going through the process. May never be heard of again.

MOLONEY: Because of the huge costs of a film?

O'RIORDAN: Absolutely; they will be looking to get a name actor or an actress before they go to the next part of the process. I was working on Catherine Dunne's four-part annotation of her novel, *In the Begin-*

ning, for RTE. The guy who commissioned that subsequently left, and it is sitting on the desk of god knows who in RTE. I'm now doing a two-parter for a company called Sallyhead—I don't know if you'd know them, Caitriona; it's a very popular detective series called *Prime Suspect.* They do that moody-broody stuff. They had a two-part idea for Helen Mirren, so I just finished the first episode of that, and she hated it; I did a second draft, so we'll see.

MOLONEY: Talking about *Involved,* in that first scene it's clear Eamon has a sexual problem and he is a very violent man. Were you positing a relationship between his sexuality and his violence?

O'RIORDAN: Yes. In that particular character, yes that was meant to be the inference; his back story would be he was very dominated by his mother, and he had a very closeted Catholic religious upbringing where sex was dirty. His mother would have given him that feeling [because] when she catches him masturbating, she threatens to chop off his dick. That would leave an impression on a child. And he has it all mixed up in his head, so sex, power, and violence merge together and come out in perverse ways like his attitude toward the prostitute.

MOLONEY: Yes, he is quite a misogynist. Except about his mother. He doesn't see the irony of that.

O'RIORDAN: Absolutely. But perhaps that's the hidden anger in him.

MOLONEY: How representative is the priest's position toward the IRA?

O'RIORDAN: I don't think it would be representative; that would make it too broad a stroke. But in the North an element of Catholic clergy, by their family's history, would be involved, and there is no denying that. But it would be actually a handful. In *Involved* the priest is related to Ma, and Eamon's father was killed in front of his eyes, so he has a very specific, particular interest.

MOLONEY: Some Irish writers are very hard on priests. There seems to be a tremendous resentment against the clergy in Ireland among intellectuals.

O'RIORDAN: Well, that will be for a very simply reason; they will have passed through their hands going to school, similarly with me and the nuns. Of my age group I don't know anybody who has had the Catholic religious upbringing who wasn't terrorized at some stage by some sadist. I don't know if the celibacy does it to them or loneliness; my husband, for example, remembers priests just beating the living crap out of him, and I remember similarly with the nuns. That will taint everything that people will have said to you.

MOLONEY: The church has also had a repressive effect on literature, banning books.

O'RIORDAN: Yes, until the 1970s. Even in the 1950s and the 1960s, the Catholic Church, including the nuns, still had a huge say. You've been to Ireland and can see for yourself that is no longer the case. And yes, literature, sex was dirty, and people were brought up with that and passed it on to next generation.

MOLONEY: Were you a Catholic in Ireland?

O'RIORDAN: Yes, but I'm not anymore. That's another one of your labels—the Catholic label. You know, once you're a Catholic, it's part of your formative years, and there would be a lot of dark memories, which is very good for literature. So maybe they did us a favor.

MOLONEY: Cotter, the sadistic teacher in *The Boy in the Moon* who is training his boys to "take back the North," is not a priest, although he sounds very like the ones you are describing.

O'RIORDAN: No, he is a married man, and he is based on someone who used to teach my husband and my brother. He was a complete and total nutter, a genuine sadist, without even being a priest. That was one of his refrains; I'm sure he was probably pissed half the time, and he was going up to take back the North, which I thought was hysterical, with all these young boys. "What are we going to do? We are going to take back the North, Sir."

MOLONEY: Have people like Carter contributed to politics in the North?

O'RIORDAN: Yes, of course, they would have. Our history books would have been totally weighted, giving a nationalist point of view, which is perfectly valid and fair, as far as I'm concerned. I'm sure in English classrooms, they would have seen the building of the empire [as] a totally glorious thing, and good luck to them. I never had a teacher that was particularly rampantly pro-IRA or anything, but I'm sure that my brothers had, in rural pockets of Ireland.

MOLONEY: How much of that is still going on?

O'RIORDAN: Precious little, I should image. Now, to be fair, I don't live there anymore, so I'm sure somebody could tell me otherwise. But the teachers I see now, so few are clergy anymore; they seem to be very young, progressive people now.

MOLONEY: In *Involved* Ma seems a prototype of Joyce's "sow that eats her farrow," a bloodthirsty maternal figure who inspires the men to violence.

O'RIORDAN: I think that would be an accepted thing in the North. Very often it would be the mother's inculcation, because the father or the brothers could be in Long Kesh or dead. So it would be up to the matriarchal figure to ensure that the struggle continues through her sons.

MOLONEY: Is Ma part of the problem with Kitty and Danny's relationship?

O'RIORDAN: Yes, her influence is huge. She has let Danny slip the net because she has so much control over the older brother. Danny is the new generation and he can go off and do his own thing. But then, she pulls him back, as any good Irish mother will do. Kitty and Danny's problems come from class and cultural things too. Danny says he's Irish—Kitty said she's Irish, but until she met him she was never up North in her life. People make assumptions about the North, the same way they would over here in England without any proper knowledge or cognition of what it is like to live there.

MOLONEY: She's Anglo-Irish but it seems like Danny's family views her as English.

O'RIORDAN: She has an English mother. But even though she is from the south, they view her as "other." Very complacently, she sees herself as Irish. But them she sees as a mongrel breed; they are not fully Irish like her, even though she has an English mother. But she is an Irish citizen. The Anglo-Irish community over here in England and in Ireland are a hybrid mix, different to anything I would consider normally Irish or English. They stick together very much as well.

MOLONEY: The ending of the book is chilling; it suggests that the IRA is going to kill Kitty in Saskatchewan. How realistic is that?

O'RIORDAN: I don't know. I think we impute things to the IRA because of the whole mythology. It's funny writing about your own people. It's very hard to take them seriously. One of the funny things about the end is the number of people who have never heard of Saskatchewan. In Northern Ireland someone asked me once, "I enjoyed the book, but is

Saskatchewan a cheese?" If you don't know that Saskatchewan is a place, the whole book ends on a cheese.

MOLONEY: Have you seen any difference in the way English and Irish readers respond to this book?

O'RIORDAN: Genuinely no. People look at it as a love story. The people in the North would look at it differently because they would look for authenticity. My Irish dialect would not always ring correctly in their ears; people have said to me, "we wouldn't say that up here." Doing an interview on BBC radio people took mortal offense to the fact that I wrote about the North at all because I'm not from there. Very protective. But the whole point of the book is about a girl from down south who knows bugger-all about the North.

MOLONEY: Are you moving away from writing about politics? *Boy in the Moon* is not very political.

O'RIORDAN: At the moment, there's something that interests me in Ireland—they're taking refugees in, for the first time ever. It's always been a country of emigration and now suddenly, people are coming in. Dublin initially didn't like it one little bit and now it's happening where I come from. The only black face the older generation may have seen was a doctor in the hospital; black people were very rare and exotic. To see black faces walking along the street is actually quite freaky to some people—they're scared, and they're worried about Africans coming and taking their jobs. I find the dilemmas facing people now fascinating.

MOLONEY: Yes, Dublin looks more and more like London; I'm staying with my cousins and one of them is a dentist. She is very petite and youthful looking, and one of her older patients said to her, "what with Packies and children, there's no real dentists any more anywhere."

O'RIORDAN: Well, you see it's payback time. All of the lovely new roads, all the fabulous new infrastructure, Ireland is much more affluent per capital than in England. Everybody has money. The New Ireland—the youngest population in Europe, under twenty-five, very well educated, free higher education—its all the stuff you don't get over here. Every classroom has a computer; you wouldn't see that over here. So all this has come from Europe. And now the Irish are being asked to take some of Europe's problems, and some people are very upset about that.

MOLONEY: *The Boy in the Moon* was a spectacular and important book, I thought. It had a surprising plot. How did you decide to put the climactic event almost at the beginning?

O'RIORDAN: Yes, that was very deliberate. You couldn't have too much of the young boy; you could only just have enough without completely alienating your reader. If you went on too much longer you're doing bad things to your reader's mind. My editor is very good; she pushes me. She'll say, raise the stakes. If you bring your big event early on in the script or the novel, you have to push your characters more, because you're not leading up to this event anymore.

MOLONEY: You give up the conventional plot.

O'RIORDAN: Or invert it, for the sake of seeing where that leaves your characters. If the young boy had died halfway through the book, then that's the story; whereas the reader knows, if it happens early on, that's horrible, but I have to deal with it.

MOLONEY: Sam comes across as a very special kid. Did you mean that to be factual or his parents' perception?

O'RIORDAN: No, I meant it to be factual. But I just meant him to be a kid you could recognize, just a nice kid. I based him on my son. *The Boy in the Moon* is his title, as he keeps reminding me. He looked up at the moon one day in the garden, and said, "it's not a man in the moon, it's a boy." And then things moved on from there. It explores my worst fear that anything could happen to him.

MOLONEY: Is her husband Brian careless or is that just her perception?

O'RIORDAN: No, he is careless, and he's negligent, but because of his own history he thinks he's being protective. The manifestation is carelessness, but the motivation—that the boy doesn't have a fear of heights, can take care of himself, will be macho—takes the father to pathological levels.

MOLONEY: Did you invent the scene at the castle wall?

O'RIORDAN: No, I didn't invent it. It happened, on a trip to Ireland. My husband put my son on top of the bridge over this river near a castle, and I was walking along with his brother. I looked back and saw him on the bridge. My whole life flashed before me. Thankfully it didn't happen, and we got him down. I told this story to women friends subsequently, and every one of them has a story like this about their husbands with their men children.

MOLONEY: Do you think it's an Oedipal thing?

O'RIORDAN: I think so; it's one of the things men like in the book. Men are not allowed as kids to say they are afraid, and they want to pass that on to their sons. Whatever you do, even if you feel afraid, you've got to confront it. You've got to do the thing. I know that sounds very simplistic, but it is very deep within the male psyche, remembering their father doing it to them. I've had this discussion with a number of men since writing the book.

MOLONEY: I read a review in the *Times Literary Supplement* titled "In Search of Forgiveness" that said the novel is a study in reconciliation. Would you say the novel is about forgiving unforgivable things?

O'RIORDAN: The possibility of love continuing without forgiveness is one of the things I never resolved in the novel, but I had to resolve it in the screenplay. I think that can happen, not on a huge scale, but in our everyday family and past. Things would have happened that are utterly unforgivable, but you still love people. But in the screenplay, she has to forgive him. If anything would have happened to my son, Jack, that day on the bridge, I would never forgive Donald.

MOLONEY: Is the time when she won't see Brian or speak to him part of a healing process?

O'RIORDAN: The power of silence is enormous. There's either words or there's silence. And one can be just as powerful as the other; for family members not talking is going back to the status quo, saying we'll preserve what is there. Because if we talk at this point, things might be said, and it might become so destructive; we won't be able to come back from that point.

MOLONEY: On the other hand, my generation is very pro-therapy, believing that talking is always therapeutic. I think psychology has replaced religion for people of my generation.

O'RIORDAN: The talk generation. It's very much what we are; any given night on any soap, there will be a character who says, "you've got to talk about it." Sometimes I feel like well, fuck off; I don't have to talk about anything.

Maura Stanton

Courtesy of Richard Cecil

Interviewed by

HELEN THOMPSON

BORN: Evanston, Illinois

EDUCATED: University of Minnesota (B.A. in journalism)
University of Iowa (M.F.A.)

RESIDES: Bloomington, Indiana

WORKS: Chair of the Creative Writing Program at Indiana State University

GENRES: Fiction, poetry

AWARDS: Pushcart Prize, PEN Syndicated Fiction Award, Lawrence Foundation Prize, and the Frances Steloff Fiction Prize.

Maura Stanton was born in Illinois and raised in Illinois and Minnesota to first-generation Irish-American parents. She has published several collections of poetry, a collection of short stories, and a novel. Her collection of short stories suggests the Irish-Americanness of her roots. For, while the title The Country I Come From *(1988) suggests the Midwest via the Bob Dylan lyric, her dedication to her father, "May the road rise to meet you. May the wind be always at your back" (1988, n.p.), suggests Ireland.*

The adolescent narrative voice that connects the stories in Stanton's collection seems appropriate because in many ways the narrator's focus on the world is like that of an immigrant moving from one culture to another. Just like a new immigrant, the narrator finds her old experience

unhelpful in her transition from youth to adulthood. The immigrant also experiences dislocation in terms of knowledge base. However, the similarity ends at the past because she is not memory-driven. She is unlike Sister Ursula in "Nijinsky," who is consumed with her friendship with the ballet dancer in Paris, and the narrator's mother in "Oz," who is consumed by memories of her experience as a nurse in London during World War II and her friend, Lucy Baxter. Contrasted with the adult memories are the Lundberg children's games in "The Sea Fairies." These self-directed stories shape the moment and put off the painful reality of a dead mother. The narrator bridges the gap between the two experiences of adulthood and childhood.

What bridges the gap between Stanton's collection of stories and her earlier novel, Molly Companion *(1977), is her tapping into the collective memory to retell old stories in new ways. In this novel she recasts the story of an Irish woman in the 1850s in war-torn Paraguay. The narrator, Molly, is a journalist, a chronicler, and a maker and shaper of history. Both Molly and Elisa Lynch, the Irish lover of Lopez, the Paraguayan dictator, are mediators between past and present, old world and new. While Molly embodies the dislocation of a traveler and a searcher, Elisa is trying to escape her past in an abusive and judgmental environment in Ireland. Both women use their relationships to men as a way to travel; both can negotiate the brutality of Lopez, even defying him. In many ways, these characters also appear to be a product of a feminist consciousness because they have mobility, agency, and self-determination.*

Maura Stanton's new collection of short stories, Do Not Forsake Me, Oh My Darling, *was published in 2002. We conducted the interview via email.*

◆   ◆   ◆

THOMPSON: I imagined that in *The Country I Come From* you were going to write about Ireland. Yet, you write about the Midwest. It was a surprise.

STANTON: *The Country I Come From* is a phrase from a Bob Dylan song, "the country I come from is called the Midwest." He grew up in Minnesota, where most of my stories are set, so the phrase seemed doubly appropriate when I was thinking about a title.

THOMPSON: Why do you think of it as a country?

STANTON: The Midwest feels like a separate country to me; I'm always relieved to get back here when I've been on the East Coast or in the south or in California. For many years, living in New York State and Virginia and northern California and Arizona, I felt I was exiled from my "country."

THOMPSON: The stereotypes of the Midwest suggest an average life that is uninteresting and boring. It seems that you tackle this picture by showing us that the average life is rich and complex.

STANTON: Yes, I'm afraid I grew up thinking that life in the Midwest was boring and uneventful. I remember telling this to Richard Yates, when I studied with him at Iowa. He insisted that I had plenty of things to write about. It didn't seem so back then (I was more interested in exotic subjects), but as I got older and lived in different parts of the country, I began to have more insight, and I wished I'd paid more attention!

THOMPSON: I think also that part of the stereotype of being average is that one's life is stable and secure, and I think these stories show us clearly that this is not the case. Is this why you chose an adolescent perspective in your stories? To look at the world differently?

STANTON: The stories are semiautobiographical. The adolescent voice seemed like a natural fit with the events. I didn't really know what I was going to say or discover until I started writing the stories.

THOMPSON: I am interested in how you meld the Irish and the Midwestern in your stories. It seems that while one is ordinary, the other is stereotypically flamboyant.

STANTON: Since I was the oldest (eventually I had four brothers and four sisters) I used to take the train to Chicago in the summers to visit my grandparents. It was always exciting to visit them. Relatives with the most beautiful accents were still coming over to Chicago in the fifties, and I remember parties where people sang and played the accordion. My grandfather had a wonderful voice. He sang "Finnegan's Wake," so I knew it as a ballad long before I [had] ever heard of Joyce's novel. I was aware of myself as an outsider on these visits. I had a flat, ordinary voice, I couldn't sing, and I didn't know all the references to people and places in Ireland that were always flying over my head. Ireland was a romantic, exotic place to me. Even Chicago, with its old-world churches, was exotic and romantic in contrast to the 1950s suburbs where I lived, where everything was brand-new. Mass in our parish in Peoria was celebrated in the gym. We didn't even have a church. The north side of Chicago (Rogers Park) was, to me, the "old world" of manners and history and beauty.

THOMPSON: Do you visit Ireland?

STANTON: I always wanted to see Ireland, but oddly, it was the last rather than the first country in Europe that I visited. And though I had a wonderful trip and met some of the nicest, friendliest people in the world (even cab drivers!), I felt more like a stranger in Ireland than I ever did in France and Italy. My American accent grated on me, and my blond hair made me look English or German. I realized that Irish-American and Irish are not the same at all, though we share some cultural things in common. I'm interested in Irish politics, but horrified by the violence.

THOMPSON: On the dedication page you quote an Irish saying, "May the road rise to meet you. May the wind be always at your back." Why did you choose this?

STANTON: I quoted from this Irish blessing because the book is dedicated to my father, who died before it saw print. We had this blessing hanging on the wall in our kitchen in Minneapolis.

THOMPSON: Is this what it means to be Irish-American, somehow dislocated from Irishness, where it exists only in memory?

STANTON: I grew up with three myths or illusions that in retrospect have turned out to be very important. I always thought that women were smarter than men (based on my observations in grade school), that most writers were women (most of the books I read were written by women), and that being Irish was the best thing you could be. I knew nothing for many years about the vexed relationship between Ireland and England. For me, being Irish (and I don't remember thinking of the hyphen Irish-American back then, I just thought of myself as Irish) was a source of great pride. It connected me to a romantic island on the edge of Europe where people were fierce and strong and spoke with beautiful lilts. It was rather a shock to grow up and read the history of Ireland.

THOMPSON: What was shocking to you?

STANTON: While I was growing up I knew nothing about the hundreds of years of poverty and oppression that Ireland had experienced. I didn't realize that the Irish had been treated by the British much like North American settlers treated Native Americans, as a dangerous subhuman population that needed to be exterminated or controlled. The Irish who came to America must have tried hard to forget that part of their history.

THOMPSON: How was the illusion of most writers being women shattered?

STANTON: It was a shock to discover that there were only three women out of hundreds in my freshman English poetry anthology. Canon reformation has been a good thing because it's brought many new writers to my attention, Langston Hughes's memoir, *The Big Sea,* for example, one of my favorite books. I was delighted to discover Katherine Mansfield, the poet Robert Hayden, and many other writers not visible when I was in college.

THOMPSON: Would you say that you are an Irish-American writer?

STANTON: I think of myself as a writer who sometimes sees the world from a feminist perspective, or from an Irish-American perspective. The concerns of my writing have changed over time. I react to things in both personal and public history.

THOMPSON: Is the dual heritage, being both Irish-American, similar to the Anglo-Irish, which is the consequence of British colonization?

STANTON: It makes a poet like Seamus Heaney feel very uneasy about writing in English, since that's the language of the oppressors, and he feels that he has to make English Irish in some way, since he doesn't write in Gaelic. But I don't have that problem. My American English belongs to me, and I love the way it's full of words that come from other cultures. I'm also lucky to be a woman writing at this time in history; I don't have to feel oppressed by blank verse, for example, which apparently weighed on Emily Dickinson and caused her to want to use the hymn meters. I feel free to use the tradition, the canon, and make it new.

THOMPSON: In what ways do you want to make the canon new?

STANTON: I don't feel oppressed by meter, for example. I often write poetry in blank verse, and feel I have something new to say in line that goes back to Shakespeare since so few women have ever written in it. I may not like D. H. Lawrence's politics, but I recognize that "The Snake" is one of the great poems of the century. I encourage my students to learn from all kinds of writers, Lady Murasaki, Colette, Katherine Mansfield, Chekhov, Raymond Carver, Hemingway, Amos Tutuola.

THOMPSON: Change on the more personal level as well as the larger social level ties the stories together. Did this emerge as you were writing?

STANTON: Yes, I think this was something I discovered in the course of writing the stories. The current arrangement of the stories, which I like, was made by my editor at Milkweed. Actually the first story written was "Scotland." "The Sea Fairies" was the last story.

THOMPSON: Did you envisage the narrator-protagonist as the same person throughout the collection?

STANTON: Yes, except for when she's part of the family voice.

THOMPSON: You must also be drawing a connection between your story "Adam's Curse" and the Yeats poem.

STANTON: Absolutely. I took the title of the story from the Yeats poem. I'd never heard of the expression "Adam's curse" before reading the poem, but it really clicked with me.

THOMPSON: If we read the narrator-protagonist's development through the stories, "Nijinksy" shows us she has learned something from her Christmas job. What does she learn exactly?

STANTON: She learns to stand up for herself, but also recognizes in herself all the dark forces that have shaped Sister Ursula.

THOMPSON: Do the dark forces help her to recognize that we are not inherently benevolent beings?

STANTON: Yes, that's part of it. And it's this recognition that will turn her into an artist.

THOMPSON: Can you explain the fantasies and the games the children play in "The Sea Fairies?"

STANTON: I loved to read when I was growing up, and children's books where extremely important to me and to all my brothers and sisters. Some of my sisters are now collecting copies of the books we used to read as kids. *The Sea Fairies* by L. Frank Baum was my favorite book growing up. But the book disappeared after I left home and it was long out of print. Now it is in print again. For Christmas I sent copies to all my sisters! I wrote "The Sea Fairies" as a way of reclaiming the book, and retelling the story. *The Wizard of Oz* was another favorite book. I loved fairy tales, mysteries, stories about magicians. I loved to escape into imaginary worlds. I found this escape empowering, and it turned me into a writer.

THOMPSON: It seems that your characters have similar versions of escape that come from their own pasts: mother's experience as a nurse during World War II in "Oz;" the uncle's story of John McCormack in "John McCormack;" Sister Ursula's life in Paris in "Nijinsky." Are these the same coping mechanisms as the children's?

STANTON: I'm not sure they're the same thing. The adults have real memories, real stories to tell; the children only have imaginary tales. The real tales of the adults—full of romance—probably encourage the children to think that their own dreams might come true, at the same time that they realize the adults are now outside of paradise, their own past, which is a scary state.

THOMPSON: Why did you choose the first-person plural point of view for the story "Scotland"?

STANTON: Two reasons. The emotional reason is that my family often seemed to think as a group about certain experiences, and still has a set of shared memories. It's always a bit shocking when someone admits to a different perspective on some past event. I guess this is the effect of having so many brothers and sisters, or maybe, as the oldest, I felt I was thinking for everyone! The other reason for the choice is literary. When I was looking for a voice for the first story I wrote I turned to Flaubert. I studied the opening of *Madame Bovary* where Charles is introduced. The voice used in the novel is "we" at first; then quickly the "we" is dropped. But I liked the intimate feel of that opening, and tried to imitate it.

THOMPSON: It's interesting that you use Flaubert as a model for your own writing. Do you offer this method to your students?

STANTON: Yes, my basic method for teaching writing is to provide good models of fine writing to my students, and to assign writing exercises based upon these models.

THOMPSON: Was teaching writing an inevitability for you?

STANTON: I was surprised to find myself a teacher. When I went off to Iowa to study writing, I assumed I'd end up with some kind of editing job to support myself. But I got a one-year visiting appointment to teach creative writing and composition. I discovered that writing and the teaching of writing were a good fit for me.

THOMPSON: Tell me about your experience at the University of Iowa.

STANTON: A creative writing class, which I signed up for in my fifth year at the University of Minnesota, was the real turning point for me. The course was taught by Vern Rutsala, a poet with an M.F.A. from Iowa, and for the first time I was introduced to contemporary poetry, and taught how to read poetry and fiction from a writer's, not a critic's, point of view. I suddenly knew what I wanted to do with my life; I wanted to write poetry and serious literary fiction. Vern told me about Iowa. I applied, and was admitted in both genres. Getting the money to go was a real struggle, but my father was wonderful. With nine children we were naturally poor, but he swallowed his pride, and asked a wealthy friend of his to loan me the money. I was lucky to have parents who loved books and valued education.

THOMPSON: How did the Iowa program help you to hone your writing skills?

STANTON: Iowa was extremely important for me. I was surrounded by dozens of other serious writers, my teachers and fellow students. I had time to dream and write and revise and read. I got connected to contemporary writing. I gained self-confidence as a writer.

THOMPSON: What compels you to write in the different genres?

STANTON: I want to invent, shape, create, make, and discover form and meaning in the world around me like other artists. My poetry is lyric but works with narrative. Fiction allows me to spread out and write longer narratives.

THOMPSON: Aside from Flaubert, which writers do you admire?

STANTON: Fiction writers I admire include Henry James, Richard Yates, Chekhov, Austen, Anita Brookner, Hemingway, David Lodge, Lady Muraski, Willa Cather, Mark Twain, Flannery O'Connor.

THOMPSON: What about canonical Irish writers, such as Joyce?

STANTON: I think that Joyce has been a major influence on my short fiction. I've learned a lot about craft from him, but he's also influenced my choice of subject matter, and his vision of the world had made me think about things—especially family—in a new way.

THOMPSON: The story of *Molly Companion* is as far away from the Midwest as it can be. Why did you choose to write about Paraguay? Is it as Calvin says, because it's the remotest place on earth?

STANTON: *Molly Companion* came out of a set of poems that appear in my first book of poetry, *Snow on Snow*. The poems are called

"Extracts from the Journal of Elisa Lynch." Elisa Lynch was the Irish-born mistress of the infamous Paraguayan dictator Francisco Solano Lopez. The fact that she was Irish had a lot to do with my fascination with her.

THOMPSON: How did you discover her?

STANTON: I discovered a biography of Elisa Lynch when I took some Latin American history and politics classes at the University of Minnesota. I was fascinated by her. She escaped poverty in Ireland, made it to Paris where she worked as a courtesan, then met Lopez, who had come over for a visit, and who dreamed of becoming the Napoleon of South America. She went back to Paraguay with Lopez, had children by him, and actually fought in the crazy war that he started with Argentina, Brazil, and Uruguay. I suppose the freezing winters in Minnesota made me long for a life of adventure in a far place with palm trees. I wrote the poems while I was a student at Iowa.

THOMPSON: How did the poems transform themselves into a novel?

STANTON: When I won a grant from the National Endowment for the Arts, my original plan was to continue with the "Extracts" and I did more research. But it quickly became clear that I had far too much material, that I really wanted to write a novel. When I started the novel, I assumed it would be about Elisa Lynch, but the more I wrote about her the more exotic she seemed. It wasn't until I invented a character more like myself, a journalist (my B.A. was in journalism, and I knew there had been some famous women reporters in the nineteenth century), that I found a voice for the novel. Elisa Lynch was relegated to a more minor role. And I began to focus on all the insane propaganda, the incredible lies, generated not just by Lopez but also by all the newspapers of the time. In my novel I was able to make use of the lies as well as whatever historical truth I could find.

THOMPSON: It's interesting that you take history and create fiction in this novel and in the short story "Nijinski." How do you work with fact and fiction?

STANTON: I used fact as a point of departure and invented many details, trying to make them consistent with the facts. But I'm a fiction writer at heart; I was willing to change any fact for the sake of the story.

THOMPSON: Writing about war has historically been the domain of male writers. Were you playing with the dynamic that women have been entrenched within a domestic tradition and have been marginalized because of it?

STANTON: The Vietnam War had just ended, so images of war were familiar to me. It did not seem strange to embark on this subject. And I had two great models, *The Red Badge of Courage* and *One Hundred Years of Solitude*. Maybe I was also playing with this dynamic, but in an unconscious way. These were questions I hadn't thought through at the time. I didn't feel any restraints as far as subject matter went. That was the subject I wanted to write about. I used Dante's *Inferno* to help me organize the book for the first draft. Later I had to go back and add a plot that had causality.

THOMPSON: How close was Vietnam to your experience?

STANTON: One of my brothers had his birthday drawn early during the televised lottery, and was drafted and sent to Vietnam. He was pulled right out of school, but because I was a girl, I was safe. It never felt right to me.

THOMPSON: The women in the novel have agency: Elisa, Molly, Pancha, Garmendia, Rosalita, even the old woman. Was this your goal, to create women characters who can survive quite well in a male-dominated environment?

STANTON: I don't think it was a goal; I think it just happened.

THOMPSON: Molly has a certain duty to her father and husband yet she is swashbuckling in the middle of a war and a rain forest in order to find her husband. How did Molly evolve as you were writing her?

STANTON: Once I found her voice, in that opening paragraph, I knew I could make her work, that she was real, and sane enough to provide a perspective on the mad world through which she travels.

THOMPSON: Why did you give Molly a rash?

STANTON: At this point in time, I have no idea why I gave her that rash, poor woman! Maybe I was trying to make her plain, like Jane Eyre. Or maybe the idea came from Dante, since the first draft was closely pinned to the chapters of the *Inferno*.

THOMPSON: I thought it might be something to do with the control she exhibits. Were you interrogating feminine stereotypes?

STANTON: I think so. I wanted strong women characters.

THOMPSON: She reminds me of some other strong women characters—the suffragettes who imagined themselves as warrior women, created uniforms, reproduced themselves and their cause in art (Sylvia Pankhurst, in particular). Did you draw inspiration from these women?

STANTON: In the back of my mind I probably had such women, and figures like Camilla in mind. But, I also had the Queen of the Sea Fairies in mind, deep down in mind, underwater in fact, something I only realized recently when I reread the children's novel by Baum, *The Sea Fairies*. And now I think that Lopez was Zog. But this was all completely unconscious when I wrote the novel. I only now see it! Amazing.

Selected Bibliography

THE FOLLOWING SELECTIONS of publications by and about the writers in this collection are not exhaustive; instead, our aim is to provide a sampling of primary and secondary sources that should serve as a starting point for students and researchers. As well as fiction, we have included writers' major publications in other genres, including poetry, drama, screenplays, biography, and literary criticism. The entries are organized alphabetically by writer and are separated into works by and about the writer in question. The tremendous variety in the lengths of bibliographies reflects the current extent of the writer's career rather than the amount of critical interest in her work. Concluding the bibliography is a list of useful websites for accessing texts, information, and publishers.

Primary texts are widely available in Europe and the United States, but not always in both. Irish publishers such as Attic, Blackstaff, and Poolbeg do not have large distribution capacities and not all of the writers have placed their work with American publishers. However, in such circumstances we are fortunate to have access to British and Irish book sources online. For example, Hanna's in Dublin, Kenny's in Galway, and Amazon in the U.K. have websites and will ship to non-European addresses. These resources make Irish women's fiction more readily available than ever before. Furthermore, for ordering larger quantities of books for classroom instruction, Dufour Editions is a useful site since it publishes and distributes a variety of foreign titles. This site also provides email access to selected Irish publishers and a catalog request form. Also, Books Britain is a source of books not usually available in the United States.

Secondary materials are becoming equally accessible, with many newspapers online with searchable archives. The *Irish Times* is a particularly useful website in this regard. Also, full text databases through Ebsco Host and Infotrac facilitate ease of access to many articles and reviews. However, some Irish periodicals are still difficult to come by in the United States.

Ivy Bannister

Primary Sources

Ivy Bannister, ed. 1980. "Sloughing Off." In *A Dream Recurring: And Other Stories and Poems*. Maxwell House Winners vol. 2. Dublin: Arlen House.

———. 1990. *The Wild Circus Show*. Newark, Del.: Proscenium.

———. 1991a. *Love Nest*, play performed by RTE.

———. 1991b. *The Road to Revolution*, play performed by RTE.

———. 1993. "Seduced." In *Virgins and Hyacinths: An Attic Press Book of Fiction*. Edited by Caroline Walsh. Dublin: Attic Press.

———. 1996a. "In My Father's Garage." *Home—An Anthology of Modern Irish Writing*. Edited by Siobhán Parkinson. Dublin: A. & A. Farmar.

———. 1996b. *Magician and Other Stories*. Dublin: Poolbeg Press.

———. 1997. *The Shavian Woman: A Study of Women in the Life and Work of George Bernard Shaw*. Dublin: Univ. Press of Ireland.

———. 2001. "The Woman Who Has Difficulty Answering the Phone." In *Loose Horses: Stories from South Dublin*. http://homepage.eircom.net/~loosehorses/stories/woman.htm

Secondary Sources

Doge, Polly. 1995. Review of *Color You Hair Red*. June 19, *Publishers Weekly*. Cork, Ireland: Mercier Press.

Sweeney, Eamon. 1997. Review of *Magician*, by Ivy Bannister. *Irish Times*, January 15, 16.

Weekes, Ann Owens. 1993. *Unveiling Treasures: The Attic Guide to the Published Works of Irish Women Literary Writers: Drama, Fiction, Poetry*, 21–22. Dublin: Attic Press.

Catherine Brady

Primary Sources

Brady, Catherine. 1981a. "In the Woodsmoke Light." *The Missouri Review* 5, no. 1: 137–46.

———. 1981b. "The Propagation of Sound through Water." *Intro* 12.

———. 1983a. "Circles." *The Greensboro Review* 33: 50–60.

———. 1983b. "Home." *Redbook*, March, 53–54+.

———. 1983c. "Myths and Realities about Short Story Writing." *The Writer* 96:11–13.

———. 1992. "Daley's Girls." In *I Know Some Things: Stories about Childhood by Contemporary Writers,* edited by Lorne Moore, 42–52. Boston: Faber and Faber.

———. 1993. "The Custom of the Country." In *The Next Parish Over: A Collection of Irish American Writing,* edited by Patricia Monaghan, 180–91. Minneapolis: New Rivers Press.

———. 1996. "Chatter." *The Kenyon Review* 18, no. 2: 136–48.

———. 1998. "Showing and Telling: The Necessary Partnership." *Associated Writing Programs Chronicle* 30, no. 6: 20–23.

———. 1999. *The End of the Class War.* Corvallis, Oreg.: Calyx.

———. 2000a. "Comfort." *Nua: Studies in Contemporary Irish Writing* 4, no. 1: 113–28.

———. 2000b. "The Last of the True Believers." *Clackamas Literary Review* 4, no. 2: 228–42.

———. 2000c. "The Loss of Green." *Water-Stone* 5, no. 1: 85–101.

———. 2000d. "Nothing to Hide." *Other Voices* 13, no. 33: 166–78.

———. 2000e. "Light, Air, Water." *Natural Bridge* 4: 120–36.

———. 2000f. "Thirteen Ways of Looking at a Blackbird." *GSU Review* (spring): 65–76.

Secondary Sources

Berman, Jenifer. 1999. Review of *The End of the Class War,* by Catherine Brady. *New York Times Book Review,* August 29, 21.

"The Editors Recommend." 1999. Review of *The End of the Class War,* by Catherine Brady. *San Francisco Chronicle,* November 28, 11.

Review of *The End of the Class War,* by Catherine Brady. 1999. *Publisher's Weekly,* May 17, 58.

Evelyn Conlon

Primary Sources

Conlon, Evelyn. 1987. *My Head Is Opening.* Dublin: Attic Press.

———. 1989a. "On the Inside of Cars." In *Wildish Things: An Anthology of New Irish Women's Writing,* edited by Ailbhe Smythe, 131–40. Dublin: Attic Press.

———. 1989b. "Park-going Days." In *Territories of the Voice: Contemporary Stories by Irish Women Writers,* edited by Louise DeSalvo, Kathleen Walsh D'Arcy, and Katherine Hogan, 164–70. Boston: Beacon Press.

———. 1990. *Stars in the Daytime.* Britain: Women's Press.

———. 1993. *Taking Scarlet as a Real Colour.* Belfast: Blackstaff Press.

———. 1998a. *A Glassful of Letters.* Belfast: Blackstaff Press.

———. 1998b. "The Mother of All Inventions." Review of *Mother of All Myths,* by Aminatta Forna. *Tribune Magazine,* July 19, 18.

———. 2000. *Telling: New and Selected Stories.* Belfast: Blackstaff Press.

———. 2001a. "When Relatives of Victims Cry Halt to Death Row." *Irish Times,* May 23.

———. 2001b. *Cutting the Night in Two: An Anthology of Short Stories.* Edited by Evelyn Conlon and Hans-Christian Oeser. Dublin: New Island Books.

———. 2002. "Telling: New and Selected Stories." In *The Field Day Anthology of Irish Writing: Irish Women's Writing and Traditions,* vol. 5, edited by Angela Bourke et al., 1227–8. Cork, Ireland: Cork Univ. Press in association with Field Day.

———. Forthcoming. *Skin of Dreams.* Dingle, Ireland: Brandon Press.

Conlon, Evelyn, ed. *Graph: A Literary Review.* Cork, Ireland: Cork Univ. Press.

Secondary Sources

Barrett, Pam. 1993. "Paperbacks." Review of *Taking Scarlet as a Real Colour,* by Evelyn Conlon. *Sunday Times,* June 27.

Beardsley, Ellen. 1998. "Winners and Losers in the Game of Life: Ellen Beardsley on New Novels From Two Irish Writers." *Irish Times,* April 18, 68.

Gaisford, Sue. 1993. "Wild Rover in a Bar: *Taking Scarlet as a Real Colour.*" Review of *Taking Scarlet as a Real Colour,* by Evelyn Conlon. *Independent* (London), August 7, 26.

Galloway, Shana Suzanne. 1994. "No Dream Is Forgotten: Marriage, Motherhood and the Irish Woman." Master's thesis, California State Univ., Long Beach.

Heller, Amanda. 1998. "A Glassful of Letters." Review of *A Glassful of Letters,* by Evelyn Conlon. *Boston Globe,* December 13, M2.

Mastin, Antoinette Mary. 1995. "The Road to the Fifth Province: Irish Women's Storytelling, 1960–1993." Ph.D. diss., Univ. of Cincinnati.

Moloney, Caitriona. 1999. "Controlling the Past." Review of *A Glassful of Letters,* by Evelyn Conlon. *Irish Literary Supplement.*

O'Brien, George. 2000. "Gripping No-oneness." Review of *Telling: New and Selected Stories,* by Evelyn Conlon. *Irish Times,* June 17, 70.

Pelan, Rebecca. 1995. "It's What Happens after You're Born That Gets It Knocked out of You: Interview with Evelyn Conlon." *Hecate* 21, no. 1: 111–13.

Potter, Jennifer. 1993. "The Women Who Are Taken as Red." Review of *Taking Scarlet as a Real Colour,* by Evelyn Conlon. *Independent* (London), July 4, 33.

"Telling Tales." 2000. *Irish Times,* May 20, 78.

Wagner, Erica. 1993. "Where Anglo-Saxons Fear to Tread." Review of *Taking Scarlet as a Real Colour,* by Evelyn Conlon. *Times,* (London), June 14, 31A.

Weekes, Ann Owens. 1993 *Unveiling Treasures: The Attic Guide to the Published Works of Irish Women Literary Writers: Drama, Fiction, Poetry,* 76–78. Dublin: Attic Press.

Emma Donoghue

Primary Sources

Donoghue, Emma. 1993a. "Imagined More Than Women: Lesbians as Hermaphrodites, 1671–1766." *Women's History Review* 2, no. 2: 199–216.

———. 1993b. " 'Out of Order': Kate O'Brien's Lesbian Fictions." In *Ordinary People Dancing.* Cork, Ireland: Cork Univ. Press.

———. [1993] 1997. *Kissing the Witch: Old Tales in New Skins.* New York: HarperCollins Publishers (Joanna Cotler Books).

———. 1994. "Going Back." In *Alternative Loves: Irish Lesbian and Gay Stories.* Dublin: Martello.

———. [1994] 1995. *Stir-fry.* Harmondsworth, England: Penguin; New York: HarperTrade.

———. [1994] 1996. *Passions Between Women: British Lesbian Culture, 1668–1801.* New York: HarperCollins; London: Scarlet Press.

———. 1995a. "Coming Out a Bit Strong." *Index on Censorship* 24, no. 1: 87–88.

———. 1995b. *Hood.* New York: HarperCollins.

———. 1997a. " 'How Could I Fear and Hold Thee by the Hand?': The Poetry of Eva Gore-Booth." In *Sex, Nation, and Dissent in Irish Writing,* edited by Éibhear Walshe, 16–42. New York: St. Martin's.

———. 1997b. *Poems Between Women: Four Centuries of Love, Romantic Friendship, and Desire.* New York: Columbia Univ. Press.

———. 1997c. *What Sappho Would Have Said: Four Centuries of Love Poems Between Women.* New York: Viking Penguin.

———. 1998a. "Counting the Days." In *Phoenix Irish Short Stories,* edited by David Marcus. Dublin: Phoenix.

———. 1998b. *Ladies and Gentlemen.* Dublin: New Island Books.

———. 1998c. *We Are Michael Field.* Bath, England: Absolute Press.

———. 1999. "Looking for Petronilla." In *Vintage Book of International Lesbian Fiction: An Anthology,* edited by Naomi Holoch and Joan Nestle, 63–75. London: Vintage.

———. 2000a. " 'Family Life, No Thanks.' " Review of *The Talented Mr. Ripley,* a film by Anthony Minghella. *Irish Times,* February 24.

———. 2000b. Unspecified story. *Ladies' Night at Finbar's Hotel,* edited by Dermot Folger. San Diego: Harcourt.

———. 2001. *Slammerkin.* London: Virago.

———. 2002. "I Know My Own Heart." In *Seen and Heard,* edited by Cathy Leeney. Dublin: Carysfort Press.

Donoghue, Emma, ed. 1999. *The Mammoth Book of Lesbian Short Stories.* New York: Carroll and Graf.

Secondary Sources

Review of *Passions Between Women.* 1997. *Eighteenth-Century Studies* 30: 319–25.

Beard, William Randall. 2000. " 'Ladies' Script Structure Makes Show Tedious." *Minneapolis Star Tribune,* April 17: 5B.

Bensyl, Stacia L. 2002. "Emma Donoghue." In *Dictionary of Literary Biography: Twenty-First-Century British and Irish Novelists,* vol. 267, edited by Michael R. Molino, 68–74. Gale: Farmington Hills, Mich.

Bergman, David. 1999. "Abbreviated Lives." *Harvard Gay and Lesbian Review* 6, no. 3: 9.

Burkhardt, Joanna M. 1994. Review of *Stir-fry. Library Journal* 119: 98.

Carton, Debbie. 1997. Review of *Kissing the Witch. Booklist* 93: 1684.

Coe, Jonathan. 1994. Review of *Stir-fry. London Review of Books* 16: 23.

DeLynn, Jane. 1994. "Lesbian Love: One from Column A 3." *Washington Post,* August 10: D2.

Dollisch, Patricia A. 1997. Review of *Kissing the Witch. School Library Journal* 43: 117.

Donoghue, Deirdre. 2001. Review of *Slammerkin. USA Today,* May 24: 5D.

Dugaw, Dianne. 1996. Review of *Passions Between Women,* by Emma Donoghue. *Women's Review of Books* 13: 5.

Dunmore, Helen. 1997. "In a Sapphic Nursery." *Times* (London), April 26.

Foster, Aisling. 1994. "Lasagne and Desire." *Times* (London), January 27.

Freeman, Lisa A. 1997. Review of *Passions Between Women,* by Emma Donoghue. *Eighteenth-Century Studies* 30: 321–22.

Hohmann, Marti. 1999. "Women's Passions of the Millennium: Emma Donoghue." *Harvard Gay and Lesbian Review* 6, no. 4: 14–16.

Hughes-Hallett, Lucy. 1994. "Liberty, Equality, Sorority." *Sunday Times* (London), January 16.

Innes, Charlotte. 1994. Review of *Stir-fry,* by Emma Donoghue. *Lambda Book Report* 4, no. 5: 28.

Jamison, Laura. 2001. "The Joy of Silks." *New York Times,* July 8, sec. 7, 23.

Joughin, Sheena. 1995. Review of *Hood,* by Emma Donoghue. *Times Literary Supplement,* April 21, no. 4803: 22.

Kuda, Marie. 1994. Review of *Stir-fry,* by Emma Donoghue. *Booklist* 90: 1663.

Lockerbie, Catherine. 1996. "Death in Dublin." Review of *Hood,* by Emma Donoghue. *New York Times Book Review,* March 24, 12.

Madden, Ed. 2000. "Poets and Lovers Ever More." Review of *We Are Michael Field,* by Emma Donoghue. *Gay and Lesbian Review* 7, no. 1: 52–53.

McEwen, Christian. 1994. Review of *Stir-fry,* by Emma Donoghue. *Ms.* 4: 76.

Mendelson, Charlotte. 1997. Review of *Kissing the Witch: Old Tales in New Skins,* by Emma Donoghue. *Times Literary Supplement,* June 27, 23.

Molino, Michael, ed. 2002. *Dictionary of Literary Biography: Twenty-First-Century British and Irish Novelists.* Vol. 267. Farmington Hills, Mich.: Gale

Nessel, Jen. 1997. Review of *Kissing the Witch: Old Tales in New Skins,* by Emma Donoghue. *New York Times Book Review,* September, 28: 28.

Neumeyer, Peter F. 1998. "Tales That Speak to Person and Time." Review of *Kissing the Witch: Old Tales in New Skins,* by Emma Donoghue. *Boston Globe,* January 4, D3.

O'Connell, Alex. 2000. Review of *Slammerkin,* by Emma Donoghue. *Times* (London), July 26.

Orleans, Ellen. 1996. Review of *Hood,* by Emma Donoghue. *Lambda Book Report* 5, no. 2: 23.

Pace, Patricia. 1997. Review of *Kissing the Witch,* by Emma Donoghue. *American Book Review* 19: 6.

Platt, Edward. 1996. Review of *Hood. Sunday Times* (London), July 28.

Quinn, Antoinette. 2000. "New Noises from the Woodshed: The Novels of Emma Donoghue." In *Contemporary Irish Fiction: Themes, Tropes, Theories,* edited by Liam Harte and Michael Parker, 145–67. Houndmills, England: Macmillan, St. Martin's.

Review of *Passions Between Women,* by Emma Donoghue. 1997. *Eighteenth-Century Studies* 30: 319–25.

Review of *Slammerkin,* by Emma Donoghue. 2001. *Times of London,* June 2.

Roberts, Michele. 1994. "Take Three Girls." *Sunday Times*, February 13.

Simon, Clea. 1994. "Untwisted Sisters Help This Cinderella Come of Age." Review of *Stir-fry*, by Emma Donoghue. *Boston Globe*, July 29, 57.

Smyth, Gerry. 1997a. *"Stir-fry."* In *The Novel and the Nation: Studies in New Irish Fiction*, 157–60. London: Pluto.

———. 1997b. *"Hood."* In *The Novel and the Nation: Studies in New Irish Fiction*, 163–65. London: Pluto.

Stevenson, Deborah. 1997. Review of *Kissing the Witch*, by Emma Donoghue. *Bulletin of the Center for Children's Books* 50: 280.

Thomas, K. L. 1999–2000. Review of *We Are Michael Field*, by Emma Donoghue. *Victorian Studies* 42, no. 2: 312–14.

Tillyard, Stella. 1996. "Gender Benders." Review of *Passions Between Women*, by Emma Donoghue. *New York Times Book Review*, February 25, sec. 7, 27.

Traub, Valerie. 1999. "The Rewards of Lesbian History." *Feminist Studies* 25, no. 2: 363.

Upchurch, Michael. 2001. "What Is Gay Fiction?" *Seattle Times*, June 24, J10.

Walter, Natasha. 1994. Review of *Stir-fry*, by Emma Donoghue. *Times Literary Supplement*, February 4, 20.

Walters, Margaret. 2000. Review of *Slammerkin*, by Emma Donoghue. *Sunday Times*, August 13.

Whitney, Scott. 1996. Review of *Hood*, by Emma Donoghue. *Booklist* 92: 1120.

Wingfield, Rachel. 1998. "Lesbian Writers in the Mainstream: Sara Maitland, Jeanette Winterson and Emma Donoghue." In *Beyond Sex and Romance? The Politics of Contemporary Lesbian Fiction*. London: Women's Press.

Catherine Dunne

Primary Sources

Dunne, Catherine. 1998a. *In the Beginning*. London: Jonathan Cape Limited.

———. 1998b. *A Name for Himself*. London: Jonathan Cape Limited.

———. 1998c. "Talking Through Her Hat." In *A Second Skin: Women Write about Clothes*. London: Women's Press.

———. [2000] 2001. *The Walled Garden*. London: Macmillan; Picador.

———. 2001. "Proof of Life." *Irish Times*, May 26.

Secondary Sources

Clifford, Susan Gene. 1998. Review of *In the Beginning,* by Catherine Dunne. *Library Journal,* March 15, 92.
Fogarty, Anne. 2000. Review of *The Walled Garden,* by Catherine Dunne. *Irish Times.*
Foster, Aisling. 1997. "Close to Home and Far Away." *Times* (London), March 27.
Grandfield, Kevin. 1998. Review of *In the Beginning,* by Catherine Dunne. *Booklist,* April, 1302–3.
Review of *In the Beginning,* by Catherine Dunne. 1998. *Publisher's Weekly,* February 23, 52.

Miriam Dunne

Primary Sources

Dunne, Miriam. 1997. *Blessed Art Thou a Monk Swimming.* London: Headline; Routledge.
———. 1998."Dragged Back by the Old Sow." *Irish Times,* August, 6.

Secondary Sources

Haverty, Anne. 1997a. Review of *Blessed Art Thou a Monk Swimming. Mail on Sunday* (London), November 30, 37.
———. 1997b. Review of *Blessed Art Thou a Monk Swimming. Sunday Tribune* (Dublin), December 7, 29.
O'Farrell, Maggie. 1997. "Bring on the Scary Nuns." *Sunday Independent* (Dublin), December 14, 33.
Perrick, Penny. 1997. "Dumb and Dumber." *Times* (London), December 13.
Power, Suzanne. 1997. Review of *Blessed Art Thou a Monk Swimming. Irish Tatler,* 44.
Redmond, Lucille. 1998. "In the Days of the Vocations." Review of *Blessed Art Thou a Monk Swimming,* by Miriam Dunne. *Irish Times,* March 5.

Anne Enright

Primary Sources

Enright, Anne. 1989. Review of *Misogynies,* by Joan Smith. *Times Literary Supplement,* May 12, 504.

———. 1990. "Smile." In *First Fictions Introduction No. 10.* New York: Faber and Faber.

———. [1991] 1995. *The Portable Virgin.* London: Random House; Secker and Warburg.

———. 1993a. "Luck Be A Lady." In *Virgins and Hyacinths: An Attic Press Book of Fiction,* edited by Caroline Walsh. Dublin: Attic Press.

———. 1993b. "Men and Angels." In *The New Picador Book of Contemporary Irish Fiction,* edited by Dermot Bolger, 481–89. London: Picador. Reprinted 1995, New York: Vintage.

———. 1996a. "Indifference," and "Smile." In *The Irish Eros: Irish Short Stories and Poems on Sexual Themes,* edited by David Marcus, 56–63; 255–58. Dublin: Gill and Macmillan.

———. 1996b. *The Wig My Father Wore.* London: Random House; New York: Grove/Atlantic Inc.

———. 1997. "You May Understand English but Can You Understand Us?" *Irish Times,* August 2.

———. 1998a. *Revenge* (screenplay). RTE.

———. 1998b. "Sentimental Journey." *Irish Times,* February 14.

———. 1998c. "Soup, Anyone?" *Irish Times,* September 27.

———. 1999a. *Waterstone's Guide to Irish Books,* edited by Cormac Kinsella, s.v. "O'Brien, Flann." Dublin: Waterstone's.

———. 1999b. "When I Met Jesus." *Irish Times,* December 24.

———. 2000a. "Anonymous Chapter." In *Finbar's Hotel,* edited by Dermot Bolger. London: Harcourt.

———. 2000b. "Taking Pictures." *The New Yorker* 76, no. 5: 116–18.

———. 2000–2001. "Pale Hands I Loved, beside the Shalimar." *The Paris Review* 42, no. 157: 269–79.

———. 2001a. "In the Bed Department." *The New Yorker* 77, no. 11: 92–95.

———. 2001 b. "Luck Be a Lady." In *Cutting the Night in Two: Short Stories by Irish Women Writers,* edited by Evelyn Conlon and Christian Oeser. Dublin: New Island.

———. 2001c. "My Milk: A Mother's Thoughts on Breast Feeding." *Harper's* 302, no. 1812: 26–29.

———. 2001d. "A Tough One to Call." *Irish Times,* June 30.

———. 2001e. *What Are You Like?* London: Random House; Jonathan Cape Limited; New York: Grove/Atlantic; Atlantic Monthly Press.

———. 2002a. "The Portable Virgin." In *The Field Day Anthology of Irish Writing: Irish Women's Writing and Traditions,* vol. 5, edited by Angela Bourke et al., 1200–2. Cork, Ireland: Cork Univ. Press in association with Field Day.

———. 2002b. *The Pleasure of Eliza Lynch.* London: Jonathan Cape.

Secondary Sources

Annan, Gabriele. 2000. Review of *What Are You Like?* by Anne Enright. *New York Review of Books* 47, no. 14: 90.

Battersby, Eileen. 2000. Review of *What Are You Like?* by Anne Enright. *Irish Times.* October 6.

"Chilling Out." 2001. *Sunday Times* (London), July 8.

Donovan, Katie. 1995. "The Astonishing Web of the Ordinary." Review of *The Wig My Father Wore,* by Anne Enright. *Irish Times,* March 18, city ed., supplement 9.

Ettler, Justine. 2000. "Books: *What Are You Like?*: The Twins of the Father." *Observer,* April 16, 13.

Fay, Liam. 1997. Review of *Finbar's Hotel. Irish Times,* October 7.

Fitzgerald, Penelope. 2000. "Bringers of Ill Luck and Bad Weather." Review of *What Are You Like?* by Anne Enright. *London Review of Books* 22, no. 5: 8.

Foster, Aisling. 2000. "When Blood Runs Thicker Than Daughters." Review of *What Are You Like?* by Anne Enright. *Times* (London), February 24.

Hallsworth, Caroline M. 2000. Review of *What Are You Like?* by Anne Enright. *Library Journal* 125, no. 13: 155.

Hogan, Robert, ed. 1996. s.v. "Anne Enright." *Dictionary of Irish Literature.* Westport, Conn.: Greenwood Press.

Kellaway, Kate. 1995. "A Hairy Tale." Review of *The Wig My Father Wore,* by Anne Enright. *Observer,* March 12, Sunday ed., 18.

Kenny, John. 2000. "Ferociously-Paced Magical Surrealism." Review of *What Are You Like?* by Anne Enright. *Irish Times,* March 4, city ed., 70.

Lister, Sam. 2001. Review of *What Are You Like?* by Anne Enright. *Times* (London), March 10.

MacFarlane, Robert. 2000. Review of *What Are You Like?* by Anne Enright. *Times Literary Supplement,* March 3, 21.

Moloney, Caitriona. 2002. *Twenty-First-Century Novelists: Dictionary of Literary Biography,* vol. 267, s.v. "Enright, Anne." Edited by Michael Molino, 88–93. Farmington Hills, Mich.: Gale.

O'Mahoney, John. 2000. "Books: To Thrill a Mockingbird." *Guardian* (London), March 11, 9.

Padel, Ruth. 2000. "The Books Interview—Anne Enright: Twin Tracks and Double Visions; Anne Enright Makes Her Own Singular and Subversive Way Through the Boys' World of Literary Ireland." *Independent* (London), February 26, 9.

Palmer, Elaine. 2000. "Green and Read." *Times* (London), March 11.

Patterson, Christina. 1995. "Books: Angel Delights." Review of *The Wig My Father Wore,* by Anne Enright. *Independent* (London), March 19 , Sunday ed., 46.

Review of *What Are You Like?* by Anne Enright. 2001. *New Statesman* 129, no. 4481: 61.

St. Peter, Christine. 2000. "Women Writing Exile." In *Changing Ireland: Strategies in Contemporary Women's Fiction,* New York: St. Martin's Press.

Taylor, Robert. 1992. Review of *The Portable Virgin. Boston Globe,* September 13, 106.

Toibin, Colm. 1999. Preface to *The Penguin Book of Irish Fiction,* edited by Colm Toibin, i-xxxiii. London: Viking.

Wallace, Richard. 2001. Review of *What Are You Like?* by Anne Enright. October 15, M14.

Weber, Katharine. 1999. "Up in the Old Hotel." Review of *Finbar's Hotel. New York Times,* May 2, sec. 7, 19.

Weekes, Ann Owens. 1993. *Unveiling Treasures: The Attic Guide to the Published Works of Irish Women Literary Writers: Drama, Fiction, Poetry.* Dublin: Attic Press.

You, Elizabeth. 1995. "Books: Grace and Favours: Wit Takes Wing in a Sparky First Novel of Women and Angels." Review of *The Wig My Father Wore,* by Anne Enright. *Guardian* (London), April 4, T7.

Jennifer Johnston

Primary Sources

Johnston, Jennifer. 1972. *The Captains and the Kings.* London: Hamish Hamilton.

———. 1973. *The Gates.* London: Hamish Hamilton.

———. 1974. *How Many Miles to Babylon.* London: Hamish Hamilton.

———. 1977. *Shadows on Our Skin.* London: Hamish Hamilton.

———. 1979. *The Old Jest.* London: Hamish Hamilton.

———. 1981a. *The Christmas Tree.* London: Hamish Hamilton.

———. 1981b. "The Nightingale and Not the Lark." *The Best Short Plays, 1981.* Selected and edited by Stanley Richards. Radnor, Pa.: Chilton Book Co.

———. 1984. *The Railway Station Man.* London: Hamish Hamilton.

———. 1986. Interview by John Quinn. In *The Portrait of the Artist As a Young Girl,* 49–62. London: Methuen.

———. 1987. *Fool's Sanctuary.* London: Hamilton.

———. 1991. *The Invisible Worm*. London: Sinclair-Stevenson.

———. 1995a. *The Illusionist*. London: Sinclair-Stevenson.

———. 1995b. *Three Monologues*. Belfast: Lagan Press.

———. 1996. *The Desert Lullaby: A Play in Two Acts*. Belfast: Lagan Press.

———. 1998. *Two Moons*. London: Review.

———. 1999. "Anonymous Chapter." In *Finbar's Hotel*, edited by Dermot Bolger. London: Harcourt.

———. 2000a. *The Essential Jennifer Johnston*. London: Review.

———. 2000b. *The Gingerbread Woman*. London: Review; Headline.

———. 2001. *Moonlight and Music*. Play written for Programme One, Fishamble Y2K Festival, Civic Theatre, Tallaght, opening February 7. Dublin Castle Crypt, opening February 14.

Secondary Sources

Backus, Margot Gayle. 1994. "Homophobia and the Imperial Demon Lover: Gothic Narrativity in Irish Representations of the Great War." *Canadian Review of Comparative Literature: Revue Canadienne de Litterature Comparée* 21, nos. 1–2: 45–63.

Baker, Phil, Pam Barrett, Ned Balfe, Ivan Hill, and Christopher Weitz. 1991. "Paperbacks." *Sunday Times* (London), June 23.

Battersby, Eileen. 2000. "How Writers Read the World." *Irish Times,* June 20.

———. 2000. "Making Sense of Life." Review of *The Gingerbread Woman. Irish Times,* September 30.

Benstock, Shari. 1982. "The Masculine World of Jennifer Johnston." In *Twentieth-Century Women Novelists*, edited by Stanley F. Thomas, 191–217. Totowa, N.J.: Barnes and Noble.

Berge, Marit. 1994. "The Big House in Jennifer Johnston's Novels." In *Excursions in Fiction: Essays in Honour of Professor Lars Hartveit on His 70th Birthday*, edited by Andrew Kennedy, 11–31. Oslo: Novus.

Bruckner, D. J. R. 1997. "In Performance: Theater." *New York Times*, April 22, 13.

Burleigh, David. 1985. "Dead and Gone: The Fiction of Jennifer Johnston and Julia O'Faolain." In *Irish Writers and Society at Large*, edited by Masaru Sekine, 1–15. Gerrards Cross: Buckinghamshire; Totowa, N.J.: Smythe; Barnes and Noble.

Cahalan, J. 1988. *The Irish Novel: A Critical History*. Dublin: Gill and Macmillan.

Callahan, Denis Joseph F. 1989. "James Joyce and the Novels of Aidan Higgins,

Jennifer Johnston, John McGahern and Brian Moore." *Dissertation Abstracts International* 49.11: 3360A. Ph.D. Univ. of Michigan.

Callahan, Mary Rose. N.d. "Johnston, Jennifer," *Dictionary of Irish Literature.*

Connelly, Joseph. 1986. "Legend and Lyric as Structure in the Selected Fiction of Jennifer Johnston." *Eire-Ireland* 21.3: 119–24.

Deane, Seamus. 1985. "Jennifer Johnston." *Ireland Today* 1015: 4–6.

DePetris, Carla. 1996. "Landing from Laputa: The Big House in Jennifer Johnston's Recent Fiction." In *The Classical World and the Mediterranean,* edited by Giuseppe Serpillo and Donatella Badin, 334–43. Cagliari, Italy: Tema.

Donnelly, Brian. 1975. "The Big House in the Recent Novel." *Studies* 64: 133–42.

Dooley, Susan. 1988. "A Sad Story of Ireland's Divided House." *Washington Post,* January 24, X10.

Dunleavy, Janet E., and Rachael Lynch. 1991. "Contemporary Irish Women Novelists." In *The British and Irish Novel Since 1960,* edited by James Acheson, 103–4. New York: St. Martin's Press.

Ellis, Walter. 1995. "Better Wait for the Film." *Times* (London), November 2.

———. 2000. "The Wretched Labours of Lost Love." *Times* (London), October 25.

Fabre, Silvia Diaz. 1997. "Rewriting the Blakeian 'Invisible Worm' in the Work of Jennifer Johnston." *Cuadernos de Literatura Inglesa y Norteamericana* 2, no. 1: 39–52.

Fauset, Eileen. 1998. "The Book and the Women's Part." *Working Papers in Irish Studies* 98, no. 3: 1–6.

Fay, Liam. 1997. Review of *Finbar's Hotel. Irish Times.* October 7.

Foster, Roy. 1990. "Moral Dilemmas and the Sins of Omission." *Sunday Times* (London), April 22.

Gonzalez, Rosa. 1998. "Jennifer Johnston." In *Ireland in Writing: Interviews with Writers and Academics,* edited by Jacqueline Hurtley et al., 7–19. Amsterdam: Rodopi.

Gordon, Giles. 1994. "The Holy Word Shines in the Bloomsday Book." *Times* (London), June 25.

Gross, John. 1988. "Books of *The Times.*" *New York Times,* January 12, C18.

Hargreaves, Tasmin. 1988. "Women's Consciousness and Identity in Four Irish Women Novelists." In *Cultural Contexts and Literary Idioms in Contemporary Irish Literature,* edited by Michael Kenneally, 290–305. Totowa, N.J.: Barnes and Noble.

Hemingway, Lorain. 1993. "A Woman's Hall of Horrors." *Washington Post,* August 26, C3.

Hynes, James. 1993. "Growing Up Nasty." *Washington Post,* May 16, X4.

Imhof, Rudiger. 1985. " 'A Little Bit of Ivory, Two Inches Wide': The Small World of Jennifer Johnston's Fiction." *Estudes Irlandaises* 10: 129–44.

Jackson, Freda Brown. 1983. *Dictionary of Literary Biography,* s.v. "Johnston, Jennifer." Vol. 14, part 2: 445–51. Detroit: Gale.

Kenny, John. 1999. "Big Houses, Little Pieces." Review of *The Essential Jennifer Johnston,* by Jennifer Johnston. *Times Literary Supplement,* December 17.

Kosok, Heinz. 1986. "The Novels of Jennifer Johnston: Festschrift fur Kurt Otten zum 60." In *Geburtstag.* Darmstadt, Germany: Wissenschaftliche Buchgesellschaft.

Lanters, Jose. 1989. "Jennifer Johnston's Divided Ireland." In *The Clash of Ireland: Literary Contrasts and Connections,* edited by C. C. Barfoot and Theo D'haen, 209–22. Amsterdam: Rodopi.

Leslie, Hazel, and Sue Gee. 1994. "The Village of Longing." *Times* (London), January 17.

Lubbers, Klaus. 1992. " 'This White Elephant of a Place': Jennifer Johnston's Uses of the Big House; A Collection of Interpretations." In *Ancestral Voices: The Big House in Anglo-Irish Literature,* edited by Michael Kenneally, 221–37. Hildesheim: Olms.

Lynch, Rachael Sealy. 2000. "Public Spaces, Private Lives: Irish Identity and Female Selfhood in the Novels of Jennifer Johnston." In *Border Crossings: Irish Women Writers and National Identities,* edited by Kathryn Kirkpatrick, 250–68. Tuscaloosa: Univ. of Alabama Press.

Macbeth, George. 1991. "Bridge over Troubled Waters." *Sunday Times* (London), March 3.

Mahon, Derek. 1996. "On the Shelf." *Sunday Times,* January 28.

Mahoney, Rosemary. 1993. "A Wry Irish Puzzle of Emotional Discovery." Review of *The Invisible Worm,* by Jennifer Johnston. *Washington Post,* August 10, part 2, 54.

McLaughlin, Barbara Ellen. 1997. "Shouting from the Bottom of the Pit": Jennifer Johnston's Dialogue with the Reductive Power of Discourse. Ph.D. diss., Marquette University. Abstract in *Dissertation Abstracts International* 57, no. 12: 5144.

McMahon, Sean. 1975. "Anglo-Irish Attitudes: The Novels of Jennifer Johnston." *Eire-Ireland* 3: 137–41.

Mortimer, Mark. 1980. "The World of Jennifer Johnston: A Look at Three Novels." *The Crane Bag* 4, no. 1, 19.

O'Byrne, Robert. 2000. "Jennifer Johnston Gives Papers to Trinity Library." *Irish Times,*November 16.

O'Faolain, Julia. 1995. Review of *The Illusionist,* by Jennifer Johnston. *Times Literary Supplement,* September 8, 5.

O'Toole, Bridget. 1985. "Three Writers of the Big House: Elizabeth Bowen, Molly Keane and Jennifer Johnston; Essays in Honour of John Hewitt." In *Across a Roaring Hill: The Protestant Imagination in Modern Ireland*, edited by Gerald Dawe and Edna Longley, 124–38. Belfast: Blackstaff.

Perrick, Penny. 1991. "A Prisoner of the Big House." *Sunday Times* (London), February 24.

———. 1995. "Now You See Him . . ." *Sunday Times,* September 10.

———. 1998. "A Breath of Fresh Eire." *Times* (London), August 29.

Raphael, Isabel. 1991. "Something Nasty in Woodshed." *Times* (London), February 28.

See, Carolyn. 1988. "A Revolution with a Wee Pinch o' Soap." *Los Angeles Times,* January 18, part 5, 4.

Stewart-Liberty, Nell. 1986. "Jennifer Johnston and the Half-People." *An Droichead: The Bridge* (spring): 31.

St. Peter, Christine. 1992. "Jennifer Johnston's Irish Troubles: A Materialist-Feminist Reading." In *Gender in Irish Writing*, edited by Toni O'Brien Johnson and David Cairns, 113–27. Buckingham: Open Univ. Press.

"Summer Books Selection—Special Offer." 2001. Review of *Two Moons*, by Jennifer Johnston. *Irish Times,* June 8.

Sutherland, John. 1991. Review of *The Invisible Worm*, by Jennifer Johnston. *London Review of Books* 13: 22.

Truss, Lynne. 2000. "Love on the Run." *Sunday Times* (London), October 8.

Wachtel, Eleanor. 1997. "Interview with Jennifer Johnston." *Queen's Quarterly* 104(2): 319–29.

Walters, Margaret. 1998. "Lessons in Avoiding Middle-Age Dread." *Sunday Times* (London), September 13.

Weber, Katharine. 1999. "Up in the Old Hotel." *New York Times,* May 2, sec. 7, 19.

Weekes, Ann Owens. 1990. *Irish Women Writers: An Uncharted Tradition,* 191–211. Lexington: Univ. Press of Kentucky.

———. 1993 *Unveiling Treasures: The Attic Guide to the Published Works of Irish Women Literary Writers: Drama, Fiction, Poetry,* 156–59. Dublin: Attic Press.

Williams, Moira, and Bernard McLaverty. 1988. *The Dawning.* Screenplay based on *The Old Jest*, by Jennifer Johnston. United Kingdom: Lawson Productions Limited.

Winner, Anthony. 1996. "Disorders of Reading Short Novels." *Kenyon Review* 18, no. 1: 117–28.

York, Richard. 1999. "A Daft Way to Earn a Living: Jennifer Johnston and the Writer's Art. An Interview" *Northern Narratives*, edited by Bill Lazenbatt, 29–47. Newtownabbey, N. Ireland: Univ. of Ulster.

Liz McManus

Primary Sources

McManus, Liz. 1986. "The Tired Trainer of Hamelin." In *Ms Muffet and Others: A Funny, Sassy, Heretical Collection of Feminist Fairytales*, 52–55. Dublin: Attic Press.

——. 1991. *Acts of Subversion*. Dublin: Poolbeg Press.

——. 1993. "Midland Jihad." In *Virgins and Hyacinths*, 65–72. Dublin: Attic Press.

——. 1995. *Report of the Task Force on the Traveling Community: With Senator Mary Kelly*. Dublin: Stationery Office.

——. 1997. "Dwelling below the Skies." In *If Only: Short Stories of Love and Divorce by Irish Women Writers*, edited by Kate Cruise O'Brien and Mary Maher, 207–14. Dublin: Poolbeg Press.

Secondary Sources

Clarity, James F. 1994. "A Changing Ireland Finds Room for a 60s Gadfly." *New York Times*, February 9, A4.

Review of *Acts of Subversion*, by Liz McManus. 1992. *Publisher's Weekly*, May 25, 48.

Smyth, Gerry. 1997. *The Novel and the Nation: Studies in New Irish Fiction*. London: Pluto.

Thompson, Sylvia. 1997. "Telling Tales about Divorce." *Irish Times*, October 16.

Weekes, Ann Owens. 1993. "Liz McManus." In *Unveiling Treasures: The Attic Guide to the Published Works of Irish Women Literary Writers*, 207–9. Dublin: Attic.

Lia Mills

Primary Sources

Mills, Lia. 1987. "Best Friends and Other Strangers." *'Teen* 31: 64+.

——. 1995. " 'I won't go back to it': Irish Women Poets and the Iconic Feminine." *Feminist Review* 50: 69–88.

——. 1996. *Another Alice*. Dublin: Poolbeg Press.

——. 2000. "Forging History: Emily Lawless's *With Essex in Ireland*." *Colby Quarterly* 36, no. 2: 132–44.

——. 2001. "Crush." *The Holly Bough*. Dec.

———. 2001. "Singing for the Bishop." In *Loose Horses: Stories from South Dublin,* edited by Lia Mills. http://homepage.eircom.net/~loosehorses/stories/bishop.htm

———. 2002. "Out of It." *The Stinging Fly.* Issue 12, April.

———. "From *Another Alice.*" In *The Field Day Anthology of Irish Writing: Irish Women's Writing and Traditions,* vol 5, edited by Angela Bourke et al., 1461–2. Cork, Ireland: Cork Univ. Press in association with Field Day.

Secondary Sources

Corcorna, Clodagh. 1996. "Switchback Story of a Shattered Childhood." Review of *Another Alice,* by Lia Mills. *Irish Times,* March 1, 14.

Macdougall, Carl. 1997. "Alice Alone in a Dark Wonderland." Review of *Another Alice,* by Lia Mills. *Herald* (Glasgow), July 19, 14.

Smyth, Gerry. 1997. "Another Alice (1996) by Lia Mills." In *The Novel and the Nation: Studies in the New Irish Fiction,* 93–98. London: Pluto.

Valerie Miner

Primary Sources

Miner, Valerie. [1978] 1980. *Tales I Tell My Mother: A Collection of Feminist Short Stories,* with Zoe Fairbairns, Sara Maitland, Michele Roberts, and Michelene Wandor. London: Journeyman Press; Boston: South End Press.

———. 1981. "Writing Feminist Fiction: Solitary Genesis or Collective Criticism?" *Frontiers: A Journal of Women Studies,* 6, nos. 1–2: 26–29.

———. 1982a. *Blood Sisters: An Examination of Conscience.* London: Women's Press Ltd.; New York: St. Martin's Press.

———. 1982b. *Movement: A Novel in Stories.* Trumansburg, N.Y. and Santa Cruz, Calif.: Crossing Press.

———. [1982] 1983. *Murder in the English Department.* Freedom, Calif.: Crossing Press; New York: St. Martin's Press.

———. [1984, 1985, 1996] 1997. *Winter's Edge.* The Crossing/Feminist Series. London: Methuen; Watsonville, Calif.: Crossing Press; New York: Feminist Press at the City Univ. of New York.

———. 1987. *More Tales I Tell My Mother: Feminist Short Stories,* with Zoe Fairbairns, Sara Maitland, Michele Roberts, and Michelene Wandor. London: Journeyman Press.

———. [1987] 1988. *All Good Women.* Freedom, Calif.: Crossing Press.

———. 1989. *Trespassing and Other Stories*. London: Methuen; Freedom, Calif.: Crossing Press.

———. 1990. "An Imaginative Collectivity of Writers and Readers." In *Lesbian Texts and Contexts: Radical Revisions*, edited by Karla Jay, Joanne Glasgow, and Catharine R. Stimpson, 13–27. New York: New York Univ. Press.

———. 1991a. *Rumors from the Cauldron: Selected Essays, Reviews, and Reportage*. Ann Arbor: Univ. of Michigan Press.

———. 1991b. "Spinning Friends: May Sarton's Literary Spinsters." In *Old Maids to Radical Spinsters: Unmarried Women in the Twentieth-Century Novel*, edited by Laura L. Doan, 15: 155–68. Urbana: Univ. of Illinois Press.

———. 1992. "A Walking Fire: Finding Cordelia's Voice as a Working-Class Hero." *Hayden's Ferry Review* 11: 26–30.

———. 1993. In *Working-Class Women in the Academy: Laborers in the Knowledge Factory*, edited by Michelle M. Tokarczyk and Elizabeth A. Fay. Amherst: Univ. of Massachusetts Press.

———. 1994a. Afterword to *Songs My Mother Taught Me: Stories, Plays and Memoir*, edited by Wakako Yamauchi and Garrett Kaoru Hongo. New York: Feminist Press at the City Univ. of New York.

———. 1994b. "On Earth." *The Virginia Quarterly Review* 70: 315–25.

———. 1994c. "A Spare Umbrella." *Ploughshares* 20: 121–28.

———. 1994d. *A Walking Fire: A Novel*. Albany: State Univ. of New York Press.

———, with Moira Ferguson and Ketu H. Hatrak. 1996a. "Feminism and Antifeminism: From Civil Rights to Culture Wars." In *Antifeminism in the Academy*, compiled and edited by Vèvè Clark et al., 35–66. New York: Routledge.

———. 1996b. "Our Life with the Windsors, 1953–1990." *Michigan Quarterly Review* 35: 329–35.

———. 1997. "Our Life with the Windsors." In *New to North America: Writing by Immigrants, Their Children and Grandchildren*. Oakland, Calif.: Burning Bush.

———. 1998a. "Neath the Pale Yellow Moon (from *The Low Road*)." *Prairie Schooner* 72, no. 3: 95–96.

———. 1998b. *Range of Light*. Cambridge, Mass.: Zoland Books.

———. 1999. "Ritual Meals (from *The Low Road*)." *Prairie Schooner* 72, no. 3: 97–101.

———. 2000a. "All the Way." *Salmagundi* 124–25: 288–301.

———. 2000b. "Legacy (from *The Low Road*)." *Prairie Schooner* 72, no. 3: 91.

———. 2000c. "(Secret Spaces)." *Michigan Quarterly Review* 39, no. 3: 471–72.

———. 2001a. *The Low Road: A Scottish Family Memoir.* East Lansing: Michigan State Univ. Press.

———. 2001b. "View from the Escalator (from *The Low Road*)." *Prairie Schooner* 72, no. 3: 92–94.

———. 2001c. "Vital Signs." *New Letters* 67, no. 2: 639–41.

———. 2002. "A Scottish Opera: Toronto, 1970–1974." *Gettysburg Review* 11: 63–71.

Miner, Valerie, and Helen E. Longino, eds. 1987. *Competition: A Feminist Taboo?* New York: Feminist Press at the City Univ. of New York.

Secondary Sources

Bass, Judy. 1988a. Review of *All Good Women,* by Valerie Miner. *Los Angeles Times,* January 10, 14.

———. 1988b. "Young Lionesses Rampant and Recumbent." Review of *All Good Women,* by Valerie Miner. *Los Angeles Times,* January 3, 9.

Becker, Alida. 1986. Review of *Winter's Edge,* by Valerie Miner. *Los Angeles Times,* January 26, 10.

Cassada, Jackie. 1982. Review of *Blood Sisters,* by Valerie Miner. *Library Journal* 107: 1345.

Coleman, Cathy A. 1994. "In Short: Fiction." Review of *A Walking Fire,* by Valerie Miner. *New York Times,* September 4, late ed., July 16.

Craig, Patricia. 1981. Review of *Blood Sisters,* by Valerie Miner. *Times Literary Supplement,* July 17, 803.

Ferrier, Carole. 1987. "Historical Fiction and Fictional History: An Interview with Valerie Miner." *Meanjin* 46, no. 4: 546–56.

Glastonbury, Marion. 1981. Review of *Blood Sisters,* by Valerie Miner. *New Statesman* 102: 20.

Gottlieb, Annie. 1982. "Women Together." Review of *Blood Sisters,* by Valerie Miner. *New York Times Book Review,* August 22, 11.

Harris, Jana. 1994. "A Walking Fire." Review of *A Walking Fire,* by Valerie Miner. *Seattle Times,* October 16, final ed., M2.

Higgins, Lisa L. 1993. "Valerie Miner." In *Contemporary Lesbian Writers of the United States: A Bio-bibliographical Critical Sourcebook,* edited by Sandra Pollack and Denise D. Knight, 40: 370–74. Westport, Conn.: Greenwood.

Hoffman, Nancy. 1988. "The Dilemma of Difference." *Change* 20: 66–69.

Leber, Michele. 1994. Review of *Range of Light,* by Valerie Miner. *Library Journal* 123, no. 5: 94.

Lundegaard, Erik. 1999. "From Valerie Miner: A Slow Starter That Turns Predictable." Review of *Range of Light,* by Valerie Miner. *Minneapolis Star Tribune,* February 7, metro ed., 19F.

Patten, Eve. 1995. "Fiction in Conflict: Northern Ireland's Prodigal Novelists."
  In *Peripheral Visions: Images of Nationhood in Contemporary British Fiction*, edited by I. A. Bell, 128–48. Cardiff: Univ. of Wales Press.
Pellegrini, Angelo. 1992. "Noted with Pleasure." Review of *Rumors from the
  Cauldron*, by Valerie Miner. *New York Times*, January 19, 31
Perry, Donna. 1993. "Valerie Miner." In *Backtalk: Women Writers Speak Out*,
  compiled by Donna Perry, 195–217. New Brunswick, N.J.: Rutgers Univ.
  Press.
———. 1996. Afterword to *Winter's Edge*, 185–201. New York: Feminist
  Press.
Quamme, Margaret. 1994. " 'Fire' Walks Line between Family, Politics: Story of
  a Homecoming Told in Rich, Realistic Detail." Review of *A Walking Fire*,
  by Valerie Miner. *Columbus Dispatch*, July 24, 7H.
———. 1999. Review of *Range of Light*, by Valerie Miner. *American Book Review* 20, no. 4: 29.
Rolston, Bill. 1989. "Mothers, Whores, and Villains: Images of Women in Novels of the Northern Ireland Conflict." *Race and Class* 31, no. 1: 40–57.
Rose, Ellen Cronan. 1982. "Lessing's Influence on Valerie Miner." *Doris Lessing
  Newsletter, Baltimore County, MD* 6, no. 2: 15.
Smiley, Jane. 1990a. "Another Twist on Jekyll-Hyde Theme." *Gannett News
  Service*, February 5.
———. 1990b. "Vivid Characters Spice Up the Life of 'Reilly.' " *USA Today*,
  January 26, 4D.
Strenski, Ivan. 1987. Review of *Competition: A Feminist Taboo*, by Valerie
  Miner. *Los Angeles Times*, September 6, 8.
Whitney, Scott. 1994. Review of *Range of Light*, by Valerie Miner. *Booklist* 94,
  no. 16: 1429.

Cláir Ní Aonghusa

Primary Sources

Ní Aonghusa, Cláir. 1997. *Four Houses and a Marriage*. Dublin: Poolbeg Press.
———. "Ambulance Days." *Electric Acorn* 4. http://acorn.dublinwriters.org/
  EA4/niaonghusastory.html.

Secondary Sources

Delap, Breandán. 1997. "Leabharmheas." *Foinse*, March, 16.
Gallagher, Djinn. 1997. Review of *Four Houses and a Marriage*, by Cláir Ní
  Aonghusa. *Sunday Tribune Magazine* (Dublin), February 23, 27.

Lahiff, Peter. 1997. "Read the Whole Shebang." *The College Tribune* (UCD), March, 13.

Redford, Carole. 1997. Review of *Four Houses and a Marriage*, by Cláir Ní Aonghusa. *Books Ireland*, October.

Review of *Four Houses and a Marriage*, by Cláir Ní Aonghusa. 1997. *RTE Gazette*, March 8–14.

Éilís Ní Dhuibhne

Primary Sources

Ní Dhuibhne, Éilís. 1983. "Dublin Modern Legends: An Intermediate Type List and Examples." *Bealoideas: The Journal of the Folklore of Ireland Society* 51: 55–70.

———. 1988a. *Blood and Water.* Dublin: Attic Press.

———. 1988b. "Blood and Water" and "Midwife to the Fairies." In *The Blackstaff Book of Short Stories*, edited by Anne Tannahill. Belfast: Blackstaff.

———. 1988c. " 'The Land of Cokaygne': A Middle English Source for Irish Food Historians." *Ulster-Folklife*, 34: 48–53.

———. 1989a. "Midwife to the Fairies." In *Territories of the Voice: Contemporary Stories by Irish Women Writers*, edited by Louise DeSalvo, Kathleen Walsh D'Arcy, and Katherine Hogan, 31–38. Boston: Beacon Press.

———. 1989b. "The Wife of Bath." In *Wildish Things: An Anthology of New Irish Women's Writing*, edited by Ailbhe Smith, 145–56. Dublin: Attic Press.

———. 1990a. *The Bray House.* Dublin: Attic Press.

———. 1990b. "Synge's Use of Popular Material in *The Shadow of the Glen*." *Bealoideas: The Journal of the Folklore of Ireland Society* 58: 141–80.

———. 1991a. *Eating Women Is Not Recommended.* Dublin: Attic Press.

———. 1991b. "The Flowering" and "The Garden of Eden." In *The Second Blackstaff Book of Short Stories*, edited by Anne Tannahill. Belfast: Blackstaff Press.

———. 1992–93. "Supernatural Legends in Nineteenth-Century Irish Writing." *Bealoideas: The Journal of the Folklore of Ireland Society* 60–61: 93–194.

———. 1993a. "Blood and Water." In *The New Picador Book of Contemporary Irish Fiction*, edited by Dermot Bolger, 481–89. London: Picador. Reprinted 1995. New York: Vintage.

———. 1993b. "The Garden of Eden." In *Virgins and Hyacinths: An Attic Press Book of Fiction*, edited by Caroline Walsh, 146–56. Dublin: Attic Press.

———. 1993c. " 'The Old Woman as Hare': Structure and Meaning in an Irish Legend (with appendix)." *Folklore*, 104, no. 1–2: 77–85.

———. 1996. "Green Fuse." In *The Irish Eros: Irish Short Stories and Poems on Sexual Themes,* edited by David Marcus, 3–5. Dublin: Gill and Macmillan.

———. 1997a. "Cruncher, Fatso, and Skyscraper Ted: Contemporary Irish Poetry for Children." In *Lion and the Unicorn: A Critical Journal of Children's Literature.* 21, no. 3: 415–25.

———. 1997b. *The Inland Ice and Other Stories.* Belfast: Blackstaff Press.

———. 1999a. "Anonymous Chapter." In *Ladies' Night at Finbar's Hotel,* edited by Dermot Bolger. London: Picador.

———. 1999b. *The Dancers Dancing.* Belfast: Blackstaff Press.

———. 1999c. "Season of Myths." Review of *Wild Decembers,* by Edna O'Brien. *Irish Times,* October 2.

———. 2001a. *The Pale Gold of Alaska.* London: Review (Headline Book Publishing).

———. 2001b. "Summer Pudding." In *Cutting the Night in Two: Short Stories by Irish Women Writers,* edited by Evelyn Conlon and Hans-Christian Oeser, 293–308. Dublin: New Island.

———. 2001c. "Wuff Wuff Wuff!" *Loose Horses: Stories from South Dublin.* http://homepage.eircom.net/~loosehorses/stories/wuff.htm

———. 2002. From "Eating Women Is Not Recommended." In *The Field Day Anthology of Irish Writing: Irish Women's Writing and Traditions,* vol. 5, edited by Angela Bourke et al., 1193–9. Cork, Ireland: Cork Univ. Press in association with Field Day.

Ní Dhuibhne, Éilís, ed. 1995. *Voices on the Wind: Women Poets of the Celtic Twilight.* Dublin: New Island Books.

Ní Dhuibhne, Éilís, ed. 2002. "International Folktales." In *The Field Day Anthology of Irish Writing: Irish Women's Writing and Traditions,* vol. 4, edited by Angela Bourke et al., 1193–9. Cork, Ireland: Cork Univ. Press in association with Field Day.

Ní Dhuibhne, Éilís, Bo Almqvist, and Saeamas O'Cathain, eds. 1991. *Viking Ale: Studies on Folklore Contacts between the Northern and the Western Worlds.* Aberystwyth, Wales: Boethius Press.

Secondary Sources

Bon, Margarita. 1995. "A Good Wif Was Ther of Biside Bath." In *Papers from the VII International Conference of the Spanish Society for Medieval English Language and Literature, Universidad de Extremadura, Caceres, 1995,* edited by B. Santano Moreno, A. R. Birtwistle, and L. G. Echevarria, 101–6. Caceres, Spain: Universidad de Extremadura.

Burke, Patrick. 1996. "A Dream of Fair Women: Marina Carr's The Mai and Ní

Dhuibhne's Dun na mBan Tri Thine." *Hungarian Journal of English and American Studies* 2: 123–27.

East, Louise. 1997. "Inland Ice." Review of *Inland Ice,* by Éilís Ní Dhuibne. *Irish Times,* July 25.

Hand, Derek. 2000. "Being Ordinary—Ireland from Elsewhere: A Reading of Éilís Ní Dhuibne's *The Bray House.*" *Irish University Review* 30, no. 1: 103–16.

Kiberd, Declan. 2001. "Gael Force." Review of *The Dancers Dancing,* by Éilís Ní Dhuibne. *Irish Times,* March 24.

Koning, Christina. 2000. "When Love Runs Out." *Times* (London), October 18.

Mastin, Antoinette Mary. 1995. "The Road to the Fifth Province: Irish Women's Storytelling, 1960–1993." Ph.D. diss., Univ. of Cincinnati.

Meaney, Geraldine. 1992. "Beyond Eco-Feminism: A Review of Éilís Ní Dhuibne's *The Bray House* and *Eating Women Is Not Recommended.*" *Irish Literary Supplement* 11, no. 2: 14.

Morris, Carol. 1996. "*The Bray House*: An Irish Critical Utopia." *Etudes Irlandaises* 21.

New York Times 1997. Editor's Choice "And Bear in Mind." December 28, sec. 7, 14.

O'Byrne, Robert. 2000. "Irish Writer Listed for Britain's Richest Prize." *Irish Times,* March 21, 3.

Perry, Donna. 1993. "Éilís Ní Dhuibne." In *Backtalk: Women Writers Speak Out,* 245–60. New Brunswick, N.J.: Rutgers Univ. Press.

Review of *The Dancers Dancing,* by Éilís Ní Dhuibne. 2001. *Times* (London), June 8.

Ruta, Suzanne. 1997. "*Inland Ice.*" Review of *Inland Ice,* by Éilís Ní Dhuibne. *New York Times,* December 21.

Smyth, Gerry. 1997. *The Novel and the Nation: Studies in the New Irish Fiction,* 166–68. London: Pluto Press.

Tallone, Giovanna. 2000. "Butter Boots and Paper Hats: The Fiction of Éilís Ní Dhuibne." In *Testi, Intertesti, Contesti: Seminario su "The Wife of Bath" di Eilis NiDhuibhne,* edited by Gianfranca Balestra and Leslie Anne Crowley, 165–68. Milan, Vita ePensiero: Universita Cattolica del Sacro Cuore.

Weekes, Ann Owens. 1993. *Unveiling Treasures: The Attic Guide to the Published Works of Irish Women Literary Writers: Drama, Fiction, Poetry,* 255–56. Dublin: Attic Press.

———. 1995. "Ordinary Women: Themes in Contemporary Fiction by Irish Writers." *Colby Quarterly* 31:88–99.

Edna O'Brien

Primary Sources

O'Brien, Edna. 1963. *The Country Girls.* Harmondsworth, England: Penguin.
———. 1964. *Girl with Green Eyes.* Harmondsworth, England: Penguin.
———. 1967a. *August Is a Wicked Month.* Middlesex, England: Penguin.
———. 1967b. *Girls in Their Married Bliss.* Harmondsworth, England: Penguin.
———. 1968a. *Casualties of Peace.* Harmondsworth, England: Penguin.
———. 1968b. *The Love Object.* Middlesex, England: Penguin.
———. 1971a. *A Pagan Place.* Middlesex, England: Penguin.
———. 1971b. *Zee and Co.* Middlesex, England: Penguin.
———. 1972. *Night.* New York: Farrar.
———. 1973. *A Pagan Place: A Play.* London: Faber.
———. 1974. *A Scandalous Woman and Other Stories.* New York: Harcourt.
———. 1977a. *Arabian Days.* New York: Quartet.
———. 1977b. *Johnny I Hardly Knew You.* London: Weidenfeld.
———. 1978. *Mother Ireland.* Middlesex, England: Penguin.
———. 1979a. *A Rose in the Heart.* Garden City, N.Y.: Doubleday.
———. 1979b. *Some Irish Loving.* Middlesex, England: Penguin.
———. 1981. *James and Nora: A Portrait of Joyce's Marriage.* London: St. John's.
———. 1982. *Returning.* London: Weidenfeld.
———. [1984] 1985. *A Fanatic Heart: Selected Short Stories of Edna O'Brien.* Middlesex, England: Penguin; Farrar, Straus & Giroux.
———. 1985. *Virginia: A Play.* Review ed. New York: Harcourt.
———. 1986a. *The Country Girls Trilogy and Epilogue.* New York: Farrar.
———. 1986b. *Tales for the Telling: Irish Folk and Fairy Stories.* New York: Atheneum.
———. 1989a. *The High Road.* New York: Plume.
———. 1989b. *On the Bone.* Warwick, England: Greville Press.
———. 1990. *Lantern Slides.* Middlesex, England: Penguin.
———. 1991. Introduction to *Dubliners,* by James Joyce, vii–xi. New York: Signet Classic.
———. 1993a. "Such a Sky (from *Lantern Slides*)." In *The Picador Book of Contemporary Irish Fiction.* London: Picador.
———. 1993b. *Time and Tide.* New York: Warner.
———. 1994. *House of Splendid Isolation.* New York: Farrar.
———. 1996. *Down by the River.* London: Weidenfeld.

————. 1997. Foreword to *Irish Women's Letters*. Compiled by Laurence Flanagan. Stroud, U.K.: Sutton.

————. 1999a. *James Joyce*. New York: Viking Penguin; Weidenfeld and Nicolson.

————. 1999b. *Wild Decembers*. London: Weidenfeld and Nicolson.

Secondary Sources

Atkins, Lucy. 1999. "Hatred over the Hedges." *Sunday Times* (London), September 26.

Baird, Jean Lorraine. 1995. "Edna O'Brien: Annotated Check-List Bibliography and Bibliography Handbook." Ph.D. diss., McMaster Univ., 1993. Abstract in *Dissertation Abstracts International* 56, no. 1: 198A.

Baker, Kenneth. 1994. "Picturing James Joyce." *San Francisco Chronicle*, September 4, 4.

Battersby, Eileen. 1999. "Life of O'Brien." *Irish Times*, October 14.

Bayle, Thierry. 1996. "Edna O'Brien: L'Irlande Inspirée." *Magazine Litteraire* 343: 92–95.

Buckley, Karen Ellen. 1991. "Homeomorphic Patterns in the Fiction of Edna O'Brien." Ph.D. diss., Southern Illinois Univ., Carbondale. Abstract in *Dissertation Abstracts International* 52, no. 5: 742A.

Cahalan, James M. 1995. "Female and Male Perspectives on Growing Up Irish in Edna O'Brien, John McGahern, and Brian Moore." *Colby Quarterly* 31, no. 1: 5–73.

————. 1997. "Her Own Private Ireland: In *Down by the River*, Edna O'Brien Imagines One Girl's Fearful Isolation." Review of *Down by the River*, by Edna O'Brien. *Boston Globe*, May 25, N13.

————. 2000. "Old Sod, Old Grudges: Edna O'Brien Sets Her Tragic Irish Tale at the Crossroads Where the Modern Meets the Rural." Review of *Wild Decembers*, by Edna O'Brien. *Boston Globe*, April 9, C1.

Campbell, Peter. 1989. Review of *The High Road*, by Edna O'Brien. *London Review of Books* 11: 4.

Carlson, Julia. 1990. "Edna O'Brien." In *Banned in Ireland: Censorship and the Irish Writer*, edited by Julia Carlson, 69–80. Athens, Ga.: Univ. of Georgia Press.

Carpenter, Humphrey. 1999. "Portrait of the Artist as a Funny Man." *Sunday Times* (London), 20 June.

Carpenter, Lynette. 1986. "Tragedies of Remembrance, Comedies of Endurance: The Novels of Edna O'Brien." In *Essays on the Contemporary British Novel*, edited by Hedwig Bock and Albert Wertheim, 263–81. Munich: Hueber.

Carriker, Kitti. 1989. "Edna O'Brien's 'The Doll': A Narrative of Abjection." *Notes on Modern Irish Literature* 1.

Cusk, Rachel. 1995. "New Lamps Outshone by Old Luminaries." *Times,* August 10.

Dallat, C. L. 1996. "After the Censor Has Gone: The Rise of the Novel as a Critique of De Valera's Ireland." *Times Literary Supplement,* September, 27: 21.

Donlon, Rita. 1999. "The Scandalous Women of Edna O'Brien: Forces against Female Authenticity." Ph.D. diss., City Univ. of New York, 1998. Abstract in *Dissertation Abstracts International, A (Humanities and Social Sciences)* 59, no. 9: 3464–65.

Doten, Patti. 1992. "Loosening the Mother Cord: In Her New Book, Edna O'Brien Wrestles with Maternal Demons." *Boston Globe,* June 8, 30.

Eckley, Grace. 1974. *Edna O'Brien.* Lewisburg, Pa.: Bucknell Univ. Press.

Foran, Charles. 1994. "Edna O'Brien's Ireland Is One Tourists Never See." *Gazette* (Montreal), December 3, 11.

Foster, Aisling. 1994. "Inside the Irish Conscience." *Times* (London), April 16.

———. 1996. "A Different Kind of Country Girl." *Times* (London), August 22.

Foster, Roy. 1999. "A Worshipper at the Shrine of the Old Master." *Times* (London), June 10.

Friedlander, Adrienne L. 1997. *Edna O'Brien: An Annotated Secondary Bibliography (1980–1995).* Working papers in Irish studies series. Fort Lauderdale, Fla.: Department of Liberal Arts, Nova Southeastern Univ.

Galloway, Shana Suzanne. 1994. "No Dream Is Forgotten: Marriage, Motherhood and the Irish Woman." Master's thesis, California State Univ., Long Beach.

Gillespie, Michael Patrick. 1996. "(S)he Was Too Scrupulous Always: Edna O'Brien and the Comic Tradition." In *The Comic Tradition in Irish Women Writers,* edited by Theresa O'Connor, 108–23. Gainesville: Univ. Press of Florida.

Gornick, Vivian. 1987. "The World and Our Mothers." *New York Times Book Review,* November 22, 1.

Graham, Amanda. 1996. " 'The Lovely Substance of the Mother': Food, Gender and Nation in the Work of Edna O'Brien." *Irish Studies Review* 15: 16–20.

Gramich, Katie. 1994. "God, Word and Nation: Language and Religion in Works by V. S. Naipaul, Edna O'Brien and Emyr Humphreys." *Swansea Review* 229–42.

Guppy, Shusha. 1989. "Edna O'Brien." In *Women Writers at Work: The Paris Review Interviews,* edited by George Plimpton, 338–59. Middlesex, England: Penguin.

Hargreaves, Tasmin. 1988. "Women's Consciousness and Identity in Four Irish

Women Novelists." In *Cultural Contexts and Literary Idioms in Contemporary Irish Literature,* edited by Michael Kenneally, 290–305. Totowa, N.J.: Barnes.

Haule, James. 1987. "Tough Luck: The Unfortunate Birth of Edna O'Brien." *Colby Library Quarterly* 23, no. 4: 216–24.

Heller, Prudence. 1997. "Abortion Debate Sparks Edna O'Brien's Gripping Novel." *Associated Press,* June 6.

Helwig, David. 2000. "Ireland Seen in a Dream." *Gazette* (Montreal), April 15.

Herman, David. 1994. "Textual 'You' and Double Deixis in Edna O'Brien's *A Pagan Place." Style* 28, no. 3: 378–411.

Jacquette, Kathleen Marie. 1996. "Irish, Catholic, and Female: The Vision of Patriarchy in the Fiction of Edna O'Brien." Ph.D. diss., City Univ. of New York, 1996. Abstract in *Dissertation Abstracts International, A (Humanities and Social Sciences)* 57, no. 5: 2032A.

Jefferson, Margo. 1994. "Edna O'Brien Takes Her Pen to a Wider Canvas." *New York Times,* July 13, C18.

Johnson, Daniel. 1992. "A Lot of Leaves to Be Desired." *Times* (London), July 11.

Keane, Mary Walkin. 1995. "O'Brien's Aging Heroine in Love with an Escaped IRA Terrorist." *Toronto Star,* January 28, J18.

Killeen, Terence. 1999. Review of *James Joyce,* by Edna O'Brien. *Irish Times,* June 1.

King, Sophia Hillan. 2000. "On the Side of Life: Edna O'Brien's Trilogy of Contemporary Ireland." *New Hibernia Review/Iris Eireannach Nua: A Quarterly Record of Irish Studies* 4, no. 2: 49–66.

Kipen, David. 1999. "O'Brien's Slim, Savory Volume on James Joyce." Review of *James Joyce,* by Edna O'Brien. *San Francisco Chronicle,* December 9, B1.

Kitchen, Judith. 1996. "Out of Place: Reading O'Brien and O'Brien." *Georgia Review* 50, no. 3: 477–95.

Lothar, Corinna. 1992. "Irish Lilt to New O'Brien Novel." *Washington Times,* June 28, B6.

Malpezzi, Frances M. 1996. "Consuming Love: Edna O'Brien's 'A Rose in the Heart of New York.' " *Studies in Short Fiction* 33, no. 3: 355–60.

Manno, Andrew Joseph. 1997. "Varieties of Exile: Culture, Patriarchy, and the Cultivation of Alienation in the Modern Irish Bildungsroman." Ph.D. diss., Lehigh Univ., 1996. Abstract in *Dissertation Abstracts International, A (Humanities and Social Sciences)* 57, no. 9: 3949.

Mastin, Antoinette Mary. 1995. "The Road to the Fifth Province: Irish Women's Storytelling, 1960–1993." Ph.D. diss., Univ. of Cincinnati.

McCormick, Marion. 1992. "More Abuse for the Battered Heart: Edna O'Brien

Is on Familiar Ground in Story of Woman Who Stands Alone." *Gazette* (Montreal), October 3, K3.

McMahon, Sean. 1966. "A Sex by Themselves: An Intermin Report on the Novels of Edna O'Brien." *Eire-Ireland* 2, no. 1: 79–87.

Morgan, Eileen M. 1999. "Reinventing the Republic: Irish Cultural Revisionism and the Legacy of Partition." Ph.D. diss., Indiana Univ., 1998. Abstract in *Dissertation Abstracts International, A (Humanities and Social Sciences)* 59, no. 9: 3467.

Murphy, Rex. 2000. "The Dubliner: Edna O'Brien Brings James Joyce to Life." Review of *James Joyce,* by Edna O'Brien. *Ottawa Citizen,* February 6.

Nicolson, Nigel, Frances Spalding, and Ann Rosen. 1981. "On Edna O'Brien's *Virginia." Virginia Woolf Miscellany* 16, 1.

Ní Dhuibhne, Éilís. 1999. "Season of Myths." Review of *Wild Decembers,* by Edna O'Brien. *Irish Times,* October 2.

Nightingale, Benedict. 1999a. "A Family Without a Prayer." *Times* (London), November 26.

———. 1999b. "Our Father." *Times* (London), December 11.

———. 2000. "Father Knows Beast." *Times* (London), July 5.

O'Brien, Darcy. 1982. "Edna O'Brien: A Kind of Irish Childhood." In *Twentieth-Century Women Novelists,* edited by Thomas F. Staley, 179–90. Totowa, N.J.: Barnes.

O'Brien, Peggy. 1987. "The Silly and the Serious: An Assessment of Edna O'Brien." *Massachusetts Review* 28, no. 3: 474–88.

O'Hara, Kiera. 1993. "Love Objects: Love and Obsession in the Stories of Edna O'Brien." *Studies in Short Fiction* 30, no. 3: 317–25.

Pearce, Sandra Manoogian. 1995. "Edna O'Brien's 'Lantern Slides' and Joyce's 'The Dead': Shadows of a Bygone Era." *Studies in Short Fiction* 32, no. 3: 437–46.

Pelan, Rebecca. 1993. "Edna O'Brien's 'Stage-Irish' Persona: An 'Act' of Resistance." *Canadian Journal of Irish Studies* 19, no. 1: 67–78.

Perrick, Penny. 1995. "Priestly Beatitudes." *Sunday Times,* May 28.

Peter, John. 1999. "Our Father." *Sunday Times* (London), December 5.

Popot, Raymonde. 1976. "Edna O'Brien's Paradise Lost." *Cahiers Irlandais* 4: 255–85.

Pouillard, M. 1971. "Ames en Peine: La Solitude dans la Trilogie d'Edna O'Brien." *Langues Modernes* 65: 365–73.

Quinn, John. 1986. "Edna O'Brien." In *The Portait of the Artist As a Young Girl.* London: Methuen.

Rafroidi, Patrick. 1977. "Bovarysm and the Irish Novel." *Irish University Review* 7: 237–43.

Review of *James Joyce*, by Edna O'Brien. 1999. *Irish Times*, September 4.

Review of *Returning*, by Edna O'Brien. 2000. *Times of London*, December 16.

Roper, Robert. 1992. "Little Nell, Unhappy Again." Review of *Time and Tide*, by Edna O'Brien. *Los Angeles Times*, June 14, 13.

Roth, Philip. 1984. "A Conversation with Edna O'Brien: The Body Contains the Life Story." *New York Times Book Review*, November 18, 38–40.

Rubin, Merle. 1997. "A Pregnant Girl's Moving, Painful Trip on the 'River.' " Review of *Down by the River*, by Edna O'Brien. *Washington Times*, 18 May, B8.

Scanlan, John Allen, Jr. 1976. "States of Exile: Alienation and Art in the Novels of Brian Moore and Edna O'Brien." Ph.D. diss., Univ. of Iowa. Abstract in *Dissertation Abstracts International* 36: 5287A–88A.

Schumaker, Jeanette Roberts. 1995. "Sacrificial Women in Short Stories by Mary Lavin and Edna O'Brien." *Studies in Short Fiction* 32: 185–97.

Senn, Fritz. 1966. "Reverberations." *James Joyce Quarterly* 3: 222.

Skenazy, Paul. 1994. "Private Battles in Ireland's War." *San Francisco Chronicle*, June 19, 1.

Snow, Lotus. 1979. " 'That Trenchant Childhood Route'?: Quest in Edna O'Brien's Novels." *Eire* 14, no. 1: 74–83.

Spencer, Charles. 1999. "The Arts: Reviews More Oirish Than Irish." *Daily Telegraph* (London), November 26, 25.

Stephens, Evelyn Delores B. 1977. "The Novel of Personal Relationships: A Study of Three Contemporary British Women Novelists." Ph.D. diss., Emory Univ. Abstract in *Dissertation Abstracts International* 38: 290A–91A.

St. Peter, Christine. 2000. "Petrifying Time: Incest Narratives from Contemporary Ireland." In *Contemporary Irish Fiction: Themes, Tropes, Theories,* edited by Liam Harte and Michael Parker, 125–44. Houndmills, England: Macmillan, St. Martin's.

Streitfeld, David. 1992. "Edna O'Brien's True Confessions: The Irish Author, Still Scarlet after All These Years." *Washington Post*, July 29, C1.

Taylor, Robert. 1999. "First-Rate Biography Furthers Joycean Scholarship." Review of *James Joyce*, by Edna O'Brien. *Boston Globe*, December 8, F5.

"Time and Tide Rolls in and out." 1994. *Associated Press*, August 21.

Thompson, Helen. 1995–96. "Edna O'Brien's Lesbian Novel." *Lesbian Review of Books* 2, no. 2: 14–15.

———. 1996. "Edna O'Brien." In *Feminist Writers*, edited by Pamela Kester-Shelton, 362–64. Detroit: St. James.

———. 1997. "Necessary Heresies: Women, Disavowal and Desire in the Works of Edna O'Brien." Ph.D. diss., Univ. of Southern Mississippi, 1996. Abstract in *Dissertation Abstracts International, A (Humanities and Social Sciences)* 57, no. 7: 3014.

———. Forthcoming. "Uncanny and Undomesticated: Lesbian Desire in Edna O'Brien's 'Sister Imelda' and *The High Road.*" *Women's Studies: An Interdisciplinary Journal.* 32, no. 1.

Veale, Scott. 2001. "New and Noteworthy Paperbacks." *New York Times,* May 6, sec. 7, 36.

Walters, Colin. 1994. "Renewal of Spirit in 'Splendid' Way." Review of *House of Splendid Isolation,* by Edna O'Brien. *Washington Times,* June 26, part C.

Weekes, Ann Owens. 1993. "Edna O'Brien." In *Unveiling Treasures: The Attic Guide to the Published Works of Irish Women Literary Writers,* 268–71. Dublin: Attic.

Wolcott, James. 1992. "The Playgirl of the Western World." *Vanity Fair,* 55: 50.

Woodward, Richard B. 1989. "Edna O'Brien: Reveling in Heartbreak." *New York Times Magazine,* March 12, 42+.

Woog, Adam. 1994. "Through Irish Eyes—Novelist Tackles the Tug of War in Her Native Land." *Seattle Times,* July 31, M2.

Zacharek, Stephanie. 2000. Review of *Wild Decembers,* by Edna O'Brien. http://www.archive.salon.com/books/review/2000/04/18/o_brien

Mary O'Donnell

Primary Sources

O'Donnell, Mary. 1991. *Strong Pagans and Other Stories.* Dublin: Poolbeg Press.

———. 1992. *The Light-Makers.* Dublin: Poolbeg Press.

———. 1993a. "In Her Own Image: An Assertion That Myths Are Made by Men, by the Poet in Transition." *Irish University Review*

———. 1996a. " 'Rough hands and a sick culture . . . ': The Writer and Cultural Tourism." *Irish University Review,* 25 no. 2, 263–74.

———. 1996b. *Virgin and the Boy.* Dublin: Poolbeg Press.

———. 1997. "Night Watch." *The Literary Review* 40: 702.

———. 1998. *Unlegendary Heroes.* Dublin: Salmon Publishing.

———. 1999. *The Elysium Testament.* London: Trident Press.

———. 2001a. "Communication Breakdown." *Irish Times,* March 31.

———. 2001b. "U.S. Sags under Weight of the Wobblies." *Irish Times,* May 10.

Secondary Sources

Browne, Carla. 1999. Review of *The Elysium Testament,* by Mary O'Donnell. *RTE Guide* Nov. 4.

Cairnduff, Maureen. 1999. Review of *The Elysium Testament,* by Mary O'Donnell. *Irish Independent,* Nov. 13.

Cremin, Kathy. 1999. "The Parent Trap." *Irish Times* Dec. 4.

Dodd, Stephen. 1993. "Women and the Writes of Sex." *Sunday Independent,* May 16: 3L+.

Fogarty, Anne. 2000. "Uncanny Families: Neo-Gothic Motifs and the Theme of Social Change in Contemporary Irish Women's Fiction." *Irish University Review* 30, no. 1: 59–81.

Hopkin, Alannah. 1996. Review of *Virgin and the Boy,* by Mary O'Donnell. *The Sunday Tribune,* August.

Houston, Nainsi Jean. 2000. "Ordinary Men: Men and Masculinity in Contemporary Irish Women's Writing (Maeve Kelly, Clare Boylan, Mary O'Donnell, Anne Haverty)." Ph.D. diss., Univ. of Tulsa.

Kelly, Shirley. 1999. "Shirley Kelly Meets Novelist, Mary O'Donnell." *Books Ireland,* 227: 351–52.

Leland, Mary. 1992. "Insightful First Novel Filled with Promise." *Sunday Tribune,* Sept. 26.

Kate O'Riordan

Primary Sources

O'Riordan, Kate. 1995. *Involved.* London: Flamingo.

———. 1997a. *The Boy in the Moon.* London: Flamingo.

———. 1997b. "Home Is Where the Hurt Is." Interview by Arminta Wallace. *Irish Times,* August 19, 6.

———. [1999] 2000. "Anonymous Chapter." In *Ladies' Night at Finbar's Hotel,* edited by Dermot Bolger. London: Picador; San Diego: Harcourt Trade Publishers.

———. 2000. *The Angel in the House.* London: Flamingo; New York: HarperCollins Publishers; San Diego: Harcourt Trade Publishers.

———. 2001. "Working to an Organic Timeframe: My Writing Day." *Irish Times,* May.

———. N.d. *The Boy In the Moon,* filmscript for BBC TV.

———. N.d. Catherine Dunne's *In the Beginning,* filmscript for RTE (Ireland).

———. N.d. For "Casualty," filmscript for BBC TV.

————. N.d. *Involved,* filmscript for HTV (Wales).

————. N.d. *Jaws of Darkness.* Unpublished play.

————. N.d. *She'll Be Wearing Silk Pyjamas.* Unpublished play.

————. Forthcoming. *Memory Stones.* London: Pocket Books.

Secondary Sources

Baker, Phil, Dan Cairns, Ian Critchley, Joanna Duckworth, and David Mills. 1995. "Paperbacks." *Sunday Times,* April 23.

Bassett, Kate. 1995. "Sporting Attempt at Tolerance." *Times* (London), March 2.

East, Louise. 1997. "The Shattering of an Idyll." Review of *The Boy in the Moon,* by Kate O'Riordan. *Irish Times,* September 19, 12.

Fogarty, Anne. 2000. "Uncanny Families: Neo-Gothic Motifs and the Theme of Social Change in Contemporary Irish Women's Fiction." *Irish University Review* 30.

Foster, Aisling. 1995. "Involved." Review of *Involved Times,* by Kate O'Riordan. *Literary Supplement,* February 17, 20C.

Hornby, Gill. "Irish Habits Die Hard." *Times* (London), May 20.

Ní Riordain, Cliona. 1998. "Visions et revisions de Belfast dans le Roman Irlandais Contemporain." *Graat: Publication des Groupes de Recherches Anglo-Americaines de L'Université Francois Rabelais De* 19: 29–37.

Patten, Eve. 1995. "Fiction in Conflict: Northern Ireland's Prodigal Novelists." In *Peripheral Visions: Images of Nationhood in Contemporary British Fiction,* edited by I. A. Bell, 129–48. Cardiff: Univ. of Wales Press.

————. 2000. "Angela's Hashes." Review of *The Angel in the House,* by Kate O'Riordan. *Irish Times.*

Perrick, Penny. 1995. "White Knuckle Sandwich." Review of *Involved,* by Kate O'Riordan. *Times* (London), February 18.

Scurr, Ruth. 1997. "In Search of Forgiveness." Review of *The Boy in the Moon,* by Kate O'Riordan. *Times Literary Supplement,* September 5, 22A.

Smyth, Gerry. 1997. *The Novel and the Nation: Studies in the New Irish Fiction,* 140–43. London: Pluto Press.

Sweeney, Eamonn. 1995. "Trouble with the Troubles." Review of *Involved,* by Kate O'Riordan. *Irish Times,* April 1, 8.

Tarien, Kersti. 2002. "Kate O'Riordan." In *Dictionary of Literary Biography: Twenty-First-Century British and Irish Novelists,* vol. 267, edited by Michael D. Molino, 279–84. Farmington Hills, Mich.: Gale.

Teeman, Tim. 1995. "IRA Up Stereotype Alley." Review of *Involved,* by Kate O'Riordan. *Independent* (London), March 26, 40.

Wallace, Arminta. 1997. Review of *The Boy in the Moon,* by Kate O'Riordan. *Irish Times,* August 19, 6.

———. 1998. Review of *The Boy in the Moon,* by Kate O'Riordan. *Irish Times,* April 4, 67.

Maura Stanton

Primary Sources

Stanton, Maura. 1975. *Snow on Snow.* New Haven: Yale Univ. Press.

———. 1977. *Molly Companion.* New York: Bobbs-Merrill.

———. 1979. "An Interview with Maura Stanton." Interview by Karla M. Hammond. *Paintbrush: A Journal of Poetry, Translations, and Letters* 6, no. 12: 34–40.

———. 1984. *Cries of Swimmers.* Salt Lake City: Univ. of Utah Press.

———. 1986. "The Sea Fairies." *Michigan Quarterly Review* 25: 642–54.

———. 1987a. "At Hemingway's House." *The American Scholar* 56: 502.

———. 1987b. "The Dance." *Michigan Quarterly Review* 26: 30–31.

———. 1987c. "Peoria." *Michigan Quarterly Review* 26: 29–30.

———. 1988a. *The Country I Come from.* Minneapolis: Milkweed Editions.

———. 1988b. *Tales of the Supernatural: Poems.* Boston: David R. Godine.

———. 1990a. "February 29." *The Antioch Review* 48: 228–29.

———. 1990b. "Otello." *The Antioch Review* 48: 226–27.

———. 1991a. "Number Seventeen." *Ploughshares* 17: 175–76.

———. 1991b. "A Portrait by Bronzino." *The American Poetry Review* 20: 21.

———. 1991c. "Train." *The American Poetry Review* 20: 20.

———. 1991d. "The Veiled Lady." *The American Poetry Review* 20: 22.

———. 1992a. "Do Not Forsake Me, Oh My Darling." In *Lovers,* edited by Amber Coverdale, 313–20. Berkeley, Calif.: Crossing Press.

———. 1992b. "The House of Cleopatra." *Ploughshares* 18: 144–61.

———. 1992–93. Review of *What Keeps Us Here,* by Maura Stanton. *Ploughshares* 18: 237–39.

———. 1993a. "The City of the Dead." *The Southern Review* 29: 286–87.

———. 1993b. "John McCormack." In *The Next Parish over: A Collection of Irish-American Writing,* edited by Patricia Monaghan, 21–31. New York: New Rivers.

———. 1993c. "Learning to Drive." *The Southern Review* 29: 284–86.

———. 1993d. "October Petunia." *The Southern Review* 29: 283–84.

———. 1993e. "The Palace." In *The Next Parish over: A Collection of Irish-*

American Writing, edited by Patricia Monaghan, 70–80. New York: New Rivers.

———. 1993f. "Pig." *The Southern Review* 29: 282.

———. 1995a. "Anne Hathaway's Cottage." *New England Review* 17: 147–48.

———. 1995b. "The Cat and the Clown." *TriQuarterly* 93: 134–44.

———. 1995c. "Labyrinth." *Chicago Review* 41, no. 1: 43–44.

———. 1997a. "Ah, Cleo." *Southwest Review* 82: 441–42.

———. 1997b. "The Last Judgment." *The Paris Review* 39: 169.

———. 1997c. "Mono Lenses." *The Southern Review* 33: 291–92.

———. 1997d. "Nijinsky." In *Cabbage and Bones: An Anthology of Irish American Women's Fiction,* edited by Caledonia Kearns, 111–28. New York: Holt.

———. 1997e. "Posthuman." *The American Poetry Review* 26: 20.

———. 1997f. "Squash Flowers." *Ploughshares* 23: 166–74.

———. 1997g. "Three Unknown Sea Creatures." *The American Poetry Review* 26: 20–21.

———. 1997h. "Winter Walk." *The Southern Review* 33: 292–93.

———. 1997–98a. "Ben Nevis." *Ploughshares* 23: 137–38.

———. 1997–98b. "Happiness." *Ploughshares* 23: 135–36.

———. 1998. *Life among the Trolls.* Pittsburgh: Carnegie Mellon Press.

———. 1999. "The Situation of American Writing 1999." *American Literary History* 11, no. 2: 320–24.

———. 2000a. "Listening to the Big Bands on New Year's Eve 1999." *Western Humanities Review* 54, no. 2: 162–63.

———. 2000b. "Tatyana." *Southwest Review* 85, no. 2: 269.

———. 2001. *Glacier Wine (Poetry Series).* Pittsburg: Carnegie Mellon Univ. Press.

———. 2002. *Do not Forsake Me, Oh My Darling.* Notre Dame, Ind.: Univ. of Notre Dame Press.

Stanton, Maura, ed. 1989. *Ploughshares Spring 1989: Stories and Poems.* Boston: Ploughshares Books.

Secondary Sources

Chernoff, Maxine. 1989. "A Childhood Cold and Wet." Review of *The Country I Come from,* by Maura Stanton. *New York Times Book Review,* February 26, 30.

Hart, Henry. 1989. Review of *Tales of the Supernatural,* by Maura Stanton. *Michigan Quarterly Review* 28: 417–36.

Kaganoff, Penny. 1988. Review of *The Country I Come from,* by Maura Stanton. *Publishers Weekly,* September 30, 60.

Lesser, Ellen. 1989. "Telling Tales: In Search of the New Short Story." Review of *The Country I Come from,* by Maura Stanton. *New England Review and Bread Loaf Quarterly* 12, no. 1: 98–108.

McMurtry, Larry. 1977. "A Poet's Novel of War." *Washington Post,* October 17, B14.

Review of *Molly Companion,* by Maura Stanton. 1977. *Publisher's Weekly,* 8 August, 63.

Ryan, Maureen. 1994. "The Other Side of Grief: American Women Writers and the Vietnam War." *Critique: Studies in Contemporary Fiction* 36, no. 1: 41–48.

Stitt, Peter. 1985. Review of *Cries of Swimmers,* by Maura Stanton. *The Georgia Review* 39: 849–63.

Electronic Sources

Personal Websites

Emma Donoghue: www.emmadonoghue.com
Valerie Miner: http://English.cla.umn.edu/faculty/MINER/miner.htm
Mary O'Donnell: www.maryodonnell.com
Maura Stanton: http://php.indiana.edu/~stanton/

Bookstores

Amazon in the U.K.: www.amazon.co.uk
Fred Hanna's: http://www.buy4now.ie/Hannas/
Kenny's in Galway: http://www.kennys.ie/
Amazon in the UK: www.amazon.co.uk
WH Smith Online: http://www.whsmith.co.uk/whs/Go.asp?menu=Books& pagedef=/books/home/index.htm

Publishers

Attic: http://www.iol.ie/~atticirl/
Blackstaff: http://www.blackstaffpress.com/
Poolbeg: http://www.poolbeg.com/
Wolfhound: http://wolfhound.ie/homepg.htm

Distributors

Books Britain (makes available British books not published in the U.S.): Books Britain, Inc., 245 West 104th Street, Suite 11D, New York, NY 10025; Tel.: 212–749–7413; Fax: 212–749–7509; http://www.Booksbritain@juno.com/

Dufour Editions (source of books by foreign publishers): http://www.dufoureditions.com/

Other Online Resources

Dublin Writer's Workshop: http://www.dublinwriters.org/welcome.html

Irish Arts Foundation: http://www.iaf.org/INDEX.htm

Irish Writer's Center: http://www.writerscentre.ie/

Irish Writers Online: http://www.irishwriters-online.com/
    http://www.writerscentre.ie/

Women's Education Research and Resource Center University College, Dublin: http://www.ucd.ie/~werrc

Index

Ireland, North of (*cont.*)
77; Republicanism, 36, 77; Royal
Ulster Constabulary, 81; Sinn Fein,
79; terrorism, 76, 82–83; "Troubles,"
xvi, 36–37, 75–76, 136; unionism,
88–89; women in, 88–89
Ireland, Republic of: Abbey Theatre, 93;
anti-British sentiments, 82; Borde
Failte (Irish Tourist Board); 38, 134;
border (between Republic and
North), 36–37, 116, 120, 121–22;
Celticism, 37; Celtic tiger, 38, 84, 89,
140; censorship, 77, 84, 120, 140,
172, 197, 199, 204; changing culture,
30, 31, 80, 96, 116, 119, 204;
childhood, 43, 200; Church and
State, 34, 47, 77, 80–81, 95, 135;
Civil Service, 76, 89; Civil War, 82;
class, 31, 40, 77, 80, 81, 139;
colonization, 37, 44, 82, 93–94, 122,
135, 141–42, 160, 172, 222–23;
conformity, 77; contraceptive train,
32; County Clare, 201, 205; critics,
199; Dail Eireann (Irish Parliament),
83; Dublin, 79, 90, 123, 134, 141,
179; Dundalk, 36; Easter Rising, 37,
82; education, 81, 92–93; emigration,
42, 48, 77, 129–30, 137, 140, 156;
and English language, 160; equal pay,
80; as environment for writers, 28,
53–54, 208; European Union, 82, 88,
119, 140; family, 36, 90; feminine
representations of, 37–38, 135, 179,
201; Galway, 86, 93; illegitimacy,
119; Labor Party, 179, 80; language,
44, 89, 102–3, 105–6, 121, 137, 198,
223; libel laws, 92; literary scene, 49;
memory, 36–37; Monaghan, 116,
120, 121–22; Mother and Child Bill,
172; motherhood, 123;
multiculturalism, 83, 98, 141–42;
national identity, xvi, xvii, 75,
122–23, 133–34, 137, 146, 157, 169;

nationalism, 36–36, 44, 81, 82, 83,
88, 93, 115, 121, 135, 136; "old"
Ireland, 129; Peacock Theatre, 93;
postindependence, 77; racism, 103,
141, 157, 160; rural West, 197, 198,
204; sex education, 48; sexuality, 48,
119; speech patterns, 176;
stereotypes, 34, 35, 37, 159, 165;
strikes (Dublin, 1913), 93; Tipperary,
90; tourism, 37, 76, 204; Tyrone
Guthrie Center, 84; and United Arab
Emirates, 126; University College,
Dublin, 79, 170, 171; Women's
Education, Research, and Resource
Center (WERRC), xv; women in, 32,
33, 47, 88–89, 90–91, 142, 197–98;
women writers, 89–90; Writers'
Week, Listowel, 86
Irish Independent, 119
Irish Press, 33
Irish Republican Army, 136, 139;
Provisional, 82
Irish Studies, xv, xvi, xvii
Irving, John, 41

James, Henry, 121, 226
Jane Eyre (C. Brontë), 228
Joanna Hayes Baby Case, 102, 108
"John McCormack" (Stanton), 225
Johnston, Jennifer, 7; on abuse of
children, 71; on Jane Austen, 72; "Big
House" tradition, 66, 72–73; on the
Booker Prize, 71; feminism, 73;
introduction to, 65–66; Irish identity,
65–66; Irish in America, 68; Irish in
England, 72; on James Joyce
(*Ulysses*), 68; on madness, 70–71;
male characters, 69; motherhood, 66;
on Julia O'Faolain, 72;
postcolonialism, 73–74; publishing,
70; reviews, 72; "Troubles," 68;
writers admired, 67–68, 72; on W. B.

responsibilities of, 21–22; stereotypes about, 18; and writing, 8, 66, 150
Mother Ireland (E. O'Brien), 201
Mother Ireland, 135, 198
Mukherjee, Bharati, 167
Multiculturalism: in Ireland, 83, 98, 141–42; in the United States, 161
Munro, Alice, 99, 167
Murasaki, Lady, 223, 226
My Head Is Opening (Conlon), 22, 23
Mythology, Irish, 101, 107–9, 184

Nabokov, Vladimir, 49
NaCopaleen, Myles. *See* O'Brien, Flann
Naipaul, V. S., 121
Name for Himself, A (C. Dunne), 30–31, 35–36, 38, 39
Narayan, R. K., 121
Narrative structure, 111–12, 216–17; and archetype, 63; epistolary style, 19; and gender, 59; point of view, 185; and writing process, 53. *See also* Lesbian narrative
National Endowment for the Arts, 227
National Endowment for the Humanities, xv
Nationalism (Irish), 36–37, 44, 81, 82, 83, 88, 93, 115, 121–22, 135, 136; and political prisoners, 18–19
National Women's Studies Association, xvi
New Irish Writing (Marcus), 85, 92
New York, 133, 138, 140, 173
New York Times, 199
Ní Aonghusa, Cláir: on Eavan Boland, 90; Catholicism, 90, 91, 95–96; Celtic tiger, 89; characters, 85–86, 88, 90, 94–99; colonialism, 89, 93; divorce, 85, 86, 87, 88, 94; domesticity, 86, 90–91; education, 92–93; European Union, 88–89; family, 85–86, 90, 96–98; feminism,

91; *The Field Day Anthology of Irish Writing* (Deane), 99; immigrants to Britain, 90; introduction to, 85–86; James Joyce, 100; Latin history, 98; lesbianism of characters, 91; libel, 92; and David Marcus, 85, 92; masculinity, 88; motherhood, 91, 94; narrative point of view, 87; and Kate Cruise O'Brien, 86–87; parents, 92; publishing, 86–87, 92; reviews of her work, 95, 99; Roman history, 98; sexuality, 93, 95–96, 99; women in Ireland, 88; women in Northern Ireland, 88–89; women writers, 89–90; writers admired, 99–100. *Works: Four Houses and a Marriage,* 85, 87, 95; *Roger Casement Is Not a Homosexual,* 95–99
Nicolson, Nigel, 203–4
Ní Dhomhnaill, Nuala, xvi, 4, 107, 113
Ní Dhuibhne, Éilís, xvii, 121, 135, 143, 145; on abuse of children, 113–14; on George Borrow *(Wild Wales),* 109; on Angela Bourke, 107; on Celebrating Irish Women Writers Conference, 110; Celtic Tiger, 107; characters, 103, 111; European Union, 104; family, 103; the Famine, 102, 109; on *The Field Day Anthology of Irish Writing* (Deane), 111; on Anne Fine, 112; Gaelic Ireland, 102; Gaelic name of, 102–3; Gaeltacht (Gaelic Ireland), 103, 106; gender inequalities, 112; Joanna Hayes Baby Case, 102, 108; infanticide, 108–9; intertextuality, 107, 110; introduction to, 101–2; Irish identity, 103, 104, 105, 114–15; Irish myth, 101, 107, 109, 110; on James Joyce, 110; male characters, 111; on David Marcus, 106; on Liz McManus, 110; on Geraldine Moane, 114; mobility, 106; narrative